William Shakespeare was born in Stratford-upon-Avon in April, 1564, and his birth is traditionally celebrated on April 23. The facts of his life, known from surviving documents, are sparse. He was one of eight children born to John Shakespeare, a merchant of some standing in his community. William probably went to the King's New School in Stratford, but he had no university education. In November 1582, at the age of eighteen, he married Anne Hathaway, eight years his senior, who was pregnant with their first child, Susanna. She was born in May, 1583. Twins, a boy, Hamnet (who would die at age eleven), and a girl, Judith, were born in 1585. By 1592 Shakespeare had gone to London, working as an actor and already known as a playwright. A rival dramatist, Robert Greene, referred to him as "an upstart crow, beautified with our feathers." Shakespeare became a principal shareholder and playwright of the successful acting troupe, the Lord Chamberlain's Men (later, under James I, called the King's Men). In 1599 the Lord Chamberlain's Men built and occupied the Globe Theatre in Southwark near the Thames River. Here many of Shakespeare's plays were performed by the most famous actors of his time, including Richard Burbage, Will Kemp, and Robert Armin. In addition to his 37 plays, Shakespeare had a hand in others, including *Sir Thomas More* and *The Two Noble Kinsmen*, and he wrote poems, including *Venus and Adonis* and *The Rape of Lucrece*. His 154 sonnets were published, probably without his authorization, in 1609. In 1611 or 1612 he gave up his lodgings in London and devoted more and more of his time to retirement in Stratford, though he continued writing such plays as *The Tempest* and *Henry VIII* until about 1613. He was buried in Holy Trinity Church, Stratford, on April 23, 1616. No collected edition of his plays was published during his lifetime, but in 1623 two members of his acting company, John Heminges and Henry Condell, put together the great collection now called the First Folio.

William Shakespeare

HAMLET, PRINCE OF DENMARK

Edited by
David Bevington
and
David Scott Kastan

BANTAM CLASSIC

HAMLET, PRINCE OF DENMARK
A Bantam Book / published by arrangement with
Pearson Education, Inc.

PUBLISHING HISTORY
Scott, Foresman edition published January 1980
Bantam edition, with newly edited text and substantially revised, edited, and
amplified notes, introduction, and other materials / February 1988
Bantam reissue with updated notes, introduction, and other materials /
February 2005

Published by Bantam Dell
A Division of Random House, Inc.
New York, New York

Valuable advice on staging matters has been provided by Richard Hosley
Collations checked by Eric Rasmussen
Additional editorial assistance by Claire McEachern

Book design by Virginia Norey

Library of Congress Catalog Card Number: 87-24096

ISBN 978-0-553-21292-1

Printed in the United States of America
Published simultaneously in Canada
www.bantamdell.com
OPM   33   32

CONTENTS

INTRODUCTION

A recurring motif in *Hamlet* is of a seemingly healthy exterior concealing an interior sickness. Mere pretense of virtue, as Hamlet warns his mother, "will but skin and film the ulcerous place, / While rank corruption, mining all within, / Infects unseen" (3.4.154–6) Polonius confesses, when he is about to use his daughter as a decoy for Hamlet, that "with devotion's visage / And pious action we do sugar o'er / The devil himself"; and his observation elicits a more anguished mea culpa from Claudius in an aside: "How smart a lash that speech doth give my conscience! / The harlot's cheek, beautied with plast'ring art, / Is not more ugly to the thing that helps it / Than is my deed to my most painted word" (3.1.47–54).

This motif of concealed evil and disease continually reminds us that, in both a specific and a broader sense, "Something is rotten in the state of Denmark" (1.4.90). The specific source of contamination is a poison: the poison with which Claudius has killed Hamlet's father, the poison in the players' enactment of "The Murder of Gonzago," and the two poisons (envenomed sword and poisoned drink) with which Claudius and Laertes plot to rid themselves of young Hamlet. More generally, the poison is an evil nature seeking to destroy humanity's better self, as in the archetypal murder of Abel by Cain. "Oh, my offense is rank! It smells to heaven," laments Claudius, "It hath the primal eldest curse upon't, / A brother's murder" (3.3.36–8). To Hamlet, his father and Claudius typify what is best and worst in humanity; one is the sun-god Hyperion and the other a satyr. Claudius is a "serpent" and a "mildewed ear, / Blasting his wholesome brother" (1.5.40; 3.4.65–6). Many a person, in Hamlet's view, is tragically destined to behold his or her better qualities corrupted by "some vicious mole of nature" over which the individual seems to have no control. "His virtues else, be they as pure as grace, / As infinite as man may undergo, / Shall in the general censure take corruption / From that particular fault." The "dram of evil" pollutes "all the noble substance" (1.4.24–37). Thus, poison spreads outward to infect the whole individual, just as bad individuals can infect an entire court or nation.

Hamlet, his mind attuned to philosophical matters, is keenly and poetically aware of humanity's fallen condition. He is, moreover, a shrewd observer of the Danish court, familiar with its ways and at the same time newly returned from abroad, looking at Denmark with a stranger's eyes. What particularly darkens his view of humanity, however, is not the general fact of corrupted human nature but rather Hamlet's knowledge of a dreadful secret. Even before he learns of his father's murder, Hamlet senses that there is something more deeply amiss than his mother's overhasty marriage to her deceased husband's brother. This is serious enough, to be sure, for it violates a taboo (parallel to the marriage of a widower to his deceased wife's sister, long regarded as incestuous by the English) and is thus understandably referred to as "incest" by Hamlet and his father's ghost. The appalling spectacle of Gertrude's "wicked speed, to post / With such dexterity to incestuous sheets" (1.2.156–7) overwhelms Hamlet with revulsion at carnal appetite and intensifies the emotional crisis any son would go through when forced to contemplate his father's death and his mother's remarriage. Still, the Ghost's revelation is of something far worse, something Hamlet has subconsciously feared and suspected. "Oh, my prophetic soul! My uncle!" (1.5.42). Now Hamlet believes he has confirming evidence for his intuition that the world itself is "an unweeded garden / That grows to seed. Things rank and gross in nature / Possess it merely" (1.2.135–7).

Something is indeed rotten in the state of Denmark. The monarch on whom the health and safety of the kingdom depend is a murderer. Yet few persons know his secret: Hamlet, Horatio only belatedly, Claudius himself, and ourselves as audience. Many ironies and misunderstandings within the play can-

not be understood without a proper awareness of this gap between Hamlet's knowledge and most others' ignorance of the
murder. For, according to their own lights, Polonius and the rest
behave as courtiers normally behave, obeying and flattering a
king who has been chosen by a constitutional process of "election" and therefore can claim to be their legitimate ruler. They
do not know that he is a murderer. Hamlet, for his part, is so ob-
sessed with the secret murder that he overreacts to those
around him, rejecting overtures of friendship and becoming
embittered, callous, brutal, and even violent. His antisocial behavior gives the others good reason to fear him as a menace to
the state. Nevertheless, we share with Hamlet a knowledge of
the truth and know that he is right, whereas the others are at
best unhappily deceived by their own blind complicity in evil.

Rosencrantz and Guildenstern, for instance, are boyhood
friends of Hamlet but are now dependent on the favor of King
Claudius. Despite their seeming concern for their one-time
comrade and Hamlet's initial pleasure in receiving them, they
are faceless courtiers whose very names, like their personalities,
are virtually interchangeable. "Thanks, Rosencrantz and gentle
Guildenstern," says the King, and "Thanks, Guildenstern and
gentle Rosencrantz," echoes the Queen (2.2.33–4). They cannot understand why Hamlet increasingly mocks their overtures
of friendship, whereas Hamlet cannot stomach their sub-
servience to the King. The secret murder divides Hamlet from
them, since only he knows of it. As the confrontation between
Hamlet and Claudius grows more deadly, Rosencrantz and
Guildenstern, not knowing the true cause, can only interpret
Hamlet's behavior as dangerous madness. The wild display he
puts on during the performance of "The Murder of Gonzago"
and then the killing of Polonius are evidence of a treasonous
threat to the crown, eliciting from them staunch assertions of
the divine right of kings. "Most holy and religious fear it is / To
keep those many many bodies safe / That live and feed upon
Your Majesty," professes Guildenstern, and Rosencrantz reiter-
ates the theme: "The cess of majesty / Dies not alone, but like a
gulf doth draw / What's near it with it" (3.3.8–17). These senti-

ments of Elizabethan orthodoxy, similar to ones frequently heard in Shakespeare's history plays, are here undercut by a devastating irony, since they are spoken unwittingly in defense of a murderer. This irony pursues Rosencrantz and Guildenstern to their graves, for they are killed performing what they see as their duty to convey Hamlet safely to England. They are as ignorant of Claudius's secret orders for the murder of Hamlet in England as they are of Claudius's real reason for wishing to be rid of his stepson. That Hamlet should ingeniously remove the secret commission from Rosencrantz and Guildenstern's packet and substitute an order for their execution is ironically fitting, even though they are guiltless of having plotted Hamlet's death. "Why, man, they did make love to this employment," says Hamlet to Horatio. "They are not near my conscience. Their defeat / Does by their own insinuation grow" (5.2.57–9). They have condemned themselves, in Hamlet's eyes, by interceding officiously in deadly affairs of which they had no comprehension. Hamlet's judgment of them is harsh, and he himself appears hardened and pitiless in his role as agent in their deaths, but he is right that they have courted their own destiny.

Polonius, too, dies for meddling. It seems an unfair fate, since he wishes no physical harm to Hamlet and is only trying to ingratiate himself with Claudius. Yet Polonius's complicity in jaded court politics is deeper than his fatuous parental sententiousness might lead one to suppose. His famous advice to his son, often quoted out of context as though it were wise counsel, is, in fact, a worldly gospel of self-interest and concern for appearances. Like his son, Laertes, he cynically presumes that Hamlet's affection for Ophelia cannot be serious, since princes are not free to marry ladies of the court; accordingly, Polonius obliges his daughter to return the love letters she so cherishes. Polonius's spies are everywhere, seeking to entrap Polonius's own son in fleshly sin or to discover symptoms of Hamlet's presumed lovesickness. Polonius may cut a ridiculous figure as a prattling busybody, but he is wily and even menacing in his intent. He has actually helped Claudius to the throne and is an essential instrument of royal policy. His ineffectuality and ignorance of the murder do not really excuse his guilty involvement.

Ophelia is more innocent than her father and brother, and more truly affectionate toward Hamlet. She earns our sympathy because she is caught between the conflicting wills of the men who are supremely important to her—her wooer, her father, and her brother. Obedient by instinct and training to patriarchal instruction, she is unprepared to cope with divided authority and so takes refuge in passivity. Nevertheless, her pitiable story suggests that weak-willed acquiescence is poisoned by the evil to which it surrenders. However passively, Ophelia becomes an instrument through which Claudius attempts to spy on Hamlet. She is much like Gertrude, for the Queen has yielded to Claudius's importunity without ever knowing fully what awful price Claudius has paid for her and for the throne. The resemblance between Ophelia and Gertrude confirms Hamlet's tendency to generalize about feminine weakness—"frailty, thy name is woman" (1.2.146)—and prompts his misogynistic outburst against Ophelia when he concludes she, too, is spying on him. His rejection of love and friendship (except for Horatio's) seems paranoid in character and yet is at least partially justified by the fact that so many of the court are in fact conspiring to learn what he is up to.

Their oversimplification of his dilemma and their facile analyses vex Hamlet as much as their meddling. When they presume to diagnose his malady, the courtiers actually reveal more about themselves than about Hamlet—something we as readers and viewers might well bear in mind. Rosencrantz and Guildenstern think in political terms, reflecting their own ambitious natures, and Hamlet takes mordant delight in leading them on. "Sir, I lack advancement," he mockingly answers Rosencrantz's questioning as to the cause of his distemper. Rosencrantz is immediately taken in: "How can that be, when you have the voice of the King himself for your succession in Denmark?" (3.2.338–41). Actually, Hamlet does hold a grudge against Claudius for having "Popped in between th'election and my hopes" (5.2.65), using the Danish custom of "election" by the chief lords of the realm to deprive young Hamlet of the succession that would normally have been his. Nevertheless, it is a gross oversimplification to suppose that political frustration is the key to Hamlet's sorrow, and to speculate thus is presumptuous. "Why, look you now, how unworthy a thing you make of me!" Hamlet protests to Rosencrantz and Guildenstern. "You would play upon me, you would seem to know my stops, you would pluck out the heart of my mystery" (3.2.362–5). An even worse offender in the distortion of complex truth is Polonius, whose facile diagnosis of lovesickness appears to have been inspired by recollections of Polonius's own far-off youth. ("Truly in my youth I suffered much extremity for love, very near this," 2.2.189–91). Polonius's fatuous complacency in his own powers of analysis—"If circumstances lead me, I will find / Where truth is hid, though it were hid indeed / Within the center" (2.2.157–9)—reads like a parody of Hamlet's struggle to discover what is true and what is not.

Thus, although Hamlet may seem to react with excessive bitterness toward those who are set to watch over him, the corruption he decries in Denmark is both real and universal. "The time is out of joint," he laments. "Oh, cursèd spite / That ever I was born to set it right!" (1.5.197–8). How is he to proceed in setting things right? Ever since the nineteenth century, it has been fashionable to discover reasons for Hamlet's delaying his revenge. The basic Romantic approach is to find a defect, or tragic flaw, in Hamlet himself. In Coleridge's words, Hamlet suffers from "an overbalance in the contemplative faculty" and is "one who vacillates from sensibility and procrastinates from thought, and loses the power of action in the energy of resolve." More recent psychological critics, such as Freud's disciple Ernest Jones, still seek answers to the Romantics' question by explaining Hamlet's failure of will. In Jones's interpretation, Hamlet is the victim of an Oedipal trauma: he has longed unconsciously to possess his mother and for that very reason cannot bring himself to punish the hated uncle who has supplanted him in his incestuous and forbidden desire. Such interpretations suggest, among other things, that Hamlet continues to serve as a mirror in which analysts who would pluck out the heart of his mystery see an image of their own concerns—just as Rosencrantz and Guildenstern read politics, and Polonius reads lovesickness, into Hamlet's distress.

We can ask, however, not only whether the explanations for Hamlet's supposed delay are valid but also whether the question they seek to answer is itself valid. Is the delay unnecessary or excessive? The question did not even arise until the nineteenth century. Earlier audiences were evidently satisfied that Hamlet must test the Ghost's credibility, since apparitions can tell half-truths to deceive people, and that, once Hamlet has confirmed the Ghost's word, he proceeds as resolutely as his canny adversary allows. More recent criticism, perhaps reflecting a modern absorption in existentialist philosophy, has proposed that Hamlet's dilemma is a matter not of personal failure, but of the absurdity of action itself in a corrupt world. Does what Hamlet is asked to do make any sense, given the bestial nature of humanity and the impossibility of knowing what is right? In part, it is a matter of style: Claudius's Denmark is crassly vulgar, and to combat this vulgarity on its own terms seems to require the sort of bad histrionics Hamlet derides in actors who mouth their lines or tear a passion to tatters. Hamlet's dilemma of action can best be studied in the play by comparing him with various characters who are obliged to act in situations similar to his own and who respond in meaningfully different ways.

Three young men—Hamlet, Laertes, and Fortinbras—are called upon to avenge their fathers' violent deaths. Ophelia, too, has lost a father by violent means, and her madness and death are another kind of reaction to such a loss. The responses of Laertes and Fortinbras offer rich parallels to Hamlet, in both cases implying the futility of positive and forceful action. Laertes thinks he has received an unambiguous mandate to take revenge, since Hamlet has undoubtedly slain Polonius and helped to deprive Ophelia of her sanity. Accordingly, Laertes comes back to Denmark in a fury, stirring the rabble with his demagoguery and spouting Senecan rant about dismissing conscience "to the profoundest pit" in his quest for vengeance

(4.5.135). When Claudius asks what Laertes would do to Hamlet "To show yourself in deed your father's son / More than in words," Laertes fires back: "To cut his throat i'th' church" (4.7.126–7). This resolution is understandable. The pity is, however, that Laertes has only superficially identified the murderer in the case. He is too easily deceived by Claudius, because he has jumped to easy and fallacious conclusions, and so is doomed to become a pawn in Claudius's sly maneuverings. Too late he sees his error and must die for it, begging and receiving Hamlet's forgiveness. Before we accuse Hamlet of thinking too deliberately before acting, we must consider that Laertes does not think enough.

Fortinbras of Norway, as his name implies ("strong in arms"), is one who believes in decisive action. At the beginning of the play, we learn that his father has been slain in battle by old Hamlet and that Fortinbras has collected an army to win back by force the territory fairly won by the Danes in that encounter. Like Hamlet, young Fortinbras does not succeed his father to the throne but must now contend with an uncle-king. When this uncle, at Claudius's instigation, forbids Fortinbras to march against the Danes and rewards him for his restraint with a huge annual income and a commission to fight the Poles instead, Fortinbras sagaciously welcomes the new opportunity. He pockets the money, marches against Poland, and waits for occasion to deliver Denmark as well into his hands. Clearly this is more of a success story than that of Laertes, and Hamlet does, after all, give his blessing to the "election" of Fortinbras to the Danish throne. Fortinbras is the man of the hour, the representative of a restored political stability. Yet Hamlet's admiration for this man on horseback is qualified by a profound reservation. Hamlet's dying prophecy that the election will light on Fortinbras (5.2.357–8) is suffused with ironies, so much so that the incongruity is sometimes made conscious and deliberate in performance. Earlier in the play, the spectacle of Fortinbras marching against Poland "to gain a little patch of ground / That hath in it no profit but the name" prompts Hamlet to berate himself for inaction, but he cannot ignore the absurdity of the effort. "Two thousand souls and twenty thousand ducats / Will not debate the question of this straw." The soldiers will risk their very lives "Even for an eggshell" (4.4.19–54). It is only one step from this view of the vanity of ambitious striving to the speculation that great Caesar or Alexander, dead and turned to dust, may one day produce the loam or clay with which to stop the bunghole of a beer barrel. Fortinbras epitomizes the ongoing political order after Hamlet's death, but is that order of any consequence to us after we have imagined with Hamlet the futility of most human endeavor?

To ask such a question is to seek passive or self-abnegating answers to the riddle of life, and Hamlet is attuned to such inquiries. Even before he learns of his father's murder, he contemplates suicide, wishing "that the Everlasting had not fixed / His canon 'gainst self-slaughter" (1.2.131–2). As with the alternative of action, other characters serve as foils to Hamlet, revealing both the attractions and perils of withdrawal. Ophelia is destroyed by meekly acquiescing in others' desires. Whether she commits suicide is uncertain, but the very possibility reminds us that Hamlet has twice considered and reluctantly rejected this despairing path as forbidden by Christian teaching—the second such occasion being his "To be, or not to be" soliloquy in 3.1. He has also playacted at the madness to which Ophelia succumbs. Gertrude identifies herself with Ophelia and like her has surrendered her will to male aggressiveness. We suspect she knows little of the actual murder (see 3.4.31) but dares not think how deeply she may be implicated. Although her death is evidently not a suicide (see 5.2.291–7), it is passive and expiatory.

A more attractive alternative to decisive action for Hamlet is acting in the theater, and he is full of exuberant advice to the visiting players. The play they perform before Claudius at Hamlet's request and with some lines added by him—a play consciously archaic in style—offers to the Danish court a kind of heightened reflection of itself, a homiletic artifact, rendering in conventional terms the taut anxieties and terrors of murder for the sake of noble passion. Structurally, the play within the play becomes not an escape for Hamlet into inaction but rather the point on which the whole drama pivots and the scene in which contemplation of past events is largely replaced with stirrings toward action. When Lucianus in the Mousetrap play turns out to be nephew rather than brother to the dead king, the audience finds itself face-to-face not with history, but with prophecy. We are not surprised when, in his conversations with the players, Hamlet openly professes his admiration for the way in which art holds "the mirror up to nature, to show virtue her feature, scorn her own image, and the very age and body of the time his form and pressure" (3.2.22–4). Hamlet admires the dramatist's ability to transmute raw human feeling into tragic art, depicting and ordering reality as Shakespeare's play of *Hamlet* does for us. Yet playacting can also be, Hamlet recognizes, a self-indulgent escape for him, a way of unpacking his heart with words and of verbalizing his situation without doing something to remedy it. Acting and talking remind him too much of Polonius, who was an actor in his youth and who continues to be, like Hamlet, an inveterate punster.

Of the passive responses in the play, the stoicism of Horatio is by far the most attractive to Hamlet. "More an antique Roman than a Dane" (5.2.343), Horatio is, as Hamlet praises him, immune to flattering or to opportunities for cheap self-advancement. He is "As one, in suffering all, that suffers nothing, / A man that Fortune's buffets and rewards / Hast ta'en with equal thanks" (3.2.65–7). Such a person has a sure defense against the worst that life can offer. Hamlet can trust and love Horatio as he can no one else. Yet even here there are limits, for Horatio's skeptical and Roman philosophy cuts him off from a Christian and metaphysical overview. "There are more things in heaven and earth, Horatio, / Than are dreamt of in your philosophy" (1.5.175–6). After they have beheld together the skulls of Yorick's graveyard, Horatio seemingly does not share with Hamlet the exulting Christian perception that, although human life is indeed vain, Providence will reveal a pattern transcending human sorrow.

Hamlet's path must lie somewhere between the rash suddenness of Laertes or the canny resoluteness of Fortinbras on the one hand, and the passivity of Ophelia or Gertrude and the stoic resignation of Horatio on the other. At first he alternates between action and inaction, finding neither satisfactory. The Ghost has commanded Hamlet to revenge but has not explained how this is to be done; indeed, Gertrude is to be left passively to heaven and her conscience. If this method will suffice for her (and Christian wisdom taught that such a purgation was as thorough as it was sure), why not for Claudius? If Claudius must be killed, should it be while he is at his sin rather than at his prayers? The play is full of questions, stemming chiefly from the enigmatic commands of the Ghost. "Say, why is this? Wherefore? What should we do?" (1.4.57). Hamlet is not incapable of action. He shows unusual strength and cunning on the pirate ship, in his duel with Laertes ("I shall win at the odds"; 5.2.209), and especially in his slaying of Polonius—an action hardly characterized by "thinking too precisely on th'event" (4.4.42). Here is forthright action of the sort Laertes espouses. Yet, when the corpse behind his mother's arras turns out to be Polonius rather than Claudius, Hamlet concludes from the mistake that he has offended heaven. Even if Polonius deserves what he got, Hamlet believes he has made himself into a cruel "scourge" of Providence who must himself suffer retribution as well as deal it out. Swift action has not accomplished what the Ghost commanded.

The Ghost does not appear to speak for Providence, in any case. His message is of revenge, a pagan concept deeply embedded in most societies but at odds with Christian teaching. His wish that Claudius be sent to hell and that Gertrude be more gently treated might, in fact, be the judgment of an impartial deity but here comes wrapped in the passionate involvement of a murdered man's restless spirit. This is not to say that Hamlet is being tempted to perform a damnable act, as he fears is possible, but that the Ghost's command cannot readily be reconciled with a complex and balanced view of justice. If Hamlet were to spring on Claudius in the fullness of his vice and cut his throat, we would pronounce Hamlet a murderer. What Hamlet believes he has learned instead is that he must become the instrument of Providence according to *its* plans, not his own. After his return from England, he senses triumphantly that all will be for the best if he allows an unseen power to decide the time and place for his final act. Under these conditions, rash action will be right. "Rashly, / And praised be rashness for it—let us know / Our indiscretion sometime serves us well / When our deep plots do pall, and that should learn us / There's a divinity that shapes our ends, / Rough-hew them how we will" (5.2.6–11). Passivity, too, is now a proper course, for Hamlet puts himself wholly at the disposal of Providence. What had seemed so impossible when Hamlet tried to formulate his own design proves elementary once he trusts to a divine justice in which he now firmly believes. Rashness and passivity are perfectly fused. Hamlet is revenged without having to commit premeditated murder and is relieved of his painful existence without having to commit suicide.

The circumstances of *Hamlet*'s catastrophe do indeed seem to accomplish all that Hamlet desires, by a route so circuitous that no one could ever have foreseen or devised it. Polonius's death, as it turns out, was instrumental after all, for it led to Laertes's angry return to Denmark and the challenge to a duel. Every seemingly unrelated event has its place; "There is special providence in the fall of a sparrow" (5.2.217–18). Repeatedly, the characters stress the role of seeming accident leading to just retribution. Even Horatio, for whom the events of the play suggest a pattern of randomness and violence, of "accidental judgments" and "casual slaughters," can see at last, "in this upshot, purposes mistook / Fall'n on th'inventors' heads" (5.2.384–7). In a similar vein, Laertes confesses himself "a woodcock to mine own springe" (5.2.309). As Hamlet had said earlier, of Rosencrantz and Guildenstern, " 'tis the sport to have the engineer / Hoist with his own petard" (3.4.213–14). Thus, too, Claudius's poisoned cup, intended for Hamlet, kills the Queen, for whom Claudius had done such evil in order to acquire her and the throne. The destiny of evil in this play is to overreach itself.

In its final resolution, *Hamlet* incorporates a broader conception of justice than its revenge formula seemed at first to make possible. Yet, in its origins, *Hamlet* is a revenge story, and these traditions have left some residual savagery in the play. In the *Historia Danica* of Saxo Grammaticus, 1180–1208, and in the rather free translation of Saxo into French by François de Belleforest, *Histoires Tragiques* (1576), Hamlet is cunning and bloodily resolute throughout. He kills an eavesdropper without a qualm during the interview with his mother and exchanges letters on his way to England with characteristic shrewdness. Ultimately, he returns to Denmark, sets fire to his uncle's hall, slays its courtly inhabitants, and claims his rightful throne from a grateful people. The Ghost, absent in this account, may well have been derived from Thomas Kyd, author of *The Spanish Tragedy* (c. 1587) and seemingly of a lost *Hamlet* play in existence by 1589. *The Spanish Tragedy* bears many resemblances to our *Hamlet* and suggests what the lost *Hamlet* may well have contained: a sensational murder, a Senecan Ghost demanding revenge, the avenger hampered by court intrigue, his resort to a feigned madness, and his difficulty in authenticating the ghostly vision. A German version of *Hamlet*, called *Der bestrafte Brudermord* (1710), based seemingly on the older *Hamlet*, includes such details as the play within the play, the sparing of the King at his prayers in order to damn his soul, Ophelia's madness, the fencing match with poisoned swords and poisoned drink, and the final catastrophe of vengeance and death. Similarly, the early unauthorized first quarto of *Hamlet* (1603) offers some passages seemingly based on the older play by Kyd.

Although this evidence suggests that Shakespeare received most of the material for the plot intact, his transformation of that material was nonetheless immeasurable. To be sure, Kyd's *The Spanish Tragedy* contains many rhetorical passages on the inadequacy of human justice, but the overall effect is still sensational and the outcome is a triumph for the pagan spirit of revenge. So, too, with the many revenge plays of the 1590s and 1600s that Kyd's dramatic genius had inspired, including Shakespeare's own *Titus Andronicus* (c. 1589–1592). *Hamlet*, written in about 1599–1601 (it is not mentioned by Frances Meres in his *Palladis Tamia: Wit's Treasury*, in 1598, and was entered in the Stationers'

Register, the official record book of the London Company of Stationers [booksellers and printers], in 1602), is unparalleled in its philosophical richness. Its ending is truly cathartic, for Hamlet dies not as a bloodied avenger, but as one who has affirmed the tragic dignity of the human race. His courage and faith, maintained in the face of great odds, atone for the dismal corruption in which Denmark has festered. His resolutely honest inquiries have taken him beyond the revulsion and doubt that express so eloquently, among other matters, the fearful response of Shakespeare's own generation to a seeming breakdown of established political, theological, and cosmological beliefs. Hamlet finally perceives that "if it be not now, yet it will come," and that "The readiness is all" (5.2.219–20). This discovery, this revelation of necessity and meaning in Hamlet's great reversal of fortune, enables him to confront the tragic circumstance of his life with understanding and heroism and to demonstrate the triumph of the human spirit even in the moment of his catastrophe.

Such an assertion of the individual will does not lessen the tragic waste with which *Hamlet* ends. Hamlet is dead, and the great promise of his life is forever lost. Few others have survived. Justice has seemingly been fulfilled in the deaths of Claudius, Gertrude, Rosencrantz and Guildenstern, Polonius, Laertes, and perhaps even Ophelia, but in a wild and extravagant way, as though Justice herself, more vengeful than providential, were unceasingly hungry for victims. Hamlet, the minister of that justice, has likewise grown indifferent to the spilling of blood, even if he submits himself at last to the will of a force he recognizes as providential. Denmark faces the kind of political uncertainty with which the play began. However much Hamlet may admire Fortinbras's resolution, the prince of Norway seems an alien choice for Denmark—even an ironic one. Horatio sees so little point in outliving the catastrophe of this play that he would choose death, were it not that he must draw his breath in pain to ensure that Hamlet's story is truly told. Still, that truth has been rescued from oblivion. Amid the ruin of the final scene, we share the artist's vision, through which we struggle to interpret and give order to the tragedy that proves inseparable from human existence.

HAMLET, PRINCE OF DENMARK
ON STAGE

Most people who know their Shakespeare are surprised and disconcerted by the cutting of so much material when they see the otherwise admirable film of *Hamlet* by Laurence Olivier (1948): all of Fortinbras's role and the negotiations with Norway, all of Rosencrantz and Guildenstern, a good deal of Act 4, and still more. The supposed reason, that a film must cut heavily to make room for visual material and to be of an acceptable length, is of course true in the main, but it overlooks the long history of the play in production. Many of the same cuts prevailed from the Restoration until the later nineteenth century as a way not only of shortening a long play but of highlighting the role of Hamlet for the lead actor.

Even in its own day, *Hamlet* (with Richard Burbage in the title role) must have been heavily cut, especially in the fourth act; the unauthorized quarto of 1603, though garbled presumably by the actors who helped to prepare a stolen copy, appears to be the report of a shortened acting text. During the Restoration, the published edition of the version that diarist Samuel Pepys saw and enjoyed five times during the 1660s was offered to its readers with a warning: "This play being too long to be conveniently acted, such places as might be least prejudicial to the plot or sense are left out upon the stage." This *Hamlet*, prepared by William Davenant and acted by Thomas Betterton at intervals from 1661 until 1709, took out some 841 lines, including most of Fortinbras's part, Polonius's advice to Laertes and instructions to Reynaldo, much of Rosencrantz and Guildenstern, the scene between Hamlet and Fortinbras's captain (4.4), and other matters, though the appearance of Fortinbras at the end was retained. Betterton's successor, Robert Wilks (active in the part until 1732), went further by removing Fortinbras from Act 5 entirely, concluding the play instead with Horatio's farewell and eulogy to his sweet prince. This ending was the only one to be seen onstage from 1732 until 1897. An operatic version of *Hamlet* in 1712 bore even less resemblance to Shakespeare's play, taking its inspiration chiefly from Saxo Grammaticus's *Historia Danica,* the twelfth-century narrative from which the history of Hamlet derives.

David Garrick used for a time a version of the Wilks text from which he also cut Hamlet's soliloquy in Act 3, scene 3 ("Now might I do it pat"), and all mention of Hamlet's voyage to England. Then, in 1772, Garrick ventured to remove nearly all of the fifth act. In Garrick's *Hamlet* the protagonist never embarks for England at all, having been prevented from doing so by the arrival of Fortinbras. Laertes, hindered by a shipwreck, never gets to France. Laertes is a more estimable person than in Shakespeare's play, since he is entirely freed of the taint of plotting to kill Hamlet with a poisoned sword. Hamlet and Laertes fight, but without the poisoned sword; Claudius tries to intervene in the duel of the two young men and is slain by Hamlet, who then runs on Laertes's sword and falls, exchanging forgiveness with Laertes as he dies. Horatio, after attempting to kill Laertes in revenge, is persuaded by the dying Hamlet to accept the will of Heaven and to rule jointly with Laertes. The gravediggers are not needed since Ophelia's burial is omitted, Gertrude is not poisoned but, we are told, is in a trance and on the verge of madness from remorse. We do not hear of the execution of Rosencrantz and Guildenstern. Garrick's intention in all this novelty seems to have been to ennoble Hamlet by pairing him in the last scene with a worthy opponent, by reducing the bloodthirstiness of his killing of Claudius, and by omitting all mention of his part in the deaths of Rosencrantz and Guildenstern. Classical decorum was served by excising long gaps of time and travels into other lands, and by refusing to countenance the comedy of the gravediggers in a tragic play. Garrick restored the soliloquy, "How all occasions do inform against me" (4.4), again enhancing the role of the protagonist, along with some of Polonius's advice to his son.

Garrick called his alterations of Hamlet "the most imprudent thing" he had ever done. Although he was "sanguine" about the results, modern audiences are more likely to feel that the Romantic era was not an auspicious time for the play. In addition to Garrick's adaptations, German actors in England at the end of the century provided the play a happy ending, with the Queen's illness warning Hamlet in time. John Philip Kemble, acting the part at various times from 1783 to 1817, cut the play back to a series of well-known theatrical vignettes, prompting critic William Hazlitt, while admiring Kemble's acting, to complain that Hamlet is better not acted at all.

As if to confirm Hazlitt's worry about the often empty theatricality of the nineteenth-century stage, a chief preoccupation of the time was to add pictorial splendor to stage production. Actor-manager William Charles Macready, at the Theatre Royal, Covent Garden, in 1838, won praise for "a series of glorious pictures." Charles Kean, who in 1838 had a great success acting Hamlet at the Theatre Royal, Drury Lane, lavished money and attention on the fortress of Elsinore in his own production of the play at the Princess's Theatre in 1850. With his customary passion for scenic elaboration, he showed, among other scenes, a guard platform of the castle and then another part of the platform, the royal court of Denmark and its handsome theater, the Queen's "closet" or chamber, and the ancient burying ground in the vicinity of the palace to which Ophelia was borne with impressive if maimed rites. Nineteenth-century illustrations of Shakespeare's plays testify to the age's interest in pictorially detailed reproductions of the play within the play, Ophelia's mad scenes, and other emotionally powerful moments in Hamlet. Ophelia became a favorite subject for the visual arts, in the theater and out of it, perhaps because she was so well suited, like the Lady of Shalott, for pre-Raphaelite interpretation. Pictorialism in the theater thus accentuated the trend, already seen among earlier actor-managers, toward highlighting the play's great iconic moments at the expense of the rest of the text. Ophelia became a leading role for actresses such as Julia Bennett, Ellen and Kate Terry, and Helena Modjeska, especially in the latter part of the century.

Charles Fechter appears to have been the first, at the Princess's Theatre in 1861 and then at the Lyceum Theatre in 1864, to garb Hamlet not in the velvet and lace of an English aristocrat, but in Viking attire appropriate to the play's Danish setting, which was matched with surrounding sets in primitive and medieval decor. His Hamlet was flaxen-haired; Rosencrantz and Guildenstern were bearded Scandinavian warriors in coarse cross-gartered leggings. Much of the action took place in the large main hall of Elsinore. Edwin Booth in America and Henry Irving in England were the leading Hamlets of the late century. Booth appeared first in the role in 1853, in San Francisco, winning instant renown both in America and abroad. In 1861, in Manchester, England, he played Hamlet to Irving's Laertes. Three years later, Irving himself first played Hamlet, and he continued in the role until 1885. Irving chose a decor of the fifth or sixth century, though not rigorously so, and his costumes retained the attractiveness of Elizabethan dress. Hamlet's first encounter with his father's ghost was impressively set in a remote part of the battlements of the castle, amid massive rocks, with the soft light of the moon filtering onto the Ghost while hints of dawn appeared over the expanse of water to be seen in the background. The scenes on the battlements showed the illuminated windows of the palace in the distance. The funeral of Ophelia took place on a hill near the palace. Irving portrayed Hamlet as deeply affected by his love for Ophelia in a sentimental interpretation that gave prominence to Ellen Terry's Ophelia. Irving made little of Hamlet's voyage to England or his encounter with Fortinbras's captain, devoting most of Act 4 instead to Ophelia's mad scenes and ending the play with "The rest is silence." These descriptions suggest the extent to which the actor-managers of that age turned to favorite scenes for their theatrical effects, cutting much else to accommodate the ponderous scenery.

Beginning with Johnston Forbes-Robertson's restoration of

the Fortinbras ending in 1897, as he was encouraged to do by George Bernard Shaw, twentieth-century directors have generally shown more respect for the play's text than did their predecessors. In 1881 at St. George's Hall, William Poel had already directed a group of amateur actors in a reading of the play based on the 1603 quarto, and in 1899 Frank Benson staged an uncut composite Folio-quarto text (something never acted in Shakespeare's day) at the Shakespeare Memorial Theatre in Stratford-upon-Avon. These were experimental performances and not rigorously followed since, though Harcourt Williams directed John Gielgud, in his first Hamlet, at the Old Vic in 1930 in a production without significant cuts. Tyrone Guthrie successfully produced the play in an uncut version, which starred Laurence Olivier, at the Old Vic in 1937, and Olivier himself directed an uncut *Hamlet* at London's National Theatre starring Peter O'Toole in 1963. At the same time, directors have turned away from the nineteenth-century sentimental focus on Hamlet's delay and love melancholy to explore ironies and conflict. *Hamlet* in modern dress, beginning with H. K. Ayliff at the Birmingham Repertory Theatre in 1925, and followed by, among others, Tyrone Guthrie in 1938, in another production at the Old Vic, explored the existential challenges of the play in the context of Europe between two world wars. Freudian interpretation played a major part in Laurence Olivier's film version of 1948, as evidenced by the camera's preoccupation with Gertrude's bedroom and by the intimate scenes between mother and son. Olivier's cutting and rearranging of scenes owed much to eighteenth- and nineteenth-century traditions, as we have seen, even while his camera work found new ways to explore the mysterious and labyrinthine corridors of Elsinore Castle. Joseph Papp's *Hamlet* (Public Theater, New York, 1968) went beyond Olivier in an iconoclastic and deliberately overstated psychological shocker, featuring a manacled Hamlet (Martin Sheen) in a coffinlike cradle at the feet of Claudius's and Gertrude's bed. Grigori Kozintsev's Russian film version of 1964, using a cut text by Boris Pasternak, found eloquent visual metaphors for Hamlet's story in the recurring images of stone, iron, fire, sea, and earth. Among the best Hamlets have been those of Richard Burton (in 1964 at New York's Lunt-Fontanne Theater, directed by John Gielgud), Nicol Williamson (in 1969 at the Roundhouse Theatre in London, directed by Tony Richardson), and Derek Jacobi (in 1979 at the Old Vic, directed by Toby Robertson) portraying the protagonist as tough and serious, capable of great tenderness in friendship and love, but faced with hard necessities and pursuing them with fierce energy.

The melancholic, pale, introspective Hamlet of Kemble and the lovestruck prince of Irving have thus seldom been seen on the modern stage, though Olivier recalls the tradition of melancholy with his voice-over soliloquies, and John Gielgud's sonorously spectral voice excels in the meditations on suicide. The play is now more apt to be satirical, even funny at times, presenting a mordant and disillusioned view of life at court, as in Peter Hall's 1965 production at Stratford-upon-Avon, or in Jonathan Miller's more austere *Hamlet* at London's Warehouse Theatre in 1982, both of which disturbingly portrayed a world in which, as Hall wrote, "politics are a game and a lie." Polonius, long regarded in the theater as little more than a "tedious old fool," as Hamlet calls him, can reveal in performances a canniness in political survival that fits well with his matter-of-fact and philistine outlook. The scenes at court lend themselves to contemporary political analogies: Claudius can become the Great Communicator, adept at public relations gimmicks, the darling of television, while the creatures who bustle about him do their part to "sell" Claudius to a complacent court and a thoroughly skeptical Hamlet. As the outsider, Hamlet is likely to be the rebel, a misfit, and justly so, in view of what he sees in Denmark. Stacy Keach, in Gerald Freedman's *Hamlet* at New York's Delacorte Theater in 1972, was neither melancholy nor vulnerable; rather, he was bitter, shrewd, and, as the drama critic of the *New York Times* wrote, "hell-bent for revenge."

In 1977, outside of Berlin, Ulrich Wildgruber's Hamlet was even more wild and unpredictable, cutting up Polonius's corpse and throwing it out the window in Peter Zadek's iconoclastic production.

The Romanian director Liviu Ciulei directed *Hamlet* at the Arena Stage in Washington, D.C., in 1978, with obvious political intent. His Denmark was a paranoid, militaristic state, where public order was literally undermined by the visible catacombs beneath the raised main stage. Hamlet came up from below to overhear Claudius praying, only the most obvious of the threats that the regime cannot prevent from arising. A very different version of the play was staged in Cologne, Germany, the following year: Hansgünter Heyme's "electronic" *Hamlet*. For Heyme, the play became an image of our disorienting technological world. The safety curtain, always down, had eighteen television monitors projecting the action on the stage from a video camera that actors turned on others or back upon themselves. An actor mimed the role of Hamlet, while his speeches, spoken by the director, were amplified through the theater. The tension between the familiar language of the play and the extraordinary visuals of the production worked to undercut the very idea of tragedy itself in a world where electronic images are more real than flesh-and-blood reality.

Heyme's production obviously influenced Heiner Müller's remarkable seven-and-a-half-hour *Hamlet/Maschine*, performed in Berlin in 1990. This combined Müller's own translation of Shakespeare's play with an original play by Müller, *Hamletmaschine*, to produce a theatrical event finally about the end of modernity itself. An almost autistic Hamlet wandered among television monitors, an alienated and isolated figure amidst the corruption of the court. A gauze replica of a giant ice block seemingly melted, its dripping amplified in the theater, as the sign of the inevitable dissolution of this world. In the second part, the action onstage in modern dress was set against a time tunnel stretching back to the Renaissance, which was understood as the point of origin of our own modernity, which itself had now reached its necessary end.

Far more traditional was Adrian Noble's *Hamlet*, which opened in London late in 1992 at the Barbican and later moved to Stratford-upon-Avon. Noble played the Q2 text almost uncut, and the performance ran well over four hours. Kenneth

Branagh's Hamlet was marked by the depth of his love for his dead father. His melancholy, like his brutal treatment of both Gertrude and Ophelia, derived from his deep sense of violation, which narcissistically he assumed he alone felt. Two years later, Peter Hall directed *Hamlet* at the Gielgud Theatre in London. Stephen Dillane's Hamlet was a brilliant mimic and angry comedian whose humor served to antagonize those who provoked it. In this production, Donald Sinden's Polonius was a shrewd and powerful politician, while Michael Pennington's Claudius was an aggressive and obviously dangerous figure whose propensity to drink made him only the more fearsome. This was a world in which Hamlet had much to fear, and his characteristic mockery seemed, if merited, all too ineffective until the very end, when he emerged in full and terrifying control. He stabbed Claudius first in the leg to immobilize him, before he finally killed him with a vicious sword thrust through his back. The same season saw another London *Hamlet*. Jonathan Kent directed Ralph Fiennes in the title role at the Almeida Theatre, in a production that eventually made its way to New York. Fiennes's Hamlet was impetuous and unreflective, impatient for the future. His soliloquies seemed less evidence of a subtle intelligence genuinely grappling with a moral problem than a sign of a mind caught up in its recurring obsessions. His callous treatment of Gertrude and Ophelia reduced both of them to some form of madness: Francesca Annis's sophisticated and stylish Gertrude became a virtual catatonic, while Tara FitzGerald's Ophelia was reduced to acting out an aggressive sexuality.

In the summer of 2000, John Caird's *Hamlet* opened at the Lyttleton Theatre in London and later transferred to the larger Olivier. Starring Simon Russell Beale, Caird's production completely cut the Fortinbras scenes and indeed most of the play's political aspects. For Caird, *Hamlet* was a play of family trauma. If the conception seemed attenuating, Beale's performance was among the most widely acclaimed of the modern era. His Hamlet was somewhat older and far less physically compelling than most Hamlets—indeed of an age with Claudius (Peter McEnery), the old King's here much younger brother. Beale's

Hamlet seemed truly depressed, meek until driven to rage by the bland unfeelingness of the Queen (Sara Kestelman). He combined a prickly disaffection with a genuine self-loathing. His was a quiet Hamlet, lacking the arrogance and the rant that have become the mark of the character, and only belatedly finding the willingness and energy to act his vengeance as the terrible toll of betrayals mounted.

As originally staged, *Hamlet* must have made good use of the handsome Globe Theatre, where it first appeared. Without scenery, the Globe offered its spectators an impressive evocation of an idea of order, with the heavens above, hell below the trapdoor, and on the main stage the ceremonial magnificence of the court of Denmark. Claudius's appearances are generally marked by ritual, by the presence of throne and crown, by an entourage of obsequious courtiers. Yet Claudius has vitiated all this seeming order by his secret murder, and Hamlet's presence is a continual reminder that all is not well in Denmark. Hamlet attires himself in black, acts strangely, insults the courtiers, makes fun of their ceremoniousness, and prefers to be alone or on the battlements with Horatio and the guard. The Ghost's appearances, too, betoken inversions of order; he reminds us of a greatness now lost to Denmark as he stalks on, usually through the stage doors, in armor and in the full light of day during an afternoon performance at the Globe. He also speaks from beneath the stage. The performance of Hamlet's "Mousetrap" play is a scene of rich panoply that is once again undercut by the secret act of murder now represented in a mimetic drama for the King who is also a murderer. The final scene of *Hamlet* is Claudius's most splendid moment of presiding over the court, until it is suddenly his last moment. The play's reflexive interest in the art of theater is everywhere evident, in Hamlet's instructions to the players and in his appraisal of himself as an actor, as he explores all that it might mean to "act." Shakespeare wrote *Hamlet* with his own theater very much in mind, and, paradoxically, precisely this has allowed it to remain so vibrantly alive on the modern stage.

HAMLET, PRINCE OF DENMARK
ON SCREEN

Shakespeare could not, of course, have imagined a world in which people would see performances of his plays projected onto large or small screens rather than acted live in theaters, but that has become the case. In the more than one hundred years since the first film of a Shakespeare play was made (in 1899, an excerpt from Sir Herbert Beerbohm Tree's production of *King John*), the screen has become Shakespeare's proper medium no less than the stage or the printed page. If Shakespeare's works are undisputedly literary classics and staples of our theatrical repertories, they have also inescapably become a part of the modern age's love affair with film. In a movie theater, on a television screen, or on a DVD player, Shakespeare's plays live for us, and thereby reach audiences much greater than those that fill our theaters.

It is, however, a development not always welcomed. Some critics complain that Shakespeare on screen is different from (and worse than) Shakespeare in the theater. Certainly it is a distinct experience to see a play in a darkened movie theater with actors larger than life. It is different, too, to see it on a television screen with actors smaller than they are in life, and where the experience of play-watching is inevitably more private than in any theater.

But there are obvious advantages as well. On screen, performances are preserved and allowed easily to circulate. If films of Shakespeare may sometimes lack the exhilarating provisionality of live theater, they gain the not insignificant benefit of easy accessibility. In a town without a theater company one can see a Shakespeare play virtually at will. Some newly filmed version of a Shakespeare play is seemingly released every year. A video or DVD can be rented even if the film itself has passed from the local cineplex. And on video we can replay—even interrupt—the performance, allowing it to repeat itself as we attend to details that might otherwise be missed.

Filmed Shakespeare is indeed different from staged Shakespeare or Shakespeare read, but it is no less valuable for being so. It provides a way—and for most of us the most convenient way—to see the plays. For people who cannot get to the theater and who find the printed text difficult to imagine as a theatrical experience, filmed Shakespeare offers easy access to a performance. For students for whom the language of a play often seems (and indeed is) stilted and archaic, the enactment clarifies the psychological and social relations of the characters. For all of us who love Shakespeare, his availability on film gives us an archive of performances to be viewed and enjoyed again and again. It is no less an authentic experience than seeing Shakespeare in the theater, for the modern theater (even the self-conscious anachronisms like the rebuilt Globe) imposes its own anachronisms upon the plays (as indeed does a modern printed edition like this one). And arguably, as many like to claim, if Shakespeare lived today he would most likely have left Stratford for Hollywood.

Not surprisingly, *Hamlet* has appeared on screen more often than any other Shakespeare play. Not only is it arguably his best-known work; with its focus on a brooding central figure and its taut narrative of murder and courtly intrigue, it provides the kind of script that filmmakers yearn for. Although in itself an immense artistic challenge, it poses few of the logistical and conceptual difficulties encountered in translating a fantasy such as *A Midsummer Night's Dream* or *The Tempest*, or the sprawling historical narratives of *Antony and Cleopatra* and the history plays, from stage to screen. Being intensely metatheatrical in its obsession with the world of actors and acting, it positively invites a bringing together and juxtaposition of the various media of theater, film, poetry, the visual arts, and music. Because it is also the perfect vehicle for a lead actor, the play has inspired a roster of film Hamlets that is essentially coexistent with the roster of great Shakespearean actors in modern times. *Hamlet* is made for television, and no less for the movie theater.

Among the fourteen or so silent *Hamlets* that precede the first talking film in 1930, the pioneer was a five-minute film of Sarah Bernhardt as Hamlet in the dueling scene, shot at the Paris Exposition of 1900. Bernhardt had played the breeches part at the Adelphi in the previous year. The famous nineteenth-century actor Johnston Forbes-Robertson is similarly recorded as a sixty-year-old and painfully sensitive Hamlet in a short feature-length silent film of 1913. The most remarkable film of the silent era is from Germany in 1920. Here the Danish star Asta Nielsen plays Hamlet not in the ordinary sort of breeches role but as a Hamlet who really is a woman and who has been raised by her mother, Gertrude, with her gender kept secret in hopes that she may live to inherit the throne. Toward Ophelia this female Hamlet feels no erotic desire. Instead, she responds with jealousy when Horatio shows an interest in Ophelia, for this Hamlet is in love with Horatio. In the closing scene, as Hamlet lies dying in the lap of her beloved Horatio, the distraught friend loosens Hamlet's neckcloth only to discover the astonishing truth: Hamlet has shapely breasts! The interpretation goes a long way toward explaining Hamlet's passivity and repressed sexual feelings, even if at the expense of bending the story a little. Nielsen's performance makes this seventy-eight-minute film worth watching.

Hamlet has been translated into widely divergent cultures worldwide: India (1935 in Hindi and 1955 in Urdu, directed by Kishore Sahu), West Germany (with Maximilian Schell, 1960), France (1962, in English, directed by Claude Chabrol), the Soviet Union (by Grigori Kozintsev, 1963–64), northern Ghana (1964, in Tongo, the home of the Frafra people), Canada (*The Trouble with Hamlet*, 1969, and a complete *Hamlet* in 1973), Brazil (*Heranca*, 1970), Japan (1977), Italy (*Amleto*, 1978), the Netherlands (1980), Poland (1981), Sweden (1984, with Stellan Skarsgård as Hamlet), and still others. In an aggressively postmodernist Spanish film of 1976, directed by Celestino Coronado, twin Hamlets (Anthony and David Meyer) soliloquize jointly in a duologue before confronting Ophelia (Helen Mirren) from the contrasting points of view of a divided sensibility.

"I did love you once," one of them insists, only to be refuted by his twin: "I loved you not" (3.1.116–20).

Hamlet has also inspired an unusually large number of spoofs. One of the earliest, entitled To Be or Not to Be, produced and directed by Ernst Lubitsch in 1942, features Jack Benny as a ham actor whose famous line "To be, or not to be?" turns out to be a secret signal that, unbeknownst to Benny himself, informs a Polish flyer (Robert Stack) sitting in the audience that Benny is now lengthily engaged in his stage performance and that the time has arrived for the flyer to hasten backstage and join Benny's wife (Carole Lombard) in her dressing room for an assignation. Hamlet Goes Business (Finnish, 1987) is about an industrial giant in modern-day Helsinki who kills his brother to gain control of a firm called Swedish Rubber Ducks, only to be foiled by his sex-starved, blithering nephew Hamlet and a chauffeur (the Horatio equivalent) who is a trade union spy. In Last Action Hero (1993), a short sequence features Arnold Schwarzenegger as Hamlet, whose meditation on the unavoidable question "To be, or not to be?" leads him to conclude that it is "Not to be." As he speaks, Elsinore Castle blows sky-high. W. S. Gilbert and G. B. Shaw had written send-ups on Hamlet earlier, but they are not recorded on film.

More seriously, Akira Kurosawa's The Bad Sleep Well (Japan, 1960) is about a thoughtful young businessman named Nishi (Toshiro Mifune) who suffers torments of conscience as he ponders the heavy assignment of avenging the death of his father in a suicide prompted by the bribe-taking of the villainous Iwabuchi (Takeshi Kato), now the powerful head of Japan Land Corporation.

Laurence Olivier's Hamlet (1948), following upon his success with Henry V in 1944, ushered in an era in which Shakespeare filmmaking rightfully belonged to this much-acclaimed star of the British stage. The film did exceptionally well in Britain and the United States, becoming the first and only Shakespeare film to win an Academy Award until the advent of Shakespeare in Love (1998). It had overcome the opprobrium of being exclusively high culture; as an underling enthusiastically reported to the film's financial backer, J. Arthur Rank, while the shooting was in progress, "Wonderful, Mr. Rank. You wouldn't even know it was Shakespeare." Olivier achieved this transformation in part by heavily cutting the script to bring it down to a digestible film length, removing the entire Fortinbras story as well as Rosencrantz and Guildenstern. The move had been made before on stage and was to be repeated in film; Hamlet is an unusually long script and probably was never acted in anything like its entirety in Shakespeare's lifetime.

Beginning with a voice-over of Olivier intoning, "This is the tragedy of a man who could not make up his mind," as the camera pans past the outside window of Gertrude's bedchamber, Olivier's Hamlet seems wedded to the notion, derived from Ernest Jones's Hamlet and Oedipus (who in turn had lifted the idea from Freud himself), that the hero is mesmerized by an Oedipal conflict compelling him to be indecisive about killing an uncle who is only doing what Hamlet himself unconsciously desires in Oedipal terms, that is, to repossess his mother as the object of his muted incestuous longing. Fortunately, Olivier does not stick to this concept as the film unfolds. He is alternately princely, despondent, furious, alienated, deeply caring, introspective, satiric, noble, rebellious, and loyal. The camera follows him through the winding passageways and staircases of Elsinore and up to the battlements as he encounters his father's ghost, arraigns Ophelia (Jean Simmons) for inconstancy, scoffs at her father, Polonius (Felix Aylmer), and confronts his mother (Eileen Herlie) with her crime of desertion. The castle is indeed a living presence in this film, seen in black and white from crane shots high and low. Olivier meditates on suicide as he looks down from "the dreadful summit of the cliff / That beetles o'er its base into the sea" (1.4.70–1). In conversation with Horatio (Norman Wooland) and the gravedigger (Stanley Holloway) about death, Olivier's Hamlet is wise, compassionate, and witty. The exciting dueling scene at the climax leads into an emblematic finale in which Claudius (Basil Sydney), mortally stricken and having been unable to prevent Gertrude from drinking from the poisoned cup, reaches out desperately toward the throne, the crown, and his queen as the guilty possessions that will now elude him forever. Hamlet dies reconciled to his mother, as Horatio, overwhelmed with grief, ends the film on the hope that "flights of angels" will sing Hamlet to his rest (5.2.362). By eliminating the Fortinbras story, Olivier is thus able to focus in conclusion on the death of a noble prince who, had he been invested in the throne, would have "proved most royal." Soldiers carry the dead Hamlet to the ramparts. In Shakespeare's text, the last words of encomium and the royal commands are given to Fortinbras; Olivier insists that the end belongs to Hamlet alone.

Grigori Kozintsev's *Hamlet* (1964), also in black and white, and starring Innokenti Smoktunovsky as the protagonist and Elza Radzina-Szolkonis as Gertrude, is, as the director has explained, a visual study in the elemental natural forces of earth, sea, stone, and fire. Based on a production staged in Leningrad in 1954 after the death of Joseph Stalin in 1953 and then filmed by the USSR's great director, who had himself been incarcerated in a prison camp during World War II, this version necessarily took on the political resonance of a struggle against oppression. By using the translation into Russian by Boris Pasternak and a powerful musical score by Dmitri Shostakovich (both of these men being identifiably defenders of artistic integrity in a totalitarian society), the director underscores Hamlet's tormented distress at what, in Kozintsev's words, "is happening in the prison state around him." An iron corset and farthingale imprison Ophelia (Anastasia Vertinskaya), emblems of lost personal freedom. The gravedigger's hammer echoes loudly as he nails down the lid of her coffin. The walls, drawbridge, and huge spiked portcullis of Elsinore are those of a state prison; iron weapons insistently call to mind the cruel oppression of war. The sea crashes ceaselessly against the shore. Amid stony fields, sand pours out of Yorick's skull. A monumental runic cross in the graveyard, battered by time and human indifference, lacks one of its transverse members. "Life's numberless trivia," said Kozintsev, render that life "senseless," "draining it of spiritual meaning." Against this hollowness stands Hamlet as existentialist rebel and sacrificial victim.

The modern-dress *Hamlet* directed by John Gielgud on Broadway in 1964 and then translated by Bill Colleran into Electronovision that same year, with Richard Burton in the title role, achieved its transformation to television by means of several handheld cameras variously positioned in the course of three performances to provide a multitudinous perspective. Having then been collated into a single show, it was broadcast four times to some 976 movie theater audiences throughout the United States. This revolutionary process resulted in a dimly lit screen and poor sound quality, since no compromises were made with the lighting of the stage production, but the cutting effects made possible by such a process were at times riveting. Burton's performance, too, though uneven, exudes power, intellect, and seriousness. Not for Burton is the brooding Hamlet of the Coleridgean tradition; this Hamlet swaggers, pouts, threatens, and brawls. A nearly uncut text also provides opportunities, not always expertly fulfilled, for Hume Cronyn as Polonius, Eileen Herlie (a veteran from Olivier's film) as Gertrude, John Gielgud as the voice of the Ghost, Alfred Drake as a particularly unsuccessful Claudius, and Linda Marsh as Ophelia. Despite these many defects, we should no doubt be thankful that not all copies of this unusual film were destroyed, as stipulated in the contract. After only two days' showing in the movie houses, to the considerable enrichment of Burton, the film is now available in voice recordings and videocassette.

Nicol Williamson's rapid-fire but crisply clear delivery of Hamlet's lines is a distinguishing feature of a 1969 film, successfully directed by Tony Richardson onstage and then shot for television at London's Roundhouse Theatre. The shadowy atmosphere of a theater space that once had been a railway locomotive-turning shed adapts itself well to an Elsinore Castle in which the bare theater walls provide the setting, devoid of scenic effects. A white spotlight evokes the presence of the Ghost. Close-up shots enhance a claustrophic sense of no exit. Williamson is brilliant, surprising, recognizably an angry young man of the late sixties protesting against the swinish epicureanism of Claudius (Anthony Hopkins) and Gertrude (Judy Parfitt) and the mindless conformity of Polonius (Mark Dignam) and his dysfunctional family (Michael Pennington as a dissolute Laertes and Marianne Faithfull as an inanimate Ophelia, incestuously attracted to each other). Williamson, frenetic and restless, ungainly, intensely physical, endowed with a thick proletarian accent, is as much antitraditional Hamlet as antiestablishment rebel. The cast should be a strong one, with Hopkins as Claudius and Pennington as Laertes, but Williamson dominates and the humor of *Hamlet* has disappeared, along with Fortinbras.

A *Hallmark Hall of Fame* production for NBC, in 1970, heavily cut for television, is noteworthy for its distinguished cast, including Richard Chamberlain as Hamlet, Michael Redgrave as Polonius, Margaret Leighton as a sensual Gertrude, Richard Johnson as an unpleasant Claudius, and John Gielgud as the Ghost. Chamberlain's passionate and idealistic Hamlet is a tortured soul, distressed as much by revulsion at his mother's sexual carrying-on with Claudius as by the Ghost's commandment of revenge. This is a highly intelligent and courageous *Hamlet*, not deserving the oblivion into which it has fallen. Gielgud, one of the great Hamlets onstage, plays the Ghost here, as he did in the Burton Electronovision *Hamlet* of 1964, which he also directed, but he never starred in a film version of this play.

Derek Jacobi, later to excel as Claudius in Branagh's 1996 film *Hamlet*, is the star of the 1980 BBC production for Time-Life Television, produced by Cedric Messina and directed by Rodney Bennett. With its nearly intact Shakespearean text and unusually strong cast, including Claire Bloom as an intelligent and sympathetic Gertrude, Patrick Stewart as a guileful Claudius, and Eric Porter as a warm and sensitive Polonius, this is one of the best of the BBC Plays of Shakespeare series. Jacobi's Hamlet is passionate, neurotic, and impetuous, by no means confined to introspection and hesitancy. A relatively uncluttered set relies on sparse details and props, keeping the focus on the actors.

Franco Zeffirelli's decision to cast Mel Gibson as Hamlet for his 1990 production, along with Alan Bates as Claudius, Glenn Close as Gertrude, Helena Bonham Carter as Ophelia, Ian Holm as Polonius, and Paul Scofield as the Ghost, was transparently a move to win audiences through celebrity appeal. And it did achieve a respectable commercial success, even if its $20 million gross in the United States (at a cost of $15 million) was far less than that of

Gibson's other action films. This, too, is an action film. Gibson is constantly on the move, athletically scaling the battlements, dealing brusquely and even violently with Rosencrantz and Guildenstern, stabbing Polonius, browbeating and nearly raping his mother, overpowering his enemies in the final duel and catastrophe. Left behind in the wake of this manly display is the brooding, introspective Hamlet of theatrical tradition. A severe cutting of the play script to less than 40 percent of its original augments the onrush toward mayhem. The other major actors' reputations are no less integral to their performances. Glenn Close, awesome as a dangerously passion-driven woman in *Fatal Attraction*, portrays Gertrude as a woman who knows what she wants. In this case she wants Claudius—as, indeed, what woman is supposed to be indifferent to the cuddly sex appeal of Alan Bates? Gertrude in this interpretation is anything but a hesitant, submissive woman who has married Claudius simply because he is importunate and accustomed to having his way; this Gertrude is almost as seriously guilty as her new husband because she so willingly embraces what fate and circumstance have given her. Claudius's desire for Gertrude is so vibrant, and his male charm is so hearty in the midst of his nearly incessant drinking, that one nearly forgets that he has murdered his brother and has stolen the throne from his nephew. Bonham Carter is familiar as the attractive, jittery, feisty sufferer of an unhappy love relationship, as in many a Merchant-Ivory film, such as *Twelfth Night* or *Howards End*. Zeffirelli is not afraid to exploit celebrity typecasting of this sort. Nor does he deny the viewer any of his celebrated lavishness in scenic effects. The film is often gorgeous, as in its depiction of the graveyard where Ophelia is laid to her eternal rest. The costumes and architecture are richly appropriate to a film intent on visual authenticity. All is quite beautiful. The characters are a little one-dimensional.

In that same year, 1990, PBS television (in WNET/Thirteen's Great Performances series) brought out a *Hamlet* directed by Kevin Kline and Kirk Browning, based on a Public Theater performance, with Kline as Hamlet. The timing was disastrous. Pitted hopelessly against the Zeffirelli-Gibson juggernaut, this version was broadcast only once and has generally been forgotten. This is a great pity. It is the opposite of its nemesis in every way: never showy or blatantly commercial, it focuses quietly on superb performances and intelligent interpretation of the script. Dana Ivey as Gertrude, Diane Venora as Ophelia, Brian Murray as Claudius, Michael Cumpsty as Laertes, Peter Francis James as Horatio, and especially Kline as Hamlet understand every word they say, and provide just the right hand and facial gestures. No doubt this version is penalized by its being a studio production that lacks physical movement, but the acting deserves to be savored.

Kenneth Branagh, having challenged Laurence Olivier with his *Henry V* (1989) and having succeeded no less well with *Much Ado About Nothing* (1993), simply had to do *Hamlet*. His great achievement, in 1996–97, was to insist on an uncut script. At four hours in length, it required an intermission for the screenings. The length manifestly has deterred some potential viewers from taking the plunge. What is so remarkable about the result, nevertheless, is that audiences can savor the entire role of Claudius, which is often severely cut by abridgments in the play's fourth act. Derek Jacobi, in a brilliant performance, realizes the part in all its chilling complexity. Julie Christie as Gertrude shows emotional range in the scene where Hamlet confronts her with her guilt, as she moves from defensive denial to terror and then to tearful penitence. Kate Winslet as Ophelia moves vast distances from the hopeful hesitancy of a young lover to distraught insanity as she is confined to a straitjacket. Richard Briers's Polonius is arrestingly original: no doddering old fool he, but a canny father and senior courtier all too aware that he is the object of Hamlet's scorn. Exterior shots of Blenheim Palace and studio interiors representing its great halls and waiting rooms provide a handsome mise-en-scène. The choice of a late-nineteenth-century time frame lends itself to elegantly handsome costuming.

At the same time, the film is plagued with erratic directorial judgments. Branagh himself, as Hamlet, is too frequently over the top; during the play within the play, he is obnoxious. Celebrity cameos, making a significant bow in the direction of commercial cachet, are sometimes briefly amusing but at other times grotesque. Robin Williams gives an offbeat performance as Osric, and Charlton Heston intones sonorously as the Player King, but Jack Lemmon as Marcellus and Gérard Depardieu as Reynaldo are disasters saved only by the brevity of their appearances. Billy Crystal as the Gravedigger, with his Brooklyn accent, seems to have wandered onto the wrong movie set. Silent appearances by John Gielgud and Judi Dench add little other than to the name-dropping roster. Branagh's decision to be visually explicit about Ophelia's loss of virginity to Hamlet seems a cheap and anachronistic way of characterizing their relationship, as though to argue that two young people like this could not be serious about each other without having gone to bed together. The earthquakelike moving of the earth in the scene with the Ghost seems concocted as a way of providing up-to-date special effects. The handsome Blenheim setting is subjected in the finale to a gratuitous invasion by Fortinbras's army, smashing windows and leaping over railings in a sequence of which the Zeffirelli-Gibson action *Hamlet* might have been proud. Still, this is an important and generally successful film. It resonates powerfully with the crisis of the British monarchy in the late 1990s—the family scandals, the sensational death of Princess Diana in 1997, the fascinated, unhealthy voyeurism about private lives made garishly public, the recent collapse of Soviet communism, the millennial apprehensiveness about an approaching apocalypse and the end of history.

Michael Almereyda's *Hamlet* (2000) demonstrates brilliantly how a low-budget, modern-setting adaptation can be made to illuminate the text that has inspired it. The story is translated to the concrete-and-steel canyons of Manhattan, where Claudius (Kyle MacLachlan) is the chief executive officer of Denmark Corporation, a multinational conglomerate headquartered near Times Square. Gertrude (Diane Venora), his recent bride, is a handsome suburban woman for whom luxurious creature comforts mean everything. Together they savor the sybaritic pleasures of stretch limousines and a private swimming pool in their luxury high-rise Elsinore Hotel. This claustrophobic world of privilege has its more menacing aspect as well, conveyed to us by images of a closed-circuit video security system. The Ghost of Hamlet's father, wonderfully portrayed by the playwright Sam Shepard, appears and vanishes on the TV system and on the high stone balconies that serve as this movie's battlements. Hamlet (Ethan Hawke), in this scenario, is a rebel with a cause. Outfitted in a Peruvian woolen hat and a studiously informal getup, he stands out as an alienated and misunderstood youth. His passion being for digital cameras and filmmaking, he naturally undertakes to shock his hated uncle with an experimental film—the equivalent of the Mousetrap play-within-the-play. Gadgetry meaningfully pervades this multimedia, reflexively metatheatrical film about film. Hamlet detects the wire that Polonius (Bill Murray) and Claudius have planted on Ophelia for her interview with Hamlet. He communicates with her on her answering machine. When Hamlet is being escorted on an overnight flight to England by Rosencrantz and Guildenstern, he takes advantage of their being sound asleep to investigate their laptop computer in the overhead luggage rack, and when he finds there the incriminating message they are carrying to the King of England ordering the execution of Hamlet, the Prince simply substitutes their names for his. These media stunts underscore the vast extent to which this *Hamlet* has been updated to the opening year of the twenty-first century. Some reviewers have been put off, but for many the wit of the visual metaphors carries the day. Murray is refreshingly intelligent as Polonius, and his children (Liev Schreiber as Laertes and Julia Stiles as Ophelia) make good sense of their scenes.

Other famous Hamlets have included Maurice Evans (NBC, April 26, 1953), John Neville (Old Vic production on CBS's *Show of the Month*, February 24, 1959), and Christopher Plummer (BBC/Danmarks Radio, 1964), taped at Elsinore Castle, Denmark.

Hamlet: Filmography (selected)

1. 1900, *Le duel d'Hamlet* (3 minutes)
   Phono-Cinéma-Théâtre
   Clément Maurice, producer-director

   Hamlet—Sarah Bernhardt

2. 1913 (59 minutes)
Gaumont
Cecil M. Hepworth, producer
E. Hay Plumb, director

   Hamlet—Johnston Forbes-Robertson
   Ophelia—Gertrude Elliot
   Marcellus—Robert Atkins
   Polonius—J. H. Barnes
   Claudius—Walter Ringham

3. 1917, *Amleto*
Rodolfi Films
Eleuterio Rodolfi, director

   Hamlet—Ruggero Ruggeri
   Ophelia—Helena Makowska

4. 1920, *Hamlet, The Drama of Vengeance*
Art-Film
Svend Gade and Heinz Schall, directors

   Hamlet—Asta Nielson
   Gertrude—Mathilde Brandt
   Ophelia—Lilly Jacobssen

5. 1933 (5 minutes, from 1.4 and 3.1)
MGM
A screen test for a film never made

   Hamlet—John Barrymore
   Marcellus—Donald Crisp

6. 1948
Two City Films
Laurence Olivier, producer and director

   Hamlet—Laurence Olivier
   Ophelia—Jean Simmons
   Marcellus—Anthony Quayle
   Polonius—Felix Aylmer

   Gertrude—Eileen Herlie
   Horatio—Norman Wooland
   Claudius—Basil Sydney
   Gravedigger—Stanley Holloway

7. 1953
   NBC TV
   Hallmark Hall of Fame
   Albert McCleery, producer
   George Schaeffer, director

   Hamlet—Maurice Evans
   Gertrude—Ruth Chatterton
   Ophelia—Sarah Churchill
   Claudius—George Schildkraut

8. 1959
   CBS TV
   Dupont Show of the Month
   Michael Benthall, producer
   Ralph Nelson, director

   Hamlet—John Neville
   Gertrude—Margaret Courtenay
   Ophelia—Barbara Jefford
   Claudius—Oliver Neville

9. 1964, *Hamlet at Elsinore*
   BBC/Danmarks Radio
   Philip Saville, director

   Hamlet—Christopher Plummer
   Claudius—Robert Shaw
   Polonius—Alec Clunes
   Horatio—Michael Caine

10. 1964
    Classic Cinemas (film of stage performance at
       Lunt-Fontanne Theatre)
    Bill Colleran, director

Hamlet—Richard Burton
Polonius—Hume Cronyn
Gertrude—Eileen Herlie
Claudius—Alfred Drake
Ophelia—Linda Marsh
Ghost—John Gielgud

11. 1964
Lenfilm (Russian trans. by Boris Pasternak,
    with English subtitles)
Grigori Kozintsev, director

Hamlet—Innokenti Smoktunovsky
Claudius—Michail Nazwanov
Ophelia—Anastasia Vertinskaya
Gertrude—Elza Radzina-Szolkonis

12. 1964, *Hamile: The Tongo Hamlet*
Ghana Films
Terry Bishop, director

Hamile/Hamlet—Kofi Middetan-Mends
Habiba/Ophelia—Mary Yirenkyi
Musa/Marcellus—Jacob Gharbin
Ibrahim/Polonius—Ernest Abbeyquaye
King/Claudius—Joe Akoror

13. 1969
Woodfall Productions/Columbia Pictures
Leslie Linder, producer
Tony Richardson, director

Hamlet—Nicol Williamson
Ophelia—Marianne Faithfull
Polonius—Mark Dignam
Claudius—Anthony Hopkins
Laertes—Michael Pennington
Gertrude—Judy Parfitt

14. 1970
    NBC TV
    Hallmark Hall of Fame
    Peter Wood, director

    > Hamlet—Richard Chamberlain
    > Ghost—John Gielgud
    > Claudius—Richard Johnson
    > Polonius—Michael Redgrave
    > Gertrude—Margaret Leighton
    > Ophelia—Clara Madden

15. 1976
    Cabochon
    Celestino Coronado, producer and director

    > Hamlet and Ghost—Anthony Meyer/David Meyer
    > Ophelia and Gertrude—Helen Mirren
    > Polonius—Quentin Crisp

16. 1980
    BBC/Time-Life Television
    Cedric Messina, producer
    Rodney Bennett, director

    > Hamlet—Derek Jacobi
    > Ophelia—Lalla Ward
    > Gertrude—Claire Bloom
    > Claudius—Patrick Stewart
    > Polonius—Eric Porter

17. 1990
    Warner Brothers
    Dyson Lovell, producer
    Franco Zeffirelli, director

    > Hamlet—Mel Gibson
    > Gertrude—Glenn Close
    > Claudius—Alan Bates
    > Polonius—Ian Holm

Ophelia—Helena Bonham Carter
Marcellus—Christian Anholt
Ghost—Paul Scofield

18. 1990
PBS Television, Great Performances
Kirk Browning and Kevin Kline, directors

Hamlet—Kevin Kline
Ophelia—Diane Venora
Laertes—Michael Cumpsty
Horatio—Peter Francis James
Gertrude—Dana Ivey
Claudius—Brian Murray

19. 1996
Columbia
David Barron, producer
Kenneth Branagh, director

Hamlet—Kenneth Branagh
Ophelia—Kate Winslet
Gertrude—Julie Christie
Polonius—Richard Briers
Claudius—Derek Jacobi
Marcellus—Jack Lemmon

20. 2000
Miramax
Jason Blum and Andrew Fierberg, producers
Michael Almereyda, director

Hamlet—Ethan Hawke
Ophelia—Julia Stiles
Gertrude—Diane Venora
Polonius—Bill Murray
Claudius—Kyle MacLachlan
Ghost—Sam Shepard
Laertes—Liev Schreiber

Adaptations:

1. 1942, *To Be or Not to Be*
   United Artists
   Ernst Lubitsch, producer and director

   > Jack Benny
   > Carole Lombard
   > Anne Bancroft

2. 1960, *The Bad Sleep Well*
   Kurosawa Productions
   Akira Kurosawa, producer and director

   > Toshiro Mifune
   > Kyoko Kagawa
   > Masyuki Mori
   > Takeshi Kato

3. 1983, *To Be or Not to Be*
   20th Century Fox
   Alan Johnson, director

   > Mel Brooks
   > Anne Bancroft
   > Charles Durning

4. 1987, *Hamlet Goes Business* (Finnish)
   Villealfa Filmproduction
   Aki Kaurismäki, director

   > Hamlet—Pirkka-Pekka Petelius
   > Ophelia—Kati Outinen
   > Gertrude—Elina Salo
   > Polonius—Esko Nikkari

5. 1995, *The Fifteen-Minute Hamlet* (by Tom Stoppard)
   Cin-Ciné 19
   Todd Louiso, director

   > Hamlet—Austin Pendleton
   > Ophelia—Todd Louiso
   > Claudius and Polonius—Ernest Perry Jr.

This early copy of a drawing by Johannes de Witt of the Swan Theatre in London (c. 1596), made by his friend Arend van Buchell, is the only surviving contemporary sketch of the interior of a public theater in the 1590s.

THE PLAYHOUSE

From other contemporary evidence, including the stage directions and dialogue of Elizabethan plays, we can surmise that the various public theaters where Shakespeare's plays were produced (the Theatre, the Curtain, the Globe) resembled the Swan in many important particulars, though there must have been some variations as well. The public playhouses were essentially round, or polygonal, and open to the sky, forming an acting arena approximately 70 feet in diameter; they did not have a large curtain with which to open and close a scene, such as we see today in opera and some traditional theater. A platform measuring approximately 43 feet across and 27 feet deep, referred to in the de Witt drawing as the *proscaenium*, projected into the yard, *planities sive arena*. The roof, *tectum*, above the stage and supported by two pillars, could contain machinery for ascents and descents, as were required in several of Shakespeare's late plays. Above this roof was a hut, shown in the drawing with a flag flying atop it and a trumpeter at its door announcing the performance of a play. The underside of the stage roof, called the heavens, was usually richly decorated with symbolic figures of the sun, the moon, and the constellations. The platform stage stood at a height of 5½ feet or so above the yard, providing room under the stage for underworldly effects. A trapdoor, which is not visible in this drawing, gave access to the space below.

The structure at the back of the platform (labeled *mimorum aedes*), known as the tiring-house because it was the actors' attiring (dressing) space, featured at least two doors, as shown here. Some theaters seem to have also had a discovery space, or curtained recessed alcove, perhaps between the two doors—in which Falstaff could have hidden from the sheriff (*1 Henry IV*, 2.4) or Polonius could have eavesdropped on Hamlet and his mother (*Hamlet*, 3.4). This discovery space probably gave the actors a means of access to and from the tiring-house. Curtains may also have been hung in front of the stage doors on occasion. The de Witt drawing shows a gallery above the doors that extends across the back and evidently contains spectators. On occasions when action "above" demanded the use of this space, as when Juliet appears at her "window" (*Romeo and Juliet*, 2.2 and 3.5), the gallery seems to have been used by the actors, but large scenes there were impractical.

The three-tiered auditorium is perhaps best described by Thomas Platter, a visitor to London in 1599 who saw on that occasion Shakespeare's *Julius Caesar* performed at the Globe:

> The playhouses are so constructed that they play on a raised platform, so that everyone has a good view. There are different galleries and places [*orchestra, sedilia, porticus*], however, where the seating is better and more comfortable and therefore more expensive. For whoever cares to stand below only pays one English penny, but if he wishes to sit, he enters by another door [*ingressus*] and pays another penny, while if he desires to sit in the most comfortable seats, which are cushioned, where he not only sees everything well but can also be seen, then he pays yet another English penny at another door. And during the performance food and drink are carried round the audience, so that for what one cares to pay one may also have refreshment.

Scenery was not used, though the theater building itself was handsome enough to invoke a feeling of order and hierarchy that lent itself to the splendor and pageantry onstage. Portable properties, such as thrones, stools, tables, and beds, could be carried or thrust on as needed. In the scene pictured here by de Witt, a lady on a bench, attended perhaps by her waiting-gentlewoman, receives the address of a male figure. If Shakespeare had written *Twelfth Night* by 1596 for performance at the Swan, we could imagine Malvolio appearing like this as he bows before the Countess Olivia and her gentlewoman, Maria.

HAMLET,
PRINCE OF DENMARK

[Dramatis Personae

GHOST of Hamlet, the former King of Denmark

CLAUDIUS, King of Denmark, the former King's brother

GERTRUDE, Queen of Denmark, widow of the former King and now wife of Claudius

HAMLET, Prince of Denmark, son of the late King and of Gertrude

POLONIUS, councillor to the King

LAERTES, his son

OPHELIA, his daughter

REYNALDO, his servant

HORATIO, Hamlet's friend and fellow student

VOLTIMAND,
CORNELIUS,
ROSENCRANTZ,
GUILDENSTERN,   members of the Danish court
OSRIC,
A GENTLEMAN,
A LORD,

BERNARDO,
FRANCISCO, } *officers and soldiers on watch*
MARCELLUS,

FORTINBRAS, *Prince of Norway*
CAPTAIN *in his army*

Three or Four PLAYERS, *taking the roles of* PROLOGUE, PLAYER
    KING, PLAYER QUEEN, *and* LUCIANUS
Two MESSENGERS
FIRST SAILOR
Two CLOWNS, *a gravedigger and his companion*
PRIEST
FIRST AMBASSADOR *from England*

*Lords, Soldiers, Attendants, Guards, other Players, Followers of
    Laertes, other Sailors, another Ambassador or Ambassadors
    from England*

SCENE: *Denmark*]

1.1 *Location: Elsinore castle. A guard platform.*

2 **me** (Francisco emphasizes that *he* is the sentry currently on watch.) **unfold yourself** reveal your identity.

14 **rivals** partners

16 **ground** country, land.

17 **liegemen to the Dane** men sworn to serve the Danish king.

18 **Give** May God give

[1.1] ❧ *Enter Bernardo and Francisco, two sentinels,*
[meeting].

BERNARDO Who's there?

FRANCISCO
Nay, answer me. Stand and unfold yourself.   2

BERNARDO Long live the King!

FRANCISCO Bernardo?

BERNARDO He.

FRANCISCO
You come most carefully upon your hour.

BERNARDO
'Tis now struck twelve. Get thee to bed, Francisco.

FRANCISCO
For this relief much thanks. 'Tis bitter cold,
And I am sick at heart.

BERNARDO Have you had quiet guard?

FRANCISCO Not a mouse stirring.

BERNARDO Well, good night.
If you do meet Horatio and Marcellus,
The rivals of my watch, bid them make haste.   14

Enter Horatio and Marcellus.

FRANCISCO
I think I hear them.—Stand, ho! Who is there?

HORATIO Friends to this ground.   16

MARCELLUS And liegemen to the Dane.   17

FRANCISCO Give you good night.   18

MARCELLUS
Oh, farewell, honest soldier. Who hath relieved you?

27 **fantasy** imagination
30 **along** to come along
31 **watch** keep watch during
33 **approve** corroborate
39 **Last . . . all** i.e., This *very* last night. (Emphatic.)
40 **pole** polestar, north star
41 **his** its.   **t'illume** to illuminate

FRANCISCO
>Bernardo hath my place. Give you good night.
>>>>>>>>>>>>>>>>>>>>>>>>>>>>>>>*Exit Francisco.*

MARCELLUS   Holla! Bernardo!

BERNARDO   Say, what, is Horatio there?

HORATIO   A piece of him.

BERNARDO
>Welcome, Horatio. Welcome, good Marcellus.

HORATIO
>What, has this thing appeared again tonight?

BERNARDO   I have seen nothing.

MARCELLUS
>Horatio says 'tis but our fantasy,   27
>And will not let belief take hold of him
>Touching this dreaded sight twice seen of us.
>Therefore I have entreated him along   30
>With us to watch the minutes of this night,   31
>That if again this apparition come
>He may approve our eyes and speak to it.   33

HORATIO
>Tush, tush, 'twill not appear.

BERNARDO   Sit down awhile
>And let us once again assail your ears,
>That are so fortified against our story,
>What we have two nights seen.

HORATIO   Well, sit we down,
>And let us hear Bernardo speak of this.

BERNARDO   Last night of all,   39
>When yond same star that's westward from the pole   40
>Had made his course t'illume that part of heaven   41
>Where now it burns, Marcellus and myself,
>The bell then beating one—

>>>>>>>>>>>>>>>>>>>>>>>>>>>>>>>>*Enter Ghost.*

46 **scholar** one learned enough to know how to question a ghost properly.

47 **'a** he

49 **It ... to** (It was commonly believed that a ghost could not speak until spoken to.)

50 **usurp'st** wrongfully takes over

52 **buried Denmark** the buried King of Denmark

53 **sometimes** formerly

59 **on't** of it.

61 **sensible** confirmed by the senses.   **avouch** warrant, evidence

MARCELLUS
    Peace, break thee off! Look where it comes again!

BERNARDO
    In the same figure like the King that's dead.

MARCELLUS
    Thou art a scholar. Speak to it, Horatio.   46

BERNARDO
    Looks 'a not like the King? Mark it, Horatio.   47

HORATIO
    Most like. It harrows me with fear and wonder.

BERNARDO
    It would be spoke to.

MARCELLUS   Speak to it, Horatio.   49

HORATIO
    What art thou that usurp'st this time of night,   50
    Together with that fair and warlike form
    In which the majesty of buried Denmark   52
    Did sometimes march? By heaven, I charge thee, speak!   53

MARCELLUS
    It is offended.

BERNARDO   See, it stalks away.

HORATIO
    Stay! Speak, speak! I charge thee, speak!   *Exit Ghost.*

MARCELLUS   'Tis gone and will not answer.

BERNARDO
    How now, Horatio? You tremble and look pale.
    Is not this something more than fantasy?
    What think you on't?   59

HORATIO
    Before my God, I might not this believe
    Without the sensible and true avouch   61
    Of mine own eyes.

MARCELLUS   Is it not like the King?

65 **Norway** King of Norway
66 **parle** parley
67 **sledded** traveling on sleds.   **Polacks** Poles
69 **jump** exactly
70 **stalk** stride
71 **to work** i.e., to collect my thoughts and try to understand this
72 **gross and scope** general drift
74 **Good now** (An expression denoting entreaty or expostulation.)
76 **toils** causes to toil.   **subject** subjects
77 **cast** casting
78 **mart** shopping
79 **impress** impressment, conscription
81 **toward** in preparation
87 **Thereto . . . pride** (Refers to old Fortinbras, not the Danish King.)   **pricked on** incited.   **emulate** emulous, ambitious
89 **this . . . world** i.e., all Europe, the Western world
90 **sealed** certified, confirmed
91 **heraldry** chivalry
93 **seized** possessed

HORATIO   As thou art to thyself.
   Such was the very armor he had on
   When he the ambitious Norway combated.   65
   So frowned he once when, in an angry parle,   66
   He smote the sledded Polacks on the ice.   67
   'Tis strange.

MARCELLUS
   Thus twice before, and jump at this dead hour,   69
   With martial stalk hath he gone by our watch.   70

HORATIO
   In what particular thought to work I know not,   71
   But in the gross and scope of mine opinion   72
   This bodes some strange eruption to our state.

MARCELLUS
   Good now, sit down, and tell me, he that knows,   74
   Why this same strict and most observant watch
   So nightly toils the subject of the land,   76
   And why such daily cast of brazen cannon   77
   And foreign mart for implements of war,   78
   Why such impress of shipwrights, whose sore task   79
   Does not divide the Sunday from the week.
   What might be toward, that this sweaty haste   81
   Doth make the night joint-laborer with the day?
   Who is't that can inform me?

HORATIO   That can I;
   At least, the whisper goes so. Our last king,
   Whose image even but now appeared to us,
   Was, as you know, by Fortinbras of Norway,
   Thereto pricked on by a most emulate pride,   87
   Dared to the combat; in which our valiant Hamlet—
   For so this side of our known world esteemed him—   89
   Did slay this Fortinbras; who by a sealed compact   90
   Well ratified by law and heraldry   91
   Did forfeit, with his life, all those his lands
   Which he stood seized of, to the conqueror;   93

94 **Against the** in return for.   **moiety competent** corresponding portion

95 **gagèd** engaged, pledged.   **had returned** would have passed

96 **inheritance** possession

97 **cov'nant** i.e., the *sealed compact* of line 90

98 **carriage . . . designed** purport of the article referred to

100 **unimprovèd mettle** untried, undisciplined spirits

101 **skirts** outlying regions, outskirts

102–4 **Sharked . . . in't** rounded up (as a shark scoops up fish) a troop of lawless desperadoes to feed and supply an enterprise of considerable daring

110 **head** source

111 **posthaste and rummage** frenetic activity and bustle

113 **Well . . . sort** That would explain why

115 **question** focus of contention

116 **mote** speck of dust

117 **palmy** flourishing

118 **Julius** Julius Caesar

119 **sheeted** shrouded

121 **As** (This abrupt transition suggests that matter is possibly omitted between lines 120 and 121.)   **trains** trails

122 **Disasters** unfavorable signs or aspects.   **moist star** i.e., moon, governing tides

123 **Neptune's . . . stands** the sea depends

124 **Was . . . eclipse** was eclipsed nearly to the cosmic darkness predicted for the second coming of Christ and the ending of the world. (See Matthew 24:29 and Revelation 6:12.)

125 **precurse** heralding, foreshadowing

126 **harbingers** forerunners.   **still** always

Against the which a moiety competent   94
Was gagèd by our king, which had returned   95
To the inheritance of Fortinbras   96
Had he been vanquisher, as, by the same cov'nant   97
And carriage of the article designed,   98
His fell to Hamlet. Now, sir, young Fortinbras,
Of unimprovèd mettle hot and full,   100
Hath in the skirts of Norway here and there   101
Sharked up a list of lawless resolutes   102
For food and diet to some enterprise   103
That hath a stomach in't, which is no other—   104
As it doth well appear unto our state—
But to recover of us, by strong hand
And terms compulsatory, those foresaid lands
So by his father lost. And this, I take it,
Is the main motive of our preparations,
The source of this our watch, and the chief head   110
Of this posthaste and rummage in the land.   111

BERNARDO
    I think it be no other but e'en so.
    Well may it sort that this portentous figure   113
    Comes armèd through our watch so like the King
    That was and is the question of these wars.   115

HORATIO
    A mote it is to trouble the mind's eye.   116
    In the most high and palmy state of Rome,   117
    A little ere the mightiest Julius fell,   118
    The graves stood tenantless, and the sheeted dead   119
    Did squeak and gibber in the Roman streets;
    As stars with trains of fire and dews of blood,   121
    Disasters in the sun; and the moist star   122
    Upon whose influence Neptune's empire stands   123
    Was sick almost to doomsday with eclipse.   124
    And even the like precurse of feared events,   125
    As harbingers preceding still the fates   126

127 **omen** calamitous event

129 **climatures** climes, regions

130 **soft** i.e., enough, break off

131 **cross** stand in its path, confront.   **blast** wither, strike with a curse.

131 **s.d.** *his* its

137 **privy to** in on the secret of

138 **happily** haply, perchance

144 **partisan** long-handled spear.

146–7 **'Tis here! / 'Tis here!** (Perhaps they attempt to strike at the Ghost, but are baffled by its seeming ability to be here and there and nowhere.)

And prologue to the omen coming on,   127
Have heaven and earth together demonstrated
Unto our climatures and countrymen.   129

    Enter Ghost.

But soft, behold! Lo, where it comes again!   130
I'll cross it, though it blast me. (*It spreads his arms.*) Stay,
  illusion!   131
If thou hast any sound or use of voice,
Speak to me!
If there be any good thing to be done
That may to thee do ease and grace to me,
Speak to me!
If thou art privy to thy country's fate,   137
Which, happily, foreknowing may avoid,   138
Oh, speak!
Or if thou hast uphoarded in thy life
Extorted treasure in the womb of earth,
For which, they say, you spirits oft walk in death,
Speak of it! (*The cock crows.*) Stay and speak!—Stop it,
  Marcellus.

MARCELLUS
Shall I strike at it with my partisan?   144

HORATIO   Do, if it will not stand.   [*They strike at it.*]

BERNARDO   'Tis here!   146

HORATIO   'Tis here!   [*Exit Ghost.*] 147

MARCELLUS   'Tis gone.
We do it wrong, being so majestical,
To offer it the show of violence,
For it is as the air invulnerable,
And our vain blows malicious mockery.

BERNARDO
It was about to speak when the cock crew.

156 **trumpet** trumpeter

160 **extravagant and erring** wandering beyond bounds.
(The words have similar meaning.)   **hies** hastens

162 **probation** proof.

164 **'gainst** just before

168 **strike** destroy by evil influence

169 **takes** bewitches.   **charm** cast a spell, control by en-
chantment

170 **gracious** full of grace

172 **russet** reddish brown

HORATIO

And then it started like a guilty thing
Upon a fearful summons. I have heard
The cock, that is the trumpet to the morn,   156
Doth with his lofty and shrill-sounding throat
Awake the god of day, and at his warning,
Whether in sea or fire, in earth or air,
Th'extravagant and erring spirit hies   160
To his confine; and of the truth herein
This present object made probation.   162

MARCELLUS

It faded on the crowing of the cock.
Some say that ever 'gainst that season comes   164
Wherein our Savior's birth is celebrated,
This bird of dawning singeth all night long,
And then, they say, no spirit dare stir abroad;
The nights are wholesome, then no planets strike,   168
No fairy takes, nor witch hath power to charm,   169
So hallowed and so gracious is that time.   170

HORATIO

So have I heard and do in part believe it.
But, look, the morn in russet mantle clad   172
Walks o'er the dew of yon high eastward hill.
Break we our watch up, and by my advice
Let us impart what we have seen tonight
Unto young Hamlet; for upon my life,
This spirit, dumb to us, will speak to him.
Do you consent we shall acquaint him with it,
As needful in our loves, fitting our duty?

MARCELLUS

Let's do't, I pray, and I this morning know
Where we shall find him most conveniently.

                                              Exeunt.

1.2 *Location: The castle.*

0.2 *as* i.e., such as, including.

0.3 *cum aliis* with others

1 **our** my. (The royal "we"; also in the following lines.)

8 **sometime** former

9 **jointress** woman possessing property with her husband

11 **With...eye** with one eye smiling and the other weeping

13 **dole** grief

17 **Now...know** Next, you need to be informed that

18 **weak supposal** low estimate

20 **disjoint...frame** in a state of total disorder

21 **Co-leaguèd...advantage** joined to his illusory sense of having the advantage over us and to his vision of future success

23 **Importing** having for its substance

24 **with...law** (See 1.1.91, "Well ratified by law and heraldry.")

[1.2]   *Flourish. Enter Claudius, King of Denmark,*
          Gertrude the Queen, [the] Council, as Polonius
          and his son Laertes, Hamlet, cum aliis [including
          Voltimand and Cornelius].

KING

Though yet of Hamlet our dear brother's death	1
The memory be green, and that it us befitted	
To bear our hearts in grief and our whole kingdom	
To be contracted in one brow of woe,	
Yet so far hath discretion fought with nature	
That we with wisest sorrow think on him	
Together with remembrance of ourselves.	
Therefore our sometime sister, now our queen,	8
Th'imperial jointress to this warlike state,	9
Have we, as 'twere with a defeated joy—	
With an auspicious and a dropping eye,	11
With mirth in funeral and with dirge in marriage,	
In equal scale weighing delight and dole—	13
Taken to wife. Nor have we herein barred	
Your better wisdoms, which have freely gone	
With this affair along. For all, our thanks.	
Now follows that you know young Fortinbras,	17
Holding a weak supposal of our worth,	18
Or thinking by our late dear brother's death	
Our state to be disjoint and out of frame,	20
Co-leaguèd with this dream of his advantage,	21
He hath not failed to pester us with message	
Importing the surrender of those lands	23
Lost by his father, with all bonds of law,	24
To our most valiant brother. So much for him.	
Now for ourself and for this time of meeting.	
Thus much the business is: we have here writ	
To Norway, uncle of young Fortinbras—	

29 **impotent** helpless

31 **His** i.e., Fortinbras's.   **gait** proceeding

31–3 **in that...subject** since the levying of troops and supplies is drawn entirely from the King of Norway's own subjects

38 **dilated** set out at length

39 **let...duty** let your swift obeying of orders, rather than mere words, express your dutifulness.

41 **nothing** not at all.

44 **the Dane** the Danish king

45 **lose your voice** waste your speech.

47 **native** closely connected, related

48 **instrumental** serviceable

51 **leave and favor** kind permission

56 **bow...pardon** entreatingly make a deep bow, asking your permission to depart.

Who, impotent and bed-rid, scarcely hears   29
Of this his nephew's purpose—to suppress
His further gait herein, in that the levies,   31
The lists, and full proportions are all made   32
Out of his subject; and we here dispatch   33
You, good Cornelius, and you, Voltimand,
For bearers of this greeting to old Norway,
Giving to you no further personal power
To business with the King more than the scope
Of these dilated articles allow.   [*He gives a paper.*]   38
Farewell, and let your haste commend your duty.   39

CORNELIUS, VOLTIMAND
In that, and all things, will we show our duty.

KING
We doubt it nothing. Heartily farewell.   41
                    [*Exeunt Voltimand and Cornelius.*]
And now, Laertes, what's the news with you?
You told us of some suit; what is't, Laertes?
You cannot speak of reason to the Dane   44
And lose your voice. What wouldst thou beg, Laertes,   45
That shall not be my offer, not thy asking?
The head is not more native to the heart,   47
The hand more instrumental to the mouth,   48
Than is the throne of Denmark to thy father.
What wouldst thou have, Laertes?

LAERTES   My dread lord,
Your leave and favor to return to France,   51
From whence though willingly I came to Denmark
To show my duty in your coronation,
Yet now I must confess, that duty done,
My thoughts and wishes bend again toward France
And bow them to your gracious leave and pardon.   56

KING
Have you your father's leave? What says Polonius?

58 **H'ath** He has

60 **sealed** (as if sealing a legal document).   **hard** reluctant

62 **Take thy fair hour** Enjoy your time of youth

63 **And . . . will** and may your time be spent in exercising your best qualities.

64 **cousin** any kin not of the immediate family

65 **A little . . . kind** Too close a blood relation, and yet we are less than kinsmen in that our relationship lacks affection and is indeed unnatural. (Hamlet plays on *kind* as [1] kindly [2] belonging to nature, suggesting that Claudius is not the same kind of being as the rest of humanity. The line is often delivered as an aside, though it need not be.)

67 **the sun** i.e., the sunshine of the King's royal favor. (With pun on *son*.)

68 **nighted color** (1) mourning garments of black (2) dark melancholy

69 **Denmark** the King of Denmark.

70 **vailèd lids** lowered eyes

72 **common** of universal occurrence. (But Hamlet plays on the sense of "vulgar" in line 74.)

75 **particular** personal

78 **customary** customary to mourning

79 **suspiration** sighing

80 **fruitful** abundant

81 **havior** expression

82 **moods** outward expression of feeling

POLONIUS

 H'ath, my lord, wrung from me my slow leave   58
 By laborsome petition, and at last
 Upon his will I sealed my hard consent.   60
 I do beseech you, give him leave to go.

KING

 Take thy fair hour, Laertes. Time be thine,   62
 And thy best graces spend it at thy will.   63
 But now, my cousin Hamlet, and my son—   64

HAMLET

 A little more than kin, and less than kind.   65

KING

 How is it that the clouds still hang on you?

HAMLET

 Not so, my lord. I am too much in the sun.   67

QUEEN

 Good Hamlet, cast thy nighted color off,   68
 And let thine eye look like a friend on Denmark. 69
 Do not forever with thy vailèd lids   70
 Seek for thy noble father in the dust.
 Thou know'st 'tis common, all that lives must die, 72
 Passing through nature to eternity.

HAMLET

 Ay, madam, it is common.

QUEEN   If it be,
 Why seems it so particular with thee?   75

HAMLET

 Seems, madam? Nay, it is. I know not "seems."
 'Tis not alone my inky cloak, good mother,
 Nor customary suits of solemn black,   78
 Nor windy suspiration of forced breath,   79
 No, nor the fruitful river in the eye,   80
 Nor the dejected havior of the visage,   81
 Together with all forms, moods, shapes of grief, 82
 That can denote me truly. These indeed seem,

92　**obsequious** suited to obsequies or funerals

93　**condolement** sorrowing

96　**unfortified** i.e., against adversity

97　**simple** ignorant

99　**As . . . sense** as the most ordinary experience

104　**still** always

105　**the first corpse** (Abel's)

107　**unprevailing** unavailing, useless

109　**most immediate** next in succession

112　**impart toward** liberally bestow on.　　**For** As for

113　**to school** i.e., to your studies.　　**Wittenberg** famous
German university founded in 1502

114　**retrograde** contrary

115　**bend you** incline yourself

For they are actions that a man might play.
But I have that within which passes show;
These but the trappings and the suits of woe.

KING
   'Tis sweet and commendable in your nature, Hamlet,
To give these mourning duties to your father.
But you must know your father lost a father,
That father lost, lost his, and the survivor bound
In filial obligation for some term
To do obsequious sorrow. But to persever   92
In obstinate condolement is a course   93
Of impious stubbornness. 'Tis unmanly grief.
It shows a will most incorrect to heaven,
A heart unfortified, a mind impatient,   96
An understanding simple and unschooled.   97
For what we know must be and is as common
As any the most vulgar thing to sense,   99
Why should we in our peevish opposition
Take it to heart? Fie, 'tis a fault to heaven,
A fault against the dead, a fault to nature,
To reason most absurd, whose common theme
Is death of fathers, and who still hath cried,   104
From the first corpse till he that died today,   105
"This must be so." We pray you, throw to earth
This unprevailing woe and think of us   107
As of a father; for let the world take note,
You are the most immediate to our throne,   109
And with no less nobility of love
Than that which dearest father bears his son
Do I impart toward you. For your intent   112
In going back to school in Wittenberg,   113
It is most retrograde to our desire,   114
And we beseech you bend you to remain   115
Here in the cheer and comfort of our eye,
Our chiefest courtier, cousin, and our son.

120 **in all my best** to the best of my ability

124 **to** i.e., at.   **grace** thanksgiving

125 **jocund** merry

127 **rouse** drinking of a draft of liquor.   **bruit again** loudly echo

128 **thunder** i.e., of trumpet and kettledrum, sounded when the King drinks; see 1.4.8–12.

129 **sullied** defiled. (The early quartos read "sallied"; the Folio, "solid.")

132 **canon** law

137 **merely** completely.

139 **to** in comparison to

140 **Hyperion** Titan sun-god, father of Helios.   **satyr** a lecherous creature of classical mythology, half-human but with a goat's legs, tail, ears, and horns

141 **beteem** allow

147 **or ere** even before

QUEEN

Let not thy mother lose her prayers, Hamlet.
I pray thee, stay with us, go not to Wittenberg.

HAMLET

I shall in all my best obey you, madam.   120

KING

Why, 'tis a loving and a fair reply.
Be as ourself in Denmark. Madam, come.
This gentle and unforced accord of Hamlet
Sits smiling to my heart, in grace whereof   124
No jocund health that Denmark drinks today   125
But the great cannon to the clouds shall tell,
And the King's rouse the heaven shall bruit again,   127
Respeaking earthly thunder. Come away.   128

                    Flourish. Exeunt all but Hamlet.

HAMLET

Oh, that this too too sullied flesh would melt,   129
Thaw, and resolve itself into a dew!
Or that the Everlasting had not fixed
His canon 'gainst self-slaughter! Oh, God, God,   132
How weary, stale, flat, and unprofitable
Seem to me all the uses of this world!
Fie on't, ah, fie! 'Tis an unweeded garden
That grows to seed. Things rank and gross in nature
Possess it merely. That it should come to this!   137
But two months dead—nay, not so much, not two.
So excellent a king, that was to this   139
Hyperion to a satyr, so loving to my mother   140
That he might not beteem the winds of heaven   141
Visit her face too roughly. Heaven and earth,
Must I remember? Why, she would hang on him
As if increase of appetite had grown
By what it fed on, and yet within a month—
Let me not think on't; frailty, thy name is woman!—
A little month, or ere those shoes were old   147
With which she followed my poor father's body,

149 **Niobe** Tantalus's daughter, Queen of Thebes, who boasted that she had more sons and daughters than Leto; for this, Apollo and Artemis, children of Leto, slew her fourteen children. She was turned by Zeus into a stone that continually dropped tears.

150 **wants . . . reason** lacks the faculty of reason

155 **gallèd** irritated, inflamed

156 **post** hasten

157 **incestuous** (In Shakespeare's day, the marriage of a man like Claudius to his deceased brother's wife was considered incestuous.)

163 **change that name** i.e., give and receive reciprocally the name of "friend" rather than talk of "servant." Or Hamlet may be saying, "No, I am *your* servant."

164 **make you from** are you doing away from

172 **To . . . of** to make it trust

Like Niobe, all tears, why she, even she—   149
Oh, God, a beast, that wants discourse of reason,   150
Would have mourned longer—married with my
   uncle,
My father's brother, but no more like my father
Than I to Hercules. Within a month,
Ere yet the salt of most unrighteous tears
Had left the flushing in her gallèd eyes,   155
She married. Oh, most wicked speed, to post   156
With such dexterity to incestuous sheets!   157
It is not, nor it cannot come to good.
But break, my heart, for I must hold my tongue.

   Enter Horatio, Marcellus, and Bernardo.

HORATIO
   Hail to Your Lordship!

HAMLET   I am glad to see you well.
   Horatio!—or I do forget myself.

HORATIO
   The same, my lord, and your poor servant ever.

HAMLET
   Sir, my good friend; I'll change that name with you.   163
   And what make you from Wittenberg, Horatio?—   164
   Marcellus.

MARCELLUS   My good lord.

HAMLET
   I am very glad to see you. [*To Bernardo*] Good even,
      sir.—
   But what in faith make you from Wittenberg?

HORATIO
   A truant disposition, good my lord.

HAMLET
   I would not hear your enemy say so,
   Nor shall you do my ear that violence
   To make it truster of your own report   172

179 **hard** close
180 **baked meats** meat pies
181 **coldly** i.e., as cold leftovers
182 **dearest** closest (and therefore deadliest)
183 **Or ever** ere, before
186 **'A** He
193 **Season your admiration** Moderate your astonishment
194 **attent** attentive

Against yourself. I know you are no truant.
But what is your affair in Elsinore?
We'll teach you to drink deep ere you depart.

HORATIO
My lord, I came to see your father's funeral.

HAMLET
I prithee, do not mock me, fellow student;
I think it was to see my mother's wedding.

HORATIO
Indeed, my lord, it followed hard upon.   179

HAMLET
Thrift, thrift, Horatio! The funeral baked meats   180
Did coldly furnish forth the marriage tables.   181
Would I had met my dearest foe in heaven   182
Or ever I had seen that day, Horatio!   183
My father!—Methinks I see my father.

HORATIO
Where, my lord?

HAMLET   In my mind's eye, Horatio.

HORATIO
I saw him once. 'A was a goodly king.   186

HAMLET
'A was a man. Take him for all in all,
I shall not look upon his like again.

HORATIO
My lord, I think I saw him yesternight.

HAMLET   Saw? Who?

HORATIO   My lord, the King your father.

HAMLET   The King my father?

HORATIO
Season your admiration for a while   193
With an attent ear till I may deliver,   194
Upon the witness of these gentlemen,
This marvel to you.

199 **dead waste** desolate stillness

201 **at point** correctly in every detail.   **cap-à-pie** from head to foot

205 **truncheon** officer's staff.   **distilled** dissolved

206 **act** action, operation

208 **dreadful** full of dread

217 **it** its

217–18 **did...speak** prepared to move as though it was about to speak

219 **even then** at that very instant

HAMLET   For God's love, let me hear!

HORATIO
Two nights together had these gentlemen,
Marcellus and Bernardo, on their watch,
In the dead waste and middle of the night,   199
Been thus encountered. A figure like your father,
Armèd at point exactly, cap-à-pie,   201
Appears before them, and with solemn march
Goes slow and stately by them. Thrice he walked
By their oppressed and fear-surprisèd eyes
Within his truncheon's length, whilst they, distilled   205
Almost to jelly with the act of fear,   206
Stand dumb and speak not to him. This to me
In dreadful secrecy impart they did,   208
And I with them the third night kept the watch,
Where, as they had delivered, both in time,
Form of the thing, each word made true and good,
The apparition comes. I knew your father;
These hands are not more like.

HAMLET   But where was this?

MARCELLUS
My lord, upon the platform where we watch.

HAMLET
Did you not speak to it?

HORATIO   My lord, I did,
But answer made it none. Yet once methought
It lifted up it head and did address   217
Itself to motion, like as it would speak;   218
But even then the morning cock crew loud,   219
And at the sound it shrunk in haste away
And vanished from our sight.

HAMLET   'Tis very strange.

HORATIO
As I do live, my honored lord, 'tis true,
And we did think it writ down in our duty
To let you know of it.

232 **beaver** visor on the helmet
233 **What** How
242 **tell** count

HAMLET
    Indeed, indeed, sirs. But this troubles me.
    Hold you the watch tonight?

ALL   We do, my lord.

HAMLET   Armed, say you?

ALL   Armed, my lord.

HAMLET   From top to toe?

ALL   My lord, from head to foot.

HAMLET   Then saw you not his face?

HORATIO
    Oh, yes, my lord, he wore his beaver up.   232

HAMLET   What looked he, frowningly?   233

HORATIO
    A countenance more in sorrow than in anger.

HAMLET   Pale or red?

HORATIO   Nay, very pale.

HAMLET   And fixed his eyes upon you?

HORATIO   Most constantly.

HAMLET   I would I had been there.

HORATIO   It would have much amazed you.

HAMLET   Very like, very like. Stayed it long?

HORATIO
    While one with moderate haste might tell a hundred.   242

MARCELLUS, BERNARDO   Longer, longer.

HORATIO   Not when I saw't.

HAMLET   His beard was grizzled—no?

HORATIO
    It was, as I have seen it in his life,
    A sable silvered.

HAMLET   I will watch tonight.
    Perchance 'twill walk again.

HORATIO   I warr'nt it will.

253 **tenable** held

259 **Your loves** i.e., Say "Your loves" to me, not just your "duty."

261 **doubt** suspect

1.3 *Location: Polonius's chambers.*

3   **convoy is assistant** means of conveyance are available

5   **For** As for

6   **toy in blood** passing amorous fancy

7   **primy** in its prime, springtime

8   **Forward** precocious

9   **suppliance** pastime, something to fill the time

HAMLET

If it assume my noble father's person,
I'll speak to it though hell itself should gape
And bid me hold my peace. I pray you all,
If you have hitherto concealed this sight,
Let it be tenable in your silence still,   253
And whatsomever else shall hap tonight,
Give it an understanding but no tongue.
I will requite your loves. So, fare you well.
Upon the platform twixt eleven and twelve
I'll visit you.

ALL   Our duty to Your Honor.

HAMLET

Your loves, as mine to you. Farewell.   259
                         Exeunt [all but Hamlet].
My father's spirit in arms! All is not well.
I doubt some foul play. Would the night were come!   261
Till then sit still, my soul. Foul deeds will rise,
Though all the earth o'erwhelm them, to men's eyes.
                                              Exit.

[1.3] ❧ *Enter Laertes and Ophelia, his sister.*

LAERTES

My necessaries are embarked. Farewell.
And, sister, as the winds give benefit
And convoy is assistant, do not sleep   3
But let me hear from you.

OPHELIA   Do you doubt that?

LAERTES

For Hamlet, and the trifling of his favor,   5
Hold it a fashion and a toy in blood,   6
A violet in the youth of primy nature,   7
Forward, not permanent, sweet, not lasting,   8
The perfume and suppliance of a minute—   9
No more.

11–14 **For nature . . . withal** For nature, as it ripens, does
not grow only in physical strength, but as the body ma-
tures the inner qualities of mind and soul grow along
with it. (Laertes warns Ophelia that the mature Hamlet
may not cling to his youthful interests.)

15 **soil nor cautel** blemish nor deceit

16 **The . . . will** the purity of his desire

17 **His greatness weighed** taking into account his high
fortune

20 **Carve** i.e., choose

23 **voice and yielding** assent, approval

26 **in . . . place** in his particular restricted circumstances

28 **main voice** general assent.   **withal** along with.

30 **credent** credulous.   **list** listen to

32 **unmastered** uncontrolled

34 **keep . . . affection** don't advance as far as your affection
might lead you. (A military metaphor.)

36 **chariest** most scrupulously modest

37 **If she unmask** if she does no more than show her
beauty.   **moon** (Symbol of chastity.)

39 **canker galls** cankerworm destroys

40 **buttons be disclosed** buds be opened

41 **liquid dew** i.e., time when dew is fresh and bright

42 **blastments** blights

44 **Youth . . . rebels** Youth yields to the rebellion of the
flesh

OPHELIA   No more but so?

LAERTES   Think it no more.
  For nature crescent does not grow alone   11
  In thews and bulk, but as this temple waxes   12
  The inward service of the mind and soul
  Grows wide withal. Perhaps he loves you now,   14
  And now no soil nor cautel doth besmirch   15
  The virtue of his will; but you must fear,   16
  His greatness weighed, his will is not his own.   17
  For he himself is subject to his birth.
  He may not, as unvalued persons do,
  Carve for himself, for on his choice depends   20
  The safety and health of this whole state,
  And therefore must his choice be circumscribed
  Unto the voice and yielding of that body   23
  Whereof he is the head. Then if he says he loves you,
  It fits your wisdom so far to believe it
  As he in his particular act and place   26
  May give his saying deed, which is no further
  Than the main voice of Denmark goes withal.   28
  Then weigh what loss your honor may sustain
  If with too credent ear you list his songs,   30
  Or lose your heart, or your chaste treasure open
  To his unmastered importunity.   32
  Fear it, Ophelia, fear it, my dear sister,
  And keep you in the rear of your affection,   34
  Out of the shot and danger of desire.
  The chariest maid is prodigal enough   36
  If she unmask her beauty to the moon.   37
  Virtue itself scapes not calumnious strokes.
  The canker galls the infants of the spring   39
  Too oft before their buttons be disclosed,   40
  And in the morn and liquid dew of youth   41
  Contagious blastments are most imminent.   42
  Be wary then; best safety lies in fear.
  Youth to itself rebels, though none else near.   44

47 **ungracious** ungodly

49 **puffed** bloated, or swollen with pride

51 **recks** heeds. **rede** counsel. **fear me not** don't worry on my account.

53–4 **A double...leave** The goddess Occasion or Opportunity smiles on the happy circumstance of being able to say good-bye twice and thus receive a second blessing.

59 **Look thou character** see to it that you inscribe.

60 **unproportioned** badly calculated, intemperate. **his** its

61 **familiar** sociable. **vulgar** common.

62 **and...tried** and their suitability to be your friends having been put to the test

64 **dull thy palm** i.e., shake hands so often as to make the gesture meaningless

65 **courage** swashbuckler.

67 **Bear't that** manage it so that

69 **censure** opinion, judgment

70 **habit** clothing

71 **fancy** excessive ornament, decadent fashion

74 **Are...that** are of a most refined and well-bred preeminence in choosing what to wear.

OPHELIA
    I shall the effect of this good lesson keep
    As watchman to my heart. But, good my brother,
    Do not, as some ungracious pastors do,   47
    Show me the steep and thorny way to heaven,
    Whiles like a puffed and reckless libertine   49
    Himself the primrose path of dalliance treads,
    And recks not his own rede.

        Enter Polonius.

LAERTES   Oh, fear me not.   51
    I stay too long. But here my father comes.
    A double blessing is a double grace;   53
    Occasion smiles upon a second leave.   54

POLONIUS
    Yet here, Laertes? Aboard, aboard, for shame!
    The wind sits in the shoulder of your sail,
    And you are stayed for. There—my blessing with thee!
    And these few precepts in thy memory
    Look thou character. Give thy thoughts no tongue,   59
    Nor any unproportioned thought his act.   60
    Be thou familiar, but by no means vulgar.   61
    Those friends thou hast, and their adoption tried,   62
    Grapple them unto thy soul with hoops of steel,
    But do not dull thy palm with entertainment   64
    Of each new-hatched, unfledged courage. Beware   65
    Of entrance to a quarrel, but being in,
    Bear't that th'opposèd may beware of thee.   67
    Give every man thy ear, but few thy voice;
    Take each man's censure, but reserve thy judgment.   69
    Costly thy habit as thy purse can buy,   70
    But not expressed in fancy; rich, not gaudy,   71
    For the apparel oft proclaims the man,
    And they in France of the best rank and station
    Are of a most select and generous chief in that.   74

77 **husbandry** thrift.
81 **season** mature
83 **invests** besieges, presses upon.   **tend** attend, wait.
91 **Marry** i.e., By the Virgin Mary. (A mild oath.)
95 **put on** impressed on, told to
98 **behooves** befits
100 **tenders** offers

Neither a borrower nor a lender be,
For loan oft loses both itself and friend,
And borrowing dulleth edge of husbandry.   77
This above all: to thine own self be true,
And it must follow, as the night the day,
Thou canst not then be false to any man.
Farewell. My blessing season this in thee!   81

LAERTES
Most humbly do I take my leave, my lord.

POLONIUS
The time invests you. Go, your servants tend.   83

LAERTES
Farewell, Ophelia, and remember well
What I have said to you.

OPHELIA   'Tis in my memory locked,
And you yourself shall keep the key of it.

LAERTES   Farewell.   *Exit Laertes.*

POLONIUS
What is't, Ophelia, he hath said to you?

OPHELIA
So please you, something touching the Lord Hamlet.

POLONIUS   Marry, well bethought.   91
'Tis told me he hath very oft of late
Given private time to you, and you yourself
Have of your audience been most free and bounteous.
If it be so—as so 'tis put on me,   95
And that in way of caution—I must tell you
You do not understand yourself so clearly
As it behooves my daughter and your honor.   98
What is between you? Give me up the truth.

OPHELIA
He hath, my lord, of late made many tenders   100
Of his affection to me.

103 **Unsifted** i.e., untried

108 **sterling** legal currency.   **Tender ... dearly**
(1) Bargain for your favors at a higher rate—i.e., hold
out for marriage (2) Show greater care of yourself

109 **crack the wind** i.e., run it until it is broken-winded

110 **tender ... fool** (1) make a fool of me (2) present me
with a *fool* or baby.

113 **fashion** mere form, pretense.   **Go to** (An expression
of impatience.)

114 **countenance** credit, confirmation

116 **springes** snares.   **woodcocks** birds easily caught;
here used to connote gullibility.

117 **prodigal** prodigally

120 **it** i.e., the promise

122 **something** somewhat

123–4 **Set ... parle** i.e., As defender of your chastity, negoti-
ate for something better than a surrender simply because the besieger requests an interview.

124 **For** As for

125 **so ... him** this much concerning him

127 **In few** Briefly

128 **brokers** go-betweens, procurers

129 **dye** color or sort.   **investments** clothes. (The vows
are not what they seem.)

POLONIUS

    Affection? Pooh! You speak like a green girl,

    Unsifted in such perilous circumstance.   103

    Do you believe his tenders, as you call them?

OPHELIA

    I do not know, my lord, what I should think.

POLONIUS

    Marry, I will teach you. Think yourself a baby

    That you have ta'en these tenders for true pay

    Which are not sterling. Tender yourself more dearly,   108

    Or—not to crack the wind of the poor phrase,   109

    Running it thus—you'll tender me a fool.   110

OPHELIA

    My lord, he hath importuned me with love

    In honorable fashion.

POLONIUS

    Ay, fashion you may call it. Go to, go to.   113

OPHELIA

    And hath given countenance to his speech, my lord,   114

    With almost all the holy vows of heaven.

POLONIUS

    Ay, springes to catch woodcocks. I do know,   116

    When the blood burns, how prodigal the soul   117

    Lends the tongue vows. These blazes, daughter,

    Giving more light than heat, extinct in both

    Even in their promise as it is a-making,   120

    You must not take for fire. From this time

    Be something scanter of your maiden presence.   122

    Set your entreatments at a higher rate   123

    Than a command to parle. For Lord Hamlet,   124

    Believe so much in him that he is young,   125

    And with a larger tether may he walk

    Than may be given you. In few, Ophelia,   127

    Do not believe his vows, for they are brokers,   128

    Not of that dye which their investments show,   129

130 **mere implorators** out-and-out solicitors
131 **Breathing** speaking
132 **for all** once for all, in sum
134 **slander** abuse, misuse.   **moment** moment's
136 **Come your ways** Come along.

1.4 *Location: The guard platform.*
  1 **shrewdly** keenly, sharply
  2 **eager** biting
  3 **lacks of** is just short of
  5 **season** time
  6 **held his wont** was accustomed
6.1 *pieces* i.e., of ordnance, cannon
  8 **wake** stay awake and hold revel.   **takes his rouse** carouses
  9 **Keeps ... reels** carouses, and riotously dances a German dance called the upspring
 10 **Rhenish** Rhine wine
 12 **The triumph ... pledge** the celebration of his offering a toast.

But mere implorators of unholy suits,   130
Breathing like sanctified and pious bawds,   131
The better to beguile. This is for all: 132
I would not, in plain terms, from this time forth
Have you so slander any moment leisure   134
As to give words or talk with the Lord Hamlet.
Look to't, I charge you. Come your ways.   136

OPHELIA   I shall obey, my lord.   *Exeunt.*

[1.4]   Enter Hamlet, Horatio, and Marcellus.

HAMLET
The air bites shrewdly; it is very cold.   1

HORATIO
It is a nipping and an eager air.   2

HAMLET
What hour now?

HORATIO   I think it lacks of twelve.   3

MARCELLUS
No, it is struck.

HORATIO   Indeed? I heard it not.
It then draws near the season   5
Wherein the spirit held his wont to walk.   6

          A flourish of trumpets, and two pieces go off
                                            [within].

What does this mean, my lord?

HAMLET
The King doth wake tonight and takes his rouse,   8
Keeps wassail, and the swagg'ring upspring reels;   9
And as he drains his drafts of Rhenish down,   10
The kettledrum and trumpet thus bray out
The triumph of his pledge.

HORATIO   Is it a custom?   12

HAMLET   Ay, marry, is't,
But to my mind, though I am native here

15 **manner** custom (of drinking)
16 **More ... observance** better neglected than followed.
17 **east and west** i.e., everywhere
18 **taxed of** censured by
19 **clepe** call.   **with swinish phrase** i.e., by calling us swine
20 **addition** reputation
21 **at height** outstandingly
22 **The pith ... attribute** the most essential part of the esteem that should be attributed to us.
24 **for ... mole** on account of some natural defect in their constitutions
26 **his** its
27 **their o'ergrowth ... complexion** the excessive growth in individuals of some natural trait
28 **pales** palings, fences (as of a fortification)
29–30 **o'erleavens ... manners** i.e., infects the way we should behave (much as bad yeast spoils the dough). *Plausive* means "pleasing."
32 **Being ... star** (that stamp of defect) being a sign identifying one as wearing the livery of, and hence being the servant to, nature (unfortunate inherited qualities) or fortune (mischance)
33 **His virtues else** i.e., the other qualities of *these men* (line 30)
34 **may undergo** can sustain
35 **in ... censure** in overall appraisal, in people's opinion generally
36–8 **The dram ... scandal** i.e., The small drop of evil blots out or works against the noble substance of the whole and brings it into disrepute. (To *dout* is to blot out. A famous crux.)
39 **ministers of grace** messengers of God
40 **Be ... health** Whether you are a good angel
41 **Bring** whether you bring
42 **Be thy intents** whether your intentions are
43 **questionable** inviting question

And to the manner born, it is a custom   15
More honored in the breach than the observance.   16
This heavy-headed revel east and west   17
Makes us traduced and taxed of other nations.   18
They clepe us drunkards, and with swinish phrase   19
Soil our addition; and indeed it takes   20
From our achievements, though performed at height,   21
The pith and marrow of our attribute.   22
So, oft it chances in particular men,
That for some vicious mole of nature in them,   24
As in their birth—wherein they are not guilty,
Since nature cannot choose his origin—   26
By their o'ergrowth of some complexion,   27
Oft breaking down the pales and forts of reason,   28
Or by some habit that too much o'erleavens   29
The form of plausive manners, that these men,   30
Carrying, I say, the stamp of one defect,
Being nature's livery or fortune's star,   32
His virtues else, be they as pure as grace,   33
As infinite as man may undergo,   34
Shall in the general censure take corruption   35
From that particular fault. The dram of evil   36
Doth all the noble substance often dout   37
To his own scandal.

     Enter Ghost.

HORATIO   Look, my lord, it comes!   38

HAMLET

Angels and ministers of grace defend us!   39
Be thou a spirit of health or goblin damned,   40
Bring with thee airs from heaven or blasts from hell,   41
Be thy intents wicked or charitable,   42
Thou com'st in such a questionable shape   43
That I will speak to thee. I'll call thee Hamlet,

47 **canonized** buried according to the canons of the church.   **hearsèd** coffined

48 **cerements** grave clothes

49 **inurned** entombed

52 **complete steel** full armor

53 **the glimpses...moon** i.e., the sublunary world, all that is beneath the moon

54 **fools of nature** mere mortals, limited to natural knowledge and subject to nature

55 **So...disposition** to distress our mental composure so violently

59 **impartment** communication

65 **fee** value

66 **for** as for

69 **flood** sea

King, father, royal Dane. Oh, answer me!
Let me not burst in ignorance, but tell
Why thy canonized bones, hearsèd in death,   47
Have burst their cerements; why the sepulcher   48
Wherein we saw thee quietly inurned   49
Hath oped his ponderous and marble jaws
To cast thee up again. What may this mean,
That thou, dead corpse, again in complete steel,   52
Revisits thus the glimpses of the moon,   53
Making night hideous, and we fools of nature   54
So horridly to shake our disposition   55
With thoughts beyond the reaches of our souls?
Say, why is this? Wherefore? What should we do?
                    [*The Ghost*] beckons [*Hamlet*].

HORATIO
It beckons you to go away with it,
As if it some impartment did desire   59
To you alone.

MARCELLUS   Look with what courteous action
It wafts you to a more removèd ground.
But do not go with it.

HORATIO   No, by no means.

HAMLET
It will not speak. Then I will follow it.

HORATIO
Do not, my lord!

HAMLET   Why, what should be the fear?
I do not set my life at a pin's fee,   65
And for my soul, what can it do to that,   66
Being a thing immortal as itself?
It waves me forth again. I'll follow it.

HORATIO
What if it tempt you toward the flood, my lord,   69
Or to the dreadful summit of the cliff

71 **beetles o'er** overhangs threateningly (like bushy eye-brows). **his** its

73 **deprive ... reason** take away the rule of reason over your mind

75 **toys of desperation** fancies of desperate acts, i.e., suicide

81 **My fate cries out** My destiny summons me

82 **petty** weak. **artery** blood vessel system through which the vital spirits were thought to have been conveyed

83 **as ... nerve** as a sinew of the huge lion slain by Hercules as the first of his twelve labors.

85 **lets** hinders

89 **Have after** Let's go after him. **issue** outcome

91 **it** i.e., the outcome.

That beetles o'er his base into the sea,   71
And there assume some other horrible form
Which might deprive your sovereignty of reason   73
And draw you into madness? Think of it.
The very place puts toys of desperation,   75
Without more motive, into every brain
That looks so many fathoms to the sea
And hears it roar beneath.

HAMLET
It wafts me still.—Go on, I'll follow thee.

MARCELLUS
You shall not go, my lord.   [*They try to stop him.*]

HAMLET   Hold off your hands!

HORATIO
Be ruled. You shall not go.

HAMLET   My fate cries out,   81
And makes each petty artery in this body   82
As hardy as the Nemean lion's nerve.   83
Still am I called. Unhand me, gentlemen.
By heaven, I'll make a ghost of him that lets me!   85
I say, away!—Go on, I'll follow thee.
                              Exeunt Ghost and Hamlet.

HORATIO
He waxes desperate with imagination.

MARCELLUS
Let's follow. 'Tis not fit thus to obey him.

HORATIO
Have after. To what issue will this come?   89

MARCELLUS
Something is rotten in the state of Denmark.

HORATIO
Heaven will direct it.

MARCELLUS   Nay, let's follow him.   *Exeunt.*   91

1.5 *Location: The battlements of the castle.*

7 **bound** (1) ready (2) obligated by duty and fate. (The Ghost, in line 8, answers in the second sense.)

12 **fast** do penance by fasting

13 **crimes** sins.   **of nature** as a mortal

14 **But that** Were it not that

17 **harrow up** lacerate, tear

18 **spheres** i.e., eye-sockets, here compared to the orbits or transparent revolving spheres in which, according to Ptolemaic astronomy, the heavenly bodies were fixed

19 **knotted . . . locks** hair neatly arranged and confined

22 **eternal blazon** revelation of the secrets of eternity

[1.5] ∾ *Enter Ghost and Hamlet.*

HAMLET
  Whither wilt thou lead me? Speak. I'll go no further.

GHOST
  Mark me.

HAMLET   I will.

GHOST   My hour is almost come,
  When I to sulf'rous and tormenting flames
  Must render up myself.

HAMLET   Alas, poor ghost!

GHOST
  Pity me not, but lend thy serious hearing
  To what I shall unfold.

HAMLET   Speak. I am bound to hear.   7

GHOST
  So art thou to revenge, when thou shalt hear.

HAMLET   What?

GHOST   I am thy father's spirit,
  Doomed for a certain term to walk the night,
  And for the day confined to fast in fires,   12
  Till the foul crimes done in my days of nature   13
  Are burnt and purged away. But that I am forbid   14
  To tell the secrets of my prison house,
  I could a tale unfold whose lightest word
  Would harrow up thy soul, freeze thy young blood,   17
  Make thy two eyes like stars start from their spheres,   18
  Thy knotted and combinèd locks to part,   19
  And each particular hair to stand on end
  Like quills upon the fretful porcupine.
  But this eternal blazon must not be   22
  To ears of flesh and blood. List, list, oh, list!
  If thou didst ever thy dear father love—

HAMLET   Oh, God!

28 **in the best** even at best
33 **shouldst thou be** you would have to be.   **fat** torpid, lethargic
34 **Lethe** the river of forgetfulness in Hades
36 **orchard** garden
38 **forgèd process** falsified account
39 **abused** deceived.
43 **adulterate** adulterous
44 **gifts** (1) talents (2) presents
50 **even with the vow** with the very vow
53 **To** compared with
54 **virtue, as it** just as virtue
55 **shape of heaven** heavenly form

GHOST
Revenge his foul and most unnatural murder.

HAMLET   Murder?

GHOST
Murder most foul, as in the best it is,   28
But this most foul, strange, and unnatural.

HAMLET
Haste me to know't, that I, with wings as swift
As meditation or the thoughts of love,
May sweep to my revenge.

GHOST   I find thee apt;
And duller shouldst thou be than the fat weed   33
That roots itself in ease on Lethe wharf,   34
Wouldst thou not stir in this. Now, Hamlet, hear.
'Tis given out that, sleeping in my orchard,   36
A serpent stung me. So the whole ear of Denmark
Is by a forgèd process of my death   38
Rankly abused. But know, thou noble youth,   39
The serpent that did sting thy father's life
Now wears his crown.

HAMLET   Oh, my prophetic soul! My uncle!

GHOST
Ay, that incestuous, that adulterate beast,   43
With witchcraft of his wit, with traitorous gifts—   44
Oh, wicked wit and gifts, that have the power
So to seduce!—won to his shameful lust
The will of my most seeming-virtuous queen.
Oh, Hamlet, what a falling off was there!
From me, whose love was of that dignity
That it went hand in hand even with the vow   50
I made to her in marriage, and to decline
Upon a wretch whose natural gifts were poor
To those of mine!   53
But virtue, as it never will be moved,   54
Though lewdness court it in a shape of heaven,   55

57 **sate . . . bed** gratify its lustful appetite to the point of re-
    vulsion or ennui, even in a virtuously lawful marriage

62 **secure hour** time of being free from worries

63 **hebona** a poison. (The word seems to be a form of
    ebony, though it is thought perhaps to be related to *hen-
    bane*, a poison, or to *ebenus*, "yew.")

64 **porches** gateways

65 **leprous distillment** distillation causing leprosylike dis-
    figurement

68 **gates** entryways

69–70 **posset . . . curd** coagulate and curdle

70 **eager** sour, acid

72 **tetter** eruption of scabs.   **barked** covered with a
    rough covering, like bark on a tree

73 **lazar-like** leperlike

76 **dispatched** suddenly deprived

78 **Unhouseled . . . unaneled** without having received the
    Sacrament or other last rites including confession, abso-
    lution, and the holy oil of extreme unction

79 **reck'ning** settling of accounts

82 **nature** i.e., the promptings of a son

84 **luxury** lechery

90 **matin** morning

So lust, though to a radiant angel linked,
Will sate itself in a celestial bed   57
And prey on garbage.
But soft, methinks I scent the morning air.
Brief let me be. Sleeping within my orchard,
My custom always of the afternoon,
Upon my secure hour thy uncle stole,   62
With juice of cursèd hebona in a vial,   63
And in the porches of my ears did pour   64
The leprous distillment, whose effect   65
Holds such an enmity with blood of man
That swift as quicksilver it courses through
The natural gates and alleys of the body,   68
And with a sudden vigor it doth posset   69
And curd, like eager droppings into milk,   70
The thin and wholesome blood. So did it mine,
And a most instant tetter barked about,   72
Most lazar-like, with vile and loathsome crust,   73
All my smooth body.
Thus was I, sleeping, by a brother's hand
Of life, of crown, of queen at once dispatched,   76
Cut off even in the blossoms of my sin,
Unhouseled, disappointed, unaneled,   78
No reck'ning made, but sent to my account   79
With all my imperfections on my head.
Oh, horrible! Oh, horrible, most horrible!
If thou hast nature in thee, bear it not.   82
Let not the royal bed of Denmark be
A couch for luxury and damnèd incest.   84
But, howsomever thou pursues this act,
Taint not thy mind nor let thy soul contrive
Against thy mother aught. Leave her to heaven
And to those thorns that in her bosom lodge,
To prick and sting her. Fare thee well at once.
The glowworm shows the matin to be near,   90

91 **his** its

94 **couple** add.   **Hold** Hold together

95 **instant** instantly

98 **globe** (1) head (2) world (3) Globe Theater.

99 **table** tablet, slate

100 **fond** foolish

101 **All ... past** all wise sayings, all shapes or images im-
    printed on the tablets of my memory, all past impres-
    sions

108 **My tables ... down** (Editors often specify that Hamlet
    makes a note in his writing tablet, but he may simply
    mean that he is making a mental observation of lasting
    impression.)

111 **there you are** i.e., there, I've noted that against you.

116 **secure him** keep him safe.

119 **Hillo ... come** (A falconer's call to a hawk in air.
    Hamlet mocks the hallooing as though it were a part of
    hawking.)

And 'gins to pale his uneffectual fire.   91
Adieu, adieu, adieu! Remember me.   [*Exit.*]

HAMLET
O all you host of heaven! O earth! What else?
And shall I couple hell? Oh, fie! Hold, hold, my heart,   94
And you, my sinews, grow not instant old,   95
But bear me stiffly up. Remember thee?
Ay, thou poor ghost, whiles memory holds a seat
In this distracted globe. Remember thee?   98
Yea, from the table of my memory   99
I'll wipe away all trivial fond records,   100
All saws of books, all forms, all pressures past   101
That youth and observation copied there,
And thy commandment all alone shall live
Within the book and volume of my brain,
Unmixed with baser matter. Yes, by heaven!
Oh, most pernicious woman!
Oh, villain, villain, smiling, damnèd villain!
My tables—meet it is I set it down   108
That one may smile, and smile, and be a villain.
At least I am sure it may be so in Denmark.
So, uncle, there you are. Now to my word: 111
It is "Adieu, adieu! Remember me."
I have sworn't.

Enter Horatio and Marcellus.

HORATIO   My lord, my lord!
MARCELLUS   Lord Hamlet!
HORATIO   Heavens secure him!   116
HAMLET   So be it.
MARCELLUS   Hillo, ho, ho, my lord!
HAMLET   Hillo, ho, ho, boy! Come, bird, come.   119
MARCELLUS   How is't, my noble lord?
HORATIO   What news, my lord?
HAMLET   Oh, wonderful!
HORATIO   Good my lord, tell it.

127 **once** ever
130 **But . . . knave** (Hamlet jokingly gives a self-evident an-
      swer: every villain is a thoroughgoing knave.)
133 **circumstance** ceremony, elaboration
142 **Saint Patrick** the keeper of Purgatory
143 **offense** (Hamlet deliberately changes Horatio's "no of-
      fense taken" to "an offense against all decency.")
144 **honest** genuine

HAMLET   No, you will reveal it.

HORATIO   Not I, my lord, by heaven.

MARCELLUS   Nor I, my lord.

HAMLET
How say you, then, would heart of man once think it?   127
But you'll be secret?

HORATIO, MARCELLUS   Ay, by heaven, my lord.

HAMLET
There's never a villain dwelling in all Denmark
But he's an arrant knave.   130

HORATIO
There needs no ghost, my lord, come from the grave
To tell us this.

HAMLET   Why, right, you are in the right.
And so, without more circumstance at all,   133
I hold it fit that we shake hands and part,
You as your business and desire shall point you—
For every man hath business and desire,
Such as it is—and for my own poor part,
Look you, I'll go pray.

HORATIO
These are but wild and whirling words, my lord.

HAMLET
I am sorry they offend you, heartily;
Yes, faith, heartily.

HORATIO   There's no offense, my lord.

HAMLET
Yes, by Saint Patrick, but there is, Horatio,   142
And much offense too. Touching this vision here,   143
It is an honest ghost, that let me tell you.   144
For your desire to know what is between us,
O'ermaster't as you may. And now, good friends,
As you are friends, scholars, and soldiers,
Give me one poor request.

153 **In faith ... I** i.e., I swear not to tell what I have seen.
   (Horatio is not refusing to swear.)

155 **sword** i.e., the hilt in the form of a cross.

156 **We ... already** i.e., We swore *in faith.*

159 **truepenny** honest old fellow.

164 **s.d. *They swear*** (Seemingly they swear here, and at lines
   170 and 190, as they lay their hands on Hamlet's sword.
   Triple oaths would have particular force; these three
   oaths deal with what they have seen, what they have
   heard, and what they promise about Hamlet's *antic disposition.*)

165 *Hic et ubique?* Here and everywhere? (Latin.)

172 **pioneer** foot soldier assigned to dig tunnels and excava-
   tions.

HORATIO   What is't, my lord? We will.

HAMLET
  Never make known what you have seen tonight.

HORATIO, MARCELLUS   My lord, we will not.

HAMLET   Nay, but swear't.

HORATIO   In faith, my lord, not I.   153

MARCELLUS   Nor I, my lord, in faith.

HAMLET   Upon my sword.   [He hold out his sword.] 155

MARCELLUS   We have sworn, my lord, already.   156

HAMLET   Indeed, upon my sword, indeed.

GHOST   (cries under the stage) Swear.

HAMLET
  Ha, ha, boy, say'st thou so? Art thou there, truepenny? 159
  Come on, you hear this fellow in the cellarage.
  Consent to swear.

HORATIO   Propose the oath, my lord.

HAMLET
  Never to speak of this that you have seen,
  Swear by my sword.

GHOST [beneath]   Swear.   [They swear.] 164

HAMLET
  Hic et ubique? Then we'll shift our ground.   165
                              [He moves to another spot.]
  Come hither, gentlemen,
  And lay your hands again upon my sword.
  Swear by my sword
  Never to speak of this that you have heard.

GHOST [beneath]   Swear by his sword.   [They swear.]

HAMLET
  Well said, old mole. Canst work i'th'earth so fast?
  A worthy pioneer!—Once more remove, good friends. 172
                              [He moves again.]

HORATIO
  Oh, day and night, but this is wondrous strange!

174 **as a stranger** i.e., needing your hospitality

176 **your philosophy** this subject that is called "natural philosophy" or "science." (*Your* is not personal.)

178 **so help you mercy** as you hope for God's mercy when you are judged

181 **antic** grotesque, strange

183 **encumbered** folded

185 **an if** if

186 **list** wished.   **There ... might** There are those who could talk if they were at liberty to do so

187 **note** indicate

188 **aught** anything

192 **commend ... you** give you my best wishes

194 **friending** friendliness

195 **lack** be lacking.

196 **still** always

197 **out of joint** in utter disorder.

199 **let's go together** (Probably they wait for him to leave first, but he refuses this ceremoniousness.)

2.1 *Location: Polonius's chambers.*

HAMLET

And therefore as a stranger give it welcome.   174
There are more things in heaven and earth, Horatio,
Than are dreamt of in your philosophy.   176
But come;
Here, as before, never, so help you mercy,   178
How strange or odd some'er I bear myself—
As I perchance hereafter shall think meet
To put an antic disposition on—   181
That you, at such times seeing me, never shall,
With arms encumbered thus, or this headshake,   183
Or by pronouncing of some doubtful phrase
As "Well, we know," or "We could, an if we would,"   185
Or "If we list to speak," or "There be, an if they
    might,"   186
Or such ambiguous giving out, to note   187
That you know aught of me—this do swear,   188
So grace and mercy at your most need help you.

GHOST *[beneath]*   Swear.   *[They swear.]*

HAMLET

Rest, rest, perturbèd spirit!—So, gentlemen,
With all my love I do commend me to you;   192
And what so poor a man as Hamlet is
May do t'express his love and friending to you,   194
God willing, shall not lack. Let us go in together,   195
And still your fingers on your lips, I pray.   196
The time is out of joint. Oh, cursèd spite   197
That ever I was born to set it right!
                        [They wait for him to leave first.]
Nay, come, let's go together.   *Exeunt.*   199

[2.1] ✒ *Enter old Polonius with his man [Reynaldo].*

POLONIUS

Give him this money and these notes, Reynaldo.
                        [He gives money and papers.]

3 **marvelous** marvelously

4 **inquire** inquiry

7 **Danskers** Danes

8 **what means** what wealth (they have).   **keep** dwell

10 **encompassment ... question** roundabout way of questioning

11–12 **come ... it** you will find out more this way than by asking pointed questions (*particular demands*).

13 **Take you** Assume, pretend

19 **put on** impute to

20 **forgeries** invented tales.   **rank** gross

22 **wanton** sportive, unrestrained

27 **drabbing** whoring

29 **season** temper, soften

REYNALDO   I will, my lord.

POLONIUS

   You shall do marvelous wisely, good Reynaldo,   3
   Before you visit him, to make inquire   4
   Of his behavior.

REYNALDO   My lord, I did intend it.

POLONIUS

   Marry, well said, very well said. Look you, sir,
   Inquire me first what Danskers are in Paris,   7
   And how, and who, what means, and where they
     keep,   8
   What company, at what expense; and finding
   By this encompassment and drift of question   10
   That they do know my son, come you more nearer   11
   Than your particular demands will touch it.   12
   Take you, as 'twere, some distant knowledge of him,   13
   As thus, "I know his father and his friends,
   And in part him." Do you mark this, Reynaldo?

REYNALDO   Ay, very well, my lord.

POLONIUS

   "And in part him, but," you may say, "not well.
   But if't be he I mean, he's very wild,
   Addicted so and so," and there put on him   19
   What forgeries you please—marry, none so rank   20
   As may dishonor him, take heed of that,
   But, sir, such wanton, wild, and usual slips   22
   As are companions noted and most known
   To youth and liberty.

REYNALDO   As gaming, my lord.

POLONIUS   Ay, or drinking, fencing, swearing,
   Quarreling, drabbing—you may go so far.   27

REYNALDO   My lord, that would dishonor him.

POLONIUS

   Faith, no, as you may season it in the charge.   29
   You must not put another scandal on him

31 **incontinency** habitual sexual excess

32 **quaintly** artfully, subtly

33 **taints of liberty** faults resulting from free living

35–6 **A savageness … assault** a wildness in untamed youth that assails all indiscriminately.

41 **fetch of warrant** legitimate trick.

43 **wi'th' working** in the process of being made, i.e., in everyday experience

45 **Your … converse** the person you are conversing with. **sound** sound out

46 **Having ever** if he has ever.   **prenominate crimes** aforenamed offenses

47 **breathe** speak

48 **closes … consequence** takes you into his confidence as follows

50 **addition** title

60 **o'ertook in 's rouse** overcome by drink

61 **falling out** quarreling

That he is open to incontinency;   31
That's not my meaning. But breathe his faults so
    quaintly   32
That they may seem the taints of liberty,   33
The flash and outbreak of a fiery mind,
A savageness in unreclaimèd blood,   35
Of general assault.   36

REYNALDO   But, my good lord—

POLONIUS   Wherefore should you do this?

REYNALDO   Ay, my lord, I would know that.

POLONIUS   Marry, sir, here's my drift,
And I believe it is a fetch of warrant.   41
You laying these slight sullies on my son,
As 'twere a thing a little soiled wi'th' working,   43
Mark you,
Your party in converse, him you would sound,   45
Having ever seen in the prenominate crimes   46
The youth you breathe of guilty, be assured   47
He closes with you in this consequence: 48
"Good sir," or so, or "friend," or "gentleman,"
According to the phrase or the addition   50
Of man and country.

REYNALDO   Very good, my lord.

POLONIUS   And then, sir, does 'a this—'a does—what
was I about to say? By the Mass, I was about to say
something. Where did I leave?

REYNALDO   At "closes in the consequence."

POLONIUS
At "closes in the consequence," ay, marry.
He closes thus: "I know the gentleman,
I saw him yesterday," or "th'other day,"
Or then, or then, with such or such, "and as you say,
There was 'a gaming," "there o'ertook in 's rouse,"   60
"There falling out at tennis," or perchance   61

63 **Videlicet** namely

64 **carp** a fish

65 **reach** capacity, ability

66 **windlasses** i.e., circuitous paths. (Literally, circuits
    made to head off the game in hunting.)   **assays of
    bias** attempts through indirection (like the curving path
    of the bowling ball, which is biased or weighted to one
    side)

67 **directions** i.e., the way things really are

68 **former lecture** just-ended set of instructions

69 **have** understand

72 **in yourself** in your own person (as well as by asking
    questions of others).

79 **closet** private chamber

80 **doublet** close-fitting jacket.   **unbraced** unfastened

82 **down-gyvèd** fallen to the ankles (like gyves or fetters)

84 **in purport** in what it expressed

"I saw him enter such a house of sale,"
Videlicet a brothel, or so forth. See you now,   63
Your bait of falsehood takes this carp of truth;   64
And thus do we of wisdom and of reach,   65
With windlasses and with assays of bias,   66
By indirections find directions out.   67
So by my former lecture and advice   68
Shall you my son. You have me, have you not?   69

REYNALDO
My lord, I have.

POLONIUS   God b'wi'ye; fare ye well.

REYNALDO   Good my lord.

POLONIUS
Observe his inclination in yourself.   72

REYNALDO   I shall, my lord.

POLONIUS   And let him ply his music.

REYNALDO   Well, my lord.

POLONIUS
Farewell.   *Exit Reynaldo.*

    Enter Ophelia.

      How now, Ophelia, what's the matter?

OPHELIA
Oh, my lord, my lord, I have been so affrighted!

POLONIUS   With what, i'th' name of God?

OPHELIA
My lord, as I was sewing in my closet,   79
Lord Hamlet, with his doublet all unbraced,   80
No hat upon his head, his stockings fouled,
Ungartered, and down-gyvèd to his ankle,   82
Pale as his shirt, his knees knocking each other,
And with a look so piteous in purport   84
As if he had been loosèd out of hell
To speak of horrors—he comes before me.

93 **As 'a** as if he
97 **As** that.   **bulk** body
104 **ecstasy** madness
105 **property fordoes** nature destroys
114 **quoted** observed

POLONIUS
Mad for thy love?

OPHELIA   My lord, I do not know,
But truly I do fear it.

POLONIUS   What said he?

OPHELIA
He took me by the wrist and held me hard.
Then goes he to the length of all his arm,
And, with his other hand thus o'er his brow
He falls to such perusal of my face
As 'a would draw it. Long stayed he so.   93
At last, a little shaking of mine arm
And thrice his head thus waving up and down,
He raised a sigh so piteous and profound
As it did seem to shatter all his bulk   97
And end his being. That done, he lets me go,
And with his head over his shoulder turned
He seemed to find his way without his eyes,
For out o' doors he went without their helps,
And to the last bended their light on me.

POLONIUS
Come, go with me. I will go seek the King.
This is the very ecstasy of love,   104
Whose violent property fordoes itself   105
And leads the will to desperate undertakings
As oft as any passion under heaven
That does afflict our natures. I am sorry.
What, have you given him any hard words of late?

OPHELIA
No, my good lord, but as you did command
I did repel his letters and denied
His access to me.

POLONIUS   That hath made him mad.
I am sorry that with better heed and judgment
I had not quoted him. I feared he did but trifle   114

115 **wrack** ruin, seduce.   **beshrew my jealousy!** a plague upon my suspicious nature!

116 **proper...age** characteristic of us (old) men

117 **cast beyond** overshoot, miscalculate. (A metaphor from hunting.)

120 **known** made known (to the King).   **close** secret

120-1 **might...love** i.e., might cause more grief (because of what Hamlet might do) by hiding the knowledge of Hamlet's strange behavior to Ophelia than unpleasantness by telling it.

2.2 *Location: The castle.*

2 **Moreover that** Besides the fact that

6 **Sith nor** since neither

7 **that** what

11-12 **That...havior** that, seeing as you were brought up with him from early youth (see 3.4.209, where Hamlet refers to Rosencrantz and Guildenstern as "my two schoolfellows"), and since you have been intimately acquainted with his youthful ways

13 **vouchsafe your rest** consent to stay

16 **occasion** opportunity

18 **opened** being revealed

And meant to wrack thee. But beshrew my jealousy! 11.
By heaven, it is as proper to our age 116
To cast beyond ourselves in our opinions 117
As it is common for the younger sort
To lack discretion. Come, go we to the King.
This must be known, which, being kept close, might
    move 120
More grief to hide than hate to utter love. 121
Come.   *Exeunt.*

[2.2] ❧ *Flourish. Enter King and Queen, Rosencrantz,
and Guildenstern [with others].*

KING
Welcome, dear Rosencrantz and Guildenstern.
Moreover that we much did long to see you, 2
The need we have to use you did provoke
Our hasty sending. Something have you heard
Of Hamlet's transformation—so call it,
Sith nor th'exterior nor the inward man 6
Resembles that it was. What it should be, 7
More than his father's death, that thus hath put him
So much from th'understanding of himself,
I cannot dream of. I entreat you both
That, being of so young days brought up with him, 11
And sith so neighbored to his youth and havior, 12
That you vouchsafe your rest here in our court 13
Some little time, so by your companies
To draw him on to pleasures, and to gather
So much as from occasion you may glean, 16
Whether aught to us unknown afflicts him thus
That, opened, lies within our remedy. 18

QUEEN
Good gentlemen, he hath much talked of you,
And sure I am two men there is not living
To whom he more adheres. If it will please you

22 **gentry** courtesy
24 **supply ... hope** aid and furtherance of what we hope for
26 **As fits ... remembrance** as would be a fitting gift of a king who rewards true service.
27 **of** over
28 **dread** inspiring awe
30 **in ... bent** to the utmost degree of our capacity. (An archery metaphor.)
38 **practices** doings
42 **still** always

To show us so much gentry and good will   22
As to expend your time with us awhile
For the supply and profit of our hope,   24
Your visitation shall receive such thanks
As fits a king's remembrance.

ROSENCRANTZ   Both Your Majesties   26
   Might, by the sovereign power you have of us,   27
   Put your dread pleasures more into command   28
   Than to entreaty.

GUILDENSTERN   But we both obey,
   And here give up ourselves in the full bent   30
   To lay our service freely at your feet,
   To be commanded.

KING
   Thanks, Rosencrantz and gentle Guildenstern.

QUEEN
   Thanks, Guildenstern and gentle Rosencrantz.
   And I beseech you instantly to visit
   My too much changèd son.—Go, some of you,
   And bring these gentlemen where Hamlet is.

GUILDENSTERN
   Heavens make our presence and our practices   38
   Pleasant and helpful to him!

QUEEN   Ay, amen!
        Exeunt Rosencrantz and Guildenstern [with some
                                    attendants].

        Enter Polonius.

POLONIUS
   Th'ambassadors from Norway, my good lord,
   Are joyfully returned.

KING
   Thou still hast been the father of good news.   42

POLONIUS
   Have I, my lord? I assure my good liege
   I hold my duty, as I hold my soul,

47 **policy** statecraft

52 **fruit** dessert

53 **grace** honor. (Punning on *grace* said before a *feast*, line
    52.)

56 **doubt** fear, suspect

58 **sift him** question Polonius (or Hamlet) closely.

59 **brother** fellow king

60 **desires** good wishes.

61 **Upon our first** At our first words on the business

66 **impotence** weakness

67 **borne in hand** deluded, taken advantage of.   **arrests**
    orders to desist

69 **in fine** in conclusion

Both to my God and to my gracious king;
And I do think, or else this brain of mine
Hunts not the trail of policy so sure   47
As it hath used to do, that I have found
The very cause of Hamlet's lunacy.

KING

Oh, speak of that! That do I long to hear.

POLONIUS

Give first admittance to th'ambassadors.
My news shall be the fruit to that great feast.   52

KING

Thyself do grace to them and bring them in.   53

[Exit Polonius.]

He tells me, my dear Gertrude, he hath found
The head and source of all your son's distemper.

QUEEN

I doubt it is no other but the main,   56
His father's death and our o'erhasty marriage.

*Enter Ambassadors [Voltimand and Cornelius,
with Polonius].*

KING

Well, we shall sift him.—Welcome, my good friends!   58
Say, Voltimand, what from our brother Norway?   59

VOLTIMAND

Most fair return of greetings and desires.   60
Upon our first, he sent out to suppress   61
His nephew's levies, which to him appeared
To be a preparation 'gainst the Polack,
But, better looked into, he truly found
It was against Your Highness. Whereat grieved
That so his sickness, age, and impotence   66
Was falsely borne in hand, sends out arrests   67
On Fortinbras, which he, in brief, obeys,
Receives rebuke from Norway, and in fine   69

71 **give th'assay** make trial of strength, challenge
79 **On ... allowance** i.e., with such considerations for the
    safety of Denmark and permission for Fortinbras
80 **likes** pleases
81 **considered** suitable for deliberation
86 **expostulate** expound, inquire into
90 **wit** sense or judgment
98 **figure** figure of speech

Makes vow before his uncle never more
To give th'assay of arms against Your Majesty.   71
Whereon old Norway, overcome with joy,
Gives him three thousand crowns in annual fee
And his commission to employ those soldiers,
So levied as before, against the Polack,
With an entreaty, herein further shown,

[giving a paper]

That it might please you to give quiet pass
Through your dominions for this enterprise
On such regards of safety and allowance   79
As therein are set down.

KING   It likes us well,   80
And at our more considered time we'll read,   81
Answer, and think upon this business.
Meantime we thank you for your well-took labor.
Go to your rest; at night we'll feast together.
Most welcome home!   *Exeunt Ambassadors.*

POLONIUS   This business is well ended.
My liege, and madam, to expostulate   86
What majesty should be, what duty is,
Why day is day, night night, and time is time,
Were nothing but to waste night, day, and time,
Therefore, since brevity is the soul of wit,   90
And tediousness the limbs and outward flourishes,
I will be brief. Your noble son is mad.
Mad call I it, for, to define true madness,
What is't but to be nothing else but mad?
But let that go.

QUEEN   More matter, with less art.

POLONIUS
Madam, I swear I use no art at all.
That he's mad, 'tis true; 'tis true 'tis pity,
And pity 'tis 'tis true—a foolish figure,   98
But farewell it, for I will use no art.

103 **For . . . cause** i.e., for this defective behavior, this madness, must have a cause.

105 **Perpend** Consider.

108 **gather and surmise** draw your own conclusions.

113 **"In . . . etc."** (The letter is poetically addressed to her heart, where a letter would be kept by a young lady.)

115 **stay . . . faithful** i.e., hold on, I will do as you wish.

118 **Doubt** suspect

120 **ill . . . numbers** unskilled at writing verses.

121 **reckon** (1) count (2) number metrically, scan

124 **machine** i.e., body

126–8 **And . . . ear** and moreover she has told me when, how, and where his solicitings of her occurred.

Mad let us grant him, then, and now remains
That we find out the cause of this effect,
Or rather say, the cause of this defect,
For this effect defective comes by cause.   103
Thus it remains, and the remainder thus.
Perpend.   105
I have a daughter—have while she is mine—
Who, in her duty and obedience, mark,
Hath given me this. Now gather and surmise.   108
[He reads the letter.]   "To the celestial and my soul's
idol, the most beautified Ophelia"—
That's an ill phrase, a vile phrase; "beautified" is a
vile phrase. But you shall hear. Thus: [He reads.]
"In her excellent white bosom, these, etc."   113

QUEEN   Came this from Hamlet to her?

POLONIUS
Good madam, stay awhile, I will be faithful.   115
                                              [He reads.]

    "Doubt thou the stars are fire,
        Doubt that the sun doth move,
    Doubt truth to be a liar,   118
        But never doubt I love.
O dear Ophelia, I am ill at these numbers. I have not   120
art to reckon my groans. But that I love thee best, O   121
most best, believe it. Adieu.
           Thine evermore, most dear lady, whilst this
              machine is to him, Hamlet."   124
This in obedience hath my daughter shown me,
And, more above, hath his solicitings,   126
As they fell out by time, by means, and place,   127
All given to mine ear.

KING   But how hath she   128
Received his love?

POLONIUS   What do you think of me?

KING
As of a man faithful and honorable.

131 **fain** gladly

136–7 **If ... dumb** if I had acted as go-between, passing love
       notes, or if I had refused to let my heart acknowledge
       what my eyes could see

138 **with idle sight** complacently or incomprehendingly.

139 **round** roundly, plainly

140 **bespeak** address

141 **out of thy star** above your sphere, position

142 **prescripts** orders

148 **watch** state of sleeplessness

149 **lightness** lightheadedness.   **declension** decline, dete-
       rioration. (With a pun on the grammatical sense.)

156 **Take this from this** (The actor probably gestures, indi-
       cating that he means his head from his shoulders, or his
       staff of office or chain from his hands or neck, or some-
       thing similar.)

POLONIUS

I would fain prove so. But what might you think,   131
When I had seen this hot love on the wing—
As I perceived it, I must tell you that,
Before my daughter told me—what might you,
Or my dear Majesty your queen here, think,
If I had played the desk or table book,   136
Or given my heart a winking, mute and dumb,   137
Or looked upon this love with idle sight?   138
What might you think? No, I went round to work,   139
And my young mistress thus I did bespeak: 140
"Lord Hamlet is a prince out of thy star;   141
This must not be." And then I prescripts gave her,   142
That she should lock herself from his resort,
Admit no messengers, receive no tokens.
Which done, she took the fruits of my advice;
And he, repellèd—a short tale to make—
Fell into a sadness, then into a fast,
Thence to a watch, thence into a weakness,   148
Thence to a lightness, and by this declension   149
Into the madness wherein now he raves,
And all we mourn for.

KING [to the Queen]   Do you think 'tis this?

QUEEN   It may be, very like.

POLONIUS

Hath there been such a time—I would fain know
    that—
That I have positively said " 'Tis so,"
When it proved otherwise?

KING   Not that I know.

POLONIUS

Take this from this, if this be otherwise.   156
If circumstances lead me, I will find
Where truth is hid, though it were hid indeed

159 **center** center of the earth, traditionally an extraordinarily inaccessible place.   **try** test

162 **loose** (As one might release an animal that is being mated.)

163 **arras** hanging, tapestry

165 **thereon** on that account

167 **carters** wagon drivers.

170 **I'll . . . leave** I'll accost him at once. Please leave us alone; leave him to me.

172 **God-a-mercy** God have mercy, i.e., thank you.

174 **fishmonger** fish merchant.

182 **a good kissing carrion** i.e., a good piece of flesh for kissing, or for the sun to kiss

Within the center.

KING   How may we try it further?   159

POLONIUS

You know sometimes he walks four hours together
Here in the lobby.

QUEEN   So he does indeed.

POLONIUS

At such a time I'll loose my daughter to him.   162
Be you and I behind an arras then.   163
Mark the encounter. If he love her not
And be not from his reason fall'n thereon,   165
Let me be no assistant for a state,
But keep a farm and carters.

KING   We will try it.   167

        Enter Hamlet [reading a book].

QUEEN

But look where sadly the poor wretch comes reading.

POLONIUS

Away, I do beseech you both, away.
I'll board him presently. Oh, give me leave.   170
        Exeunt King and Queen [with attendants].
How does my good Lord Hamlet?

HAMLET   Well, God-a-mercy.   172

POLONIUS   Do you know me, my lord?

HAMLET   Excellent well. You are a fishmonger.   174

POLONIUS   Not I, my lord.

HAMLET   Then I would you were so honest a man.

POLONIUS   Honest, my lord?

HAMLET   Ay, sir. To be honest, as this world goes, is to
be one man picked out of ten thousand.

POLONIUS   That's very true, my lord.

HAMLET   For if the sun breed maggots in a dead dog,
being a good kissing carrion—Have you a daughter?   182

184 **i'th' sun** in public. (With additional implication of the sunshine of princely favors.) **Conception** (1) Understanding (2) Pregnancy

194 **matter** substance. (But Hamlet plays on the sense of "basis for a dispute.")

199 **purging** discharging. **amber** i.e., resin, like the resinous *plum-tree gum*

200 **wit** understanding

203 **honesty** decency, decorum

204 **old** as old

206 **out of the air** (The open air was considered dangerous for sick people.)

209 **pregnant** quick-witted, full of meaning. **happiness** felicity of expression

211 **prosperously** successfully

212 **suddenly** immediately

216 **withal** with

POLONIUS I have, my lord.

HAMLET Let her not walk i'th' sun. Conception is a 184
blessing, but as your daughter may conceive, friend,
look to't.

POLONIUS [*aside*] How say you by that? Still harping
on my daughter. Yet he knew me not at first; 'a said
I was a fishmonger. 'A is far gone. And truly in my
youth I suffered much extremity for love, very near
this. I'll speak to him again.—What do you read,
my lord?

HAMLET Words, words, words.

POLONIUS What is the matter, my lord?   194

HAMLET Between who?

POLONIUS I mean, the matter that you read, my lord.

HAMLET Slanders, sir; for the satirical rogue says here
that old men have gray beards, that their faces are wrin-
kled, their eyes purging thick amber and plum-tree 199
gum, and that they have a plentiful lack of wit, to- 200
gether with most weak hams. All which, sir, though I
most powerfully and potently believe, yet I hold it not
honesty to have it thus set down, for yourself, sir, shall 203
grow old as I am, if like a crab you could go backward. 204

POLONIUS [*aside*] Though this be madness, yet there is
method in't.—Will you walk out of the air, my lord? 206

HAMLET Into my grave.

POLONIUS Indeed, that's out of the air. [*Aside*] How
pregnant sometimes his replies are! A happiness that 209
often madness hits on, which reason and sanity could
not so prosperously be delivered of. I will leave him 211
and suddenly contrive the means of meeting between 212
him and my daughter.—My honorable lord, I will
most humbly take my leave of you.

HAMLET You cannot, sir, take from me anything that I
will more willingly part withal—except my life, except 216
my life, except my life.

227 **indifferent** ordinary, at neither extreme of fortune or
    misfortune

232–3 **the middle ... favors** i.e., her genitals.

234 **her privates we** (1) we dwell in her privates, her geni-
    tals, in the middle of her favors (2) we are her ordinary
    footsoldiers.

236 **strumpet** (Fortune was proverbially thought of as
    fickle.)

Enter Guildenstern and Rosencrantz.

POLONIUS   Fare you well, my lord.

HAMLET   These tedious old fools!

POLONIUS   You go to seek the Lord Hamlet. There he is.

ROSENCRANTZ   [*to Polonius*]   God save you, sir!

[*Exit Polonius.*]

GUILDENSTERN   My honored lord!

ROSENCRANTZ   My most dear lord!

HAMLET   My excellent good friends! How dost thou,
Guildenstern? Ah, Rosencrantz! Good lads, how do
you both?

ROSENCRANTZ
As the indifferent children of the earth.   227

GUILDENSTERN
Happy in that we are not overhappy.
On Fortune's cap we are not the very button.

HAMLET   Nor the soles of her shoe?

ROSENCRANTZ   Neither, my lord.

HAMLET   Then you live about her waist, or in the mid-   232
dle of her favors?   233

GUILDENSTERN   Faith, her privates we.   234

HAMLET   In the secret parts of Fortune? Oh, most true,
she is a strumpet. What news?   236

ROSENCRANTZ   None, my lord, but the world's grown
honest.

HAMLET   Then is doomsday near. But your news is not
true. Let me question more in particular. What have
you, my good friends, deserved at the hands of
Fortune that she sends you to prison hither?

GUILDENSTERN   Prison, my lord?

HAMLET   Denmark's a prison.

ROSENCRANTZ   Then is the world one.

247 **confines** places of confinement

259 **the very ... ambitious** that seemingly very substantial thing that the ambitious pursue

264–5 **Then ... shadows** (Hamlet pursues their argument about ambition to its absurd extreme: if ambition is only a shadow of a shadow, then beggars (who are presumably without ambition) must be real, whereas monarchs and heroes are only their shadows—*outstretched* like elongated shadows, made to look bigger than they are.)

266 **fay** faith

267 **wait upon** accompany, attend. (But Hamlet uses the phrase in the sense of providing menial service.)

268 **sort** class, categorize

270 **dreadfully attended** waited upon in slovenly fashion.

271 **beaten way** familiar path, tried-and-true course. **make** do

275 **too dear a halfpenny** (1) too expensive at even a halfpenny, i.e., of little worth (2) too expensive by a halfpenny in return for worthless kindness.

276 **free** voluntary

279 **Anything but to th' purpose** Anything except a straightforward answer. (Said ironically.)

HAMLET   A goodly one, in which there are many
confines, wards, and dungeons, Denmark being one   247
o'th' worst.

ROSENCRANTZ   We think not so, my lord.

HAMLET   Why then 'tis none to you, for there is nothing
either good or bad but thinking makes it so. To me it
is a prison.

ROSENCRANTZ   Why then, your ambition makes it one.
'Tis too narrow for your mind.

HAMLET   Oh, God, I could be bounded in a nutshell and
count myself a king of infinite space, were it not that
I have bad dreams.

GUILDENSTERN   Which dreams indeed are ambition, for
the very substance of the ambitious is merely the   259
shadow of a dream.

HAMLET   A dream itself is but a shadow.

ROSENCRANTZ   Truly, and I hold ambition of so airy
and light a quality that it is but a shadow's shadow.

HAMLET   Then are our beggars bodies, and our mon-   264
archs and outstretched heroes the beggars' shadows.   265
Shall we to th' court? For, by my fay, I cannot reason.   266

ROSENCRANTZ, GUILDENSTERN   We'll wait upon you.   267

HAMLET   No such matter. I will not sort you with the   268
rest of my servants, for, to speak to you like an honest
man, I am most dreadfully attended. But, in the   270
beaten way of friendship, what make you at Elsinore?   271

ROSENCRANTZ   To visit you, my lord, no other occasion.

HAMLET   Beggar that I am, I am even poor in thanks;
but I thank you, and sure, dear friends, my thanks are
too dear a halfpenny. Were you not sent for? Is it your   275
own inclining? Is it a free visitation? Come, come, deal   276
justly with me. Come, come. Nay, speak.

GUILDENSTERN   What should we say, my lord?

HAMLET   Anything but to th' purpose. You were sent   279

281 **color** disguise.

284 **conjure** adjure, entreat

285-6 **the consonancy of our youth** our closeness in our younger days

287 **better** more skillful

288 **charge** urge.   **even** straight, honest

291 **of** on

292 **hold not off** don't hold back.

294-5 **so . . . discovery** in that way my saying it first will spare you from having to reveal the truth

296 **molt no feather** i.e., not diminish in the least.

301 **brave** splendid

302 **fretted** adorned (with fretwork, as in a vaulted ceiling)

304 **congregation** mass.   **piece of work** masterpiece

306 **express** well-framed, exact, expressive

307 **apprehension** power of comprehending

309 **quintessence** very essence. (Literally, the fifth essence beyond earth, water, air, and fire, supposed to be extractable from them.)

for, and there is a kind of confession in your looks
which your modesties have not craft enough to color. 281
I know the good King and Queen have sent for you.

ROSENCRANTZ   To what end, my lord?

HAMLET   That you must teach me. But let me conjure 284
you, by the rights of our fellowship, by the consonancy 285
of our youth, by the obligation of our ever-preserved 286
love, and by what more dear a better proposer 287
could charge you withal, be even and direct with me 288
whether you were sent for or no.

ROSENCRANTZ   [aside to Guildenstern]   What say you?

HAMLET   [aside]   Nay, then, I have an eye of you.—If 291
you love me, hold not off. 292

GUILDENSTERN   My lord, we were sent for.

HAMLET   I will tell you why; so shall my anticipation 294
prevent your discovery, and your secrecy to the King 295
and Queen molt no feather. I have of late—but 296
wherefore I know not—lost all my mirth, forgone all
custom of exercises; and indeed it goes so heavily with
my disposition that this goodly frame, the earth,
seems to me a sterile promontory; this most excellent
canopy, the air, look you, this brave o'erhanging 301
firmament, this majestical roof fretted with golden 302
fire, why, it appeareth nothing to me but a foul and
pestilent congregation of vapors. What a piece of work 304
is a man! How noble in reason, how infinite in faculties,
in form and moving how express and admirable, in 306
action how like an angel, in apprehension how like a 307
god! The beauty of the world, the paragon of animals!
And yet, to me, what is this quintessence of dust? 309
Man delights not me—no, nor woman neither,
though by your smiling you seem to say so.

ROSENCRANTZ   My lord, there was no such stuff in my
thoughts.

HAMLET   Why did you laugh, then, when I said man
delights not me?

317 **Lenten entertainment** meager reception (appropriate to Lent)

318 **coted** overtook and passed by

321 **tribute** (1) applause (2) homage paid in money.   **of** from

322 **foil and target** sword and shield

323 **gratis** for nothing.   **humorous man** eccentric character, dominated by one trait or "humor"

323–4 **in peace** i.e., with full license

325 **tickle o'th' sear** hair trigger, ready to laugh easily. (A *sear* is part of a gun-lock.)

326 **halt** limp

329 **tragedians** actors

330 **residence** remaining in their usual place, i.e., in the city

332 **inhibition** formal prohibition (from acting plays in the city)

333 **late innovation** i.e., recent new fashion in satirical plays performed by boy actors in the "private" theaters; or the Earl of Essex's abortive rebellion in 1601 against Elizabeth's government. (A much debated passage of seemingly topical reference.)

337 **How . . . rusty?** Have they lost their polish, gone out of fashion? (This passage, through line 362, alludes to the rivalry between the children's companies and the adult actors, given strong impetus by the reopening of the Children of the Chapel at the Blackfriars Theater in late 1600.)

338 **keeps . . . wonted** continues in the usual

339 **aerie** nest.   **eyases** young hawks

340 **cry . . . question** speak shrilly, dominating the controversy (in decrying the public theaters)

340–1 **tyrannically** vehemently

342 **berattle . . . stages** clamor against the public theaters

343 **many wearing rapiers** i.e., many men of fashion, afraid to patronize the common players for fear of being satirized by the poets writing for the boy actors.   **goose quills** i.e., pens of satirists

346 **escotted** maintained.   **quality** (acting) profession

346–7 **no longer . . . sing** i.e., only until their voices change.

348 **common** regular, adult

ROSENCRANTZ   To think, my lord, if you delight not in
man, what Lenten entertainment the players shall 317
receive from you. We coted them on the way, and 318
hither are they coming to offer you service.

HAMLET   He that plays the king shall be welcome; His
Majesty shall have tribute of me. The adventurous 321
knight shall use his foil and target, the lover shall not 322
sigh gratis, the humorous man shall end his part in 323
peace, the clown shall make those laugh whose lungs 324
are tickle o'th' sear, and the lady shall say her mind 325
freely, or the blank verse shall halt for't What players 326
are they?

ROSENCRANTZ   Even those you were wont to take such
delight in, the tragedians of the city.   329

HAMLET   How chances it they travel? Their residence, 330
both in reputation and profit, was better both ways.

ROSENCRANTZ   I think their inhibition comes by the 332
means of the late innovation.   333

HAMLET   Do they hold the same estimation they did
when I was in the city? Are they so followed?

ROSENCRANTZ   No, indeed are they not.

HAMLET   How does it? Do they grow rusty?   337

ROSENCRANTZ   Nay, their endeavor keeps in the wonted 338
pace. But there is, sir, an aerie of children, little eyases, 339
that cry out on the top of question and are most tyran- 340
nically clapped for't. These are now the fashion, and 341
so berattle the common stages—so they call them— 342
that many wearing rapiers are afraid of goose quills 343
and dare scarce come thither.

HAMLET   What, are they children? Who maintains 'em?
How are they escotted? Will they pursue the quality no 346
longer than they can sing? Will they not say after- 347
wards, if they should grow themselves to common 348

349 **like** likely

349-50 **if ... better** if they find no better way to support themselves

351 **succession** i.e., future careers.

352 **to-do** ado

353 **tar** incite (as in inciting dogs to attack a chained bear)

354-6 **There ... question** i.e., For a while, no money was offered by the acting companies to playwrights for the plot to a play unless the satirical poets who wrote for the boys and the adult actors came to blows in the play itself.

360 **carry it away** i.e., win the day.

361-2 **Hercules ... load** (Thought to be an allusion to the sign of the Globe Theatre, which allegedly was Hercules bearing the world on his shoulders.)

364 **mouths** faces

366 **ducats** gold coins.   **in little** in miniature.   **'Sblood** By God's (Christ's) blood

371 **Th'appurtenance** The proper accompaniment

372 **comply** observe the formalities of courtesy

373 **garb** i.e., manner.   **my extent** that which I extend, i.e., my polite behavior

374 **show fairly outwards** show every evidence of cordiality

375 **entertainment** a (warm) reception.

378 **north-north-west** just off true north, only partly.

379 **I ... handsaw** (Speaking in his mad guise, Hamlet perhaps suggests that he can tell true from false. A *handsaw* may be a *hernshaw* or heron. Still, a supposedly mad disposition might compare hawks and handsaws.)

players—as it is most like, if their means are no 349
better—their writers do them wrong to make them 350
exclaim against their own succession?   351

ROSENCRANTZ   Faith, there has been much to-do on 352
both sides, and the nation holds it no sin to tar them to 353
controversy. There was for a while no money bid for 354
argument unless the poet and the player went to cuffs 355
in the question.   356

HAMLET   Is't possible?

GUILDENSTERN   Oh, there has been much throwing
about of brains.

HAMLET   Do the boys carry it away?   360

ROSENCRANTZ   Ay, that they do, my lord—Hercules 361
and his load too.   362

HAMLET   It is not very strange; for my uncle is King of
Denmark, and those that would make mouths at him 364
while my father lived give twenty, forty, fifty, a
hundred ducats apiece for his picture in little. 'Sblood, 366
there is something in this more than natural, if philosophy could find it out.

A flourish [of trumpets within].

GUILDENSTERN   There are the players.

HAMLET   Gentlemen, you are welcome to Elsinore. Your
hands, come then. Th'appurtenance of welcome is 371
fashion and ceremony. Let me comply with you in this 372
garb, lest my extent to the players, which, I tell you, 373
must show fairly outwards, should more appear like 374
entertainment than yours. You are welcome. But my 375
uncle-father and aunt-mother are deceived.

GUILDENSTERN   In what, my dear lord?

HAMLET   I am but mad north-north-west. When the 378
wind is southerly I know a hawk from a handsaw.   379

Enter Polonius.

POLONIUS   Well be with you, gentlemen!

383 **swaddling clouts** cloths in which to wrap a newborn baby.

384 **Haply** Perhaps

387-8 **You say...then indeed** (Said to impress upon Polonius the idea that Hamlet is in serious conversation with his friends.)

390 **Roscius** a famous Roman actor who died in 62 B.C.

393 **Buzz** (An interjection used to denote stale news.)

399-400 **scene...unlimited** plays that are unclassifiable and all-inclusive. (An absurdly catchall conclusion to Polonius's pompous list of categories.)

400 **Seneca** writer of Latin tragedies.   **Plautus** writer of Latin comedies

401 **law...liberty** dramatic composition both according to the rules and disregarding the rules.   **these** i.e., the actors

403 **Jephthah...Israel** (Jephthah had to sacrifice his daughter; see Judges 11. Hamlet goes on to quote from a ballad on the theme.)

408 **passing** surpassingly

413 **that follows not** i.e., just because you resemble Jephthah in having a daughter does not logically prove that you love her.

HAMLET   Hark you, Guildenstern, and you too; at each
ear a hearer. That great baby you see there is not yet
out of his swaddling clouts.   383

ROSENCRANTZ   Haply he is the second time come to 384
them, for they say an old man is twice a child.

HAMLET   I will prophesy he comes to tell me of the
players. Mark it.—You say right, sir, o' Monday 387
morning, 'twas then indeed.   388

POLONIUS   My lord, I have news to tell you.

HAMLET   My lord, I have news to tell you. When Roscius 390
was an actor in Rome—

POLONIUS   The actors are come hither, my lord.

HAMLET   Buzz, buzz!   393

POLONIUS   Upon my honor—

HAMLET   Then came each actor on his ass.

POLONIUS   The best actors in the world, either for
tragedy, comedy, history, pastoral, pastoral-comical,
historical-pastoral, tragical-historical, tragical-comical-
historical-pastoral, scene individable, or poem unlim 399
ited. Seneca cannot be too heavy, nor Plautus too 400
light. For the law of writ and the liberty, these are the 401
only men.

HAMLET   O Jephthah, judge of Israel, what a treasure 403
hadst thou!

POLONIUS   What a treasure had he, my lord?

HAMLET   Why,
      "One fair daughter, and no more,
      The which he lovèd passing well."   408

POLONIUS [aside]   Still on my daughter.

HAMLET   Am I not i'th' right, old Jephthah?

POLONIUS   If you call me Jephthah, my lord, I have a
daughter that I love passing well.

HAMLET   Nay, that follows not.   413

414 **What ... lord?** What does follow logically? (But Hamlet, pretending madness, answers with a fragment of a ballad, as if Polonius had asked, "What comes next?" See 419n.)

416 **lot** chance.   **wot** knows

418 **like** likely, probable

419 **the first ... more** the first stanza of this biblically based ballad will satisfy your stated desire to know *what follows* (line 414).

420 **my abridgment** something that cuts short my conversation; also, a diversion

421 **masters** good sirs

423 **valanced** fringed (with a beard)

424 **beard** confront, challenge. (With obvious pun.)
    young lady i.e., boy playing women's parts

425 **By'r Lady** By Our Lady

425–6 **nearer to heaven** i.e., taller

427 **chopine** thick-soled shoe of Italian fashion.

427–8 **uncurrent** not passable as lawful coinage

428 **cracked ... ring** i.e., changed from adolescent to male voice, no longer suitable for women's roles. (Coins featured rings enclosing the sovereign's head; if the coin was sufficiently clipped to invade within this ring, it was unfit for currency.)

429 **e'en to't** go at it

430 **straight** at once.

431 **quality** professional skill.

436–7 **caviar to the general** i.e., an expensive delicacy not generally palatable to uneducated tastes.

438–9 **cried in the top of** i.e., spoke with greater authority than

439 **digested** arranged, ordered

440 **modesty** moderation, restraint.   **cunning** skill.

441 **sallets** i.e., something savory, spicy improprieties

443 **indict** convict

445 **handsome** well-proportioned.   **fine** elaborately ornamented, showy.

POLONIUS What follows then, my lord?   414

HAMLET Why,
    "As by lot, God wot,"   416
and then, you know,
    "It came to pass, as most like it was"—   418
the first row of the pious chanson will show you more,   419
for look where my abridgement comes.   420

    Enter the Players.

You are welcome, masters; welcome, all. I am glad to   421
see thee well. Welcome, good friends. Oh, old friend!
Why, thy face is valanced since I saw thee last. Com'st   423
thou to beard me in Denmark? What, my young lady   424
and mistress! By'r Lady, Your Ladyship is nearer to   425
heaven than when I saw you last, by the altitude of a   426
chopine. Pray God your voice, like a piece of uncur-   427
rent gold, be not cracked within the ring. Masters, you   428
are all welcome. We'll e'en to't like French falconers,   429
fly at anything we see. We'll have a speech straight.   430
Come, give us a taste of your quality. Come, a   431
passionate speech.

FIRST PLAYER What speech, my good lord?

HAMLET I heard thee speak me a speech once, but it
was never acted, or if it was, not above once, for the
play, I remember, pleased not the million; 'twas cav-   436
iar to the general. But it was—as I received it, and   437
others, whose judgments in such matters cried in the   438
top of mine—an excellent play, well digested in the   439
scenes, set down with as much modesty as cunning. I   440
remember one said there were no sallets in the lines to   441
make the matter savory, nor no matter in the phrase
that might indict the author of affectation, but called it   443
an honest method, as wholesome as sweet, and by very
much more handsome than fine. One speech in't I   445
chiefly loved: 'twas Aeneas' tale to Dido, and there-

447–8 **Priam's slaughter** the slaying of the ruler of Troy, when the Greeks finally took the city

450 **Pyrrhus** a Greek hero in the Trojan War, also known as Neoptolemus, son of Achilles—another avenging son. **th' Hyrcanian beast** i.e., the tiger. (On the death of Priam, see Virgil, *Aeneid*, 2.506 ff.; compare the whole speech with Marlowe's *Dido Queen of Carthage*, 2.1.214 ff. On the *Hyrcanian* tiger, see *Aeneid*, 4.366–7. Hyrcania is on the Caspian Sea.)

452 **rugged** shaggy, savage.   **sable** black (for reasons of camouflage during the episode of the Trojan horse)

454 **couchèd** concealed.   **ominous horse** fateful Trojan horse, by which the Greeks gained access to Troy

456 **dismal** calamitous.

457 **total gules** entirely red. (A heraldic term.)   **tricked** spotted and smeared. (Heraldic.)

459 **Baked...streets** roasted and encrusted, like a thick paste, by the parching heat of the streets (because of the fires everywhere)

460 **tyrannous** cruel

461 **their lord's** i.e., Priam's

462 **o'ersizèd** covered as with size or glue

463 **carbuncles** large fiery-red precious stones thought to emit their own light

469 **antique** ancient, long-used

471 **Repugnant** disobedient, resistant

473 **fell** cruel

474 **Th' unnervèd** the strengthless.   **senseless Ilium** inanimate citadel of Troy

476 **his** its

478 **declining** descending.   **milky** white-haired

480 **painted** motionless, as in a painting

481 **like...matter** i.e., as though suspended between his intention and its fulfillment

about of it especially when he speaks of Priam's 447
slaughter. If it live in your memory, begin at this line: 448
let me see, let me see—

    "The rugged Pyrrhus, like th'Hyrcanian beast"— 450
'Tis not so. It begins with Pyrrhus:

    "The rugged Pyrrhus, he whose sable arms, 452
    Black as his purpose, did the night resemble
    When he lay couchèd in th' ominous horse, 454
    Hath now this dread and black complexion
      smeared
    With heraldry more dismal. Head to foot 456
    Now is he total gules, horridly tricked 457
    With blood of fathers, mothers, daughters, sons,
    Baked and impasted with the parching streets, 459
    That lend a tyrannous and a damnèd light 460
    To their lord's murder. Roasted in wrath and fire, 461
    And thus o'ersizèd with coagulate gore, 462
    With eyes like carbuncles, the hellish Pyrrhus 463
    Old grandsire Priam seeks."

So proceed you.

POLONIUS 'Fore God, my lord, well spoken, with good
accent and good discretion.

FIRST PLAYER   "Anon he finds him
Striking too short at Greeks. His antique sword, 469
Rebellious to his arm, lies where it falls,
Repugnant to command. Unequal matched, 471
Pyrrhus at Priam drives, in rage strikes wide,
But with the whiff and wind of his fell sword 473
Th'unnervèd father falls. Then senseless Ilium, 474
Seeming to feel this blow, with flaming top
Stoops to his base, and with a hideous crash 476
Takes prisoner Pyrrhus' ear. For, lo! His sword,
Which was declining on the milky head 478
Of reverend Priam, seemed i'th'air to stick.
So as a painted tyrant Pyrrhus stood, 480
And, like a neutral to his will and matter, 481

483 **against** just before

484 **rack** mass of clouds

485 **orb** globe, earth

487 **region** sky

489 **Cyclops** giant armor makers in the smithy of Vulcan

490 **proof** proven or tested resistance to assault

491 **remorse** pity

494 **synod** assembly

495 **fellies** pieces of wood forming the rim of a wheel

496 **nave** hub.   **hill of heaven** Mount Olympus

500 **jig** comic song and dance often given at the end of a
   play

501 **Hecuba** wife of Priam.

502 **who...had** anyone who had. (Also in line 510.)
   moblèd muffled

505 **threat'ning the flames** i.e., weeping hard enough to
   dampen the flames

506 **bisson rheum** blinding tears.   **clout** cloth

507 **late** lately

508 **all o'erteemèd** utterly worn out with bearing children

511 **state** rule, managing.   **pronounced** proclaimed.

Did nothing.
But as we often see against some storm   483
A silence in the heavens, the rack stand still,   484
The bold winds speechless, and the orb below   485
As hush as death, anon the dreadful thunder
Doth rend the region, so, after Pyrrhus' pause,   487
A rousèd vengeance sets him new a-work,
And never did the Cyclops' hammers fall   489
On Mars's armor forged for proof eterne   490
With less remorse than Pyrrhus' bleeding sword   491
Now falls on Priam.
Out, out, thou strumpet Fortune! All you gods
In general synod take away her power!   494
Break all the spokes and fellies from her wheel,   495
And bowl the round nave down the hill of heaven   496
As low as to the fiends!"

POLONIUS   This is too long.

HAMLET   It shall to the barber's with your beard.—Prithee, say on. He's for a jig or a tale of bawdry, or he   500
sleeps. Say on; come to Hecuba.   501

FIRST PLAYER
"But who, ah woe! had seen the moblèd queen"—   502

HAMLET   "The moblèd queen"?

POLONIUS   That's good. "Moblèd queen" is good.

FIRST PLAYER
"Run barefoot up and down, threat'ning the flames   505
With bisson rheum, a clout upon that head   506
Where late the diadem stood, and, for a robe,   507
About her lank and all o'erteemèd loins   508
A blanket, in the alarm of fear caught up—
Who this had seen, with tongue in venom steeped,
'Gainst Fortune's state would treason have
    pronounced.   511
But if the gods themselves did see her then
When she saw Pyrrhus make malicious sport
In mincing with his sword her husband's limbs,

517 **milch** milky, moist with tears.   **burning eyes of heaven** i.e., stars, heavenly bodies

518 **passion** overpowering emotion

519 **whe're** whether

523 **bestowed** lodged.

524 **abstract** summary account

529 **God's bodikin** By God's (Christ's) little body, *bodykin*. (Not to be confused with *bodkin*, "dagger.")

531 **after** according to

540 **ha 't** have it

541 **study** memorize

The instant burst of clamor that she made,
Unless things mortal move them not at all,
Would have made milch the burning eyes of heaven,   517
And passion in the gods."   518

POLONIUS   Look whe'er he has not turned his color and   519
has tears in 's eyes. Prithee, no more.

HAMLET   'Tis well; I'll have thee speak out the rest of
this soon.—Good my lord, will you see the players well
bestowed? Do you hear, let them be well used, for they   523
are the abstract and brief chronicles of the time. After   524
your death you were better have a bad epitaph than
their ill report while you live.

POLONIUS   My lord, I will use them according to their
desert.

HAMLET   God's bodikin, man, much better. Use every   529
man after his desert, and who shall scape whipping?
Use them after your own honor and dignity. The less   531
they deserve, the more merit is in your bounty. Take
them in.

POLONIUS   Come, sirs.   [Exit.]

HAMLET   Follow him, friends. We'll hear a play tomor-
row. [As they start to leave, Hamlet detains the First
Player.] Dost thou hear me, old friend? Can you play
The Murder of Gonzago?

FIRST PLAYER   Ay, my lord.

HAMLET   We'll ha 't tomorrow night. You could, for a   540
need, study a speech of some dozen or sixteen lines   541
which I would set down and insert in't, could you not?

FIRST PLAYER   Ay, my lord.

HAMLET   Very well. Follow that lord, and look you mock
him not.   Exeunt players.
My good friends, I'll leave you till night. You are welcome to Elsinore.

ROSENCRANTZ   Good my lord!
                    Exeunt [Rosencrantz and Guildenstern].

552 **But** merely

553 **force . . . conceit** bring his innermost being so entirely
     into accord with his conception (of the role)

554 **from her working** as a result of, or in response to, his
     soul's activity.   **wanned** grew pale

555 **aspect** look, glance

556–7 **his whole . . . conceit** all his bodily powers respond-
     ing with actions to suit his thought.

563 **the general ear** everyone's ear.   **horrid** horrible

564 **appall** (Literally, make pale.)   **free** innocent

565 **Confound the ignorant** i.e., dumbfound those who
     know nothing of the crime that has been committed.
     amaze stun

567 **muddy-mettled** dull-spirited

567–8 **peak . . . cause** mope, like a dreaming idler, not quick-
     ened by my cause

570 **property** person and function

571 **damned defeat** damnable act of destruction

572 **pate** head

574 **Gives . . . throat** Calls me an out-and-out liar

576 **'swounds** by his (Christ's) wounds

577 **pigeon-livered** (The pigeon or dove was popularly sup-
     posed to be mild because it secreted no gall.)

578 **To . . . bitter** to make things bitter for oppressors

579 **region kites** kites (birds of prey) of the air

580 **offal** entrails.

581 **Remorseless** Pitiless.   **kindless** unnatural

583 **brave** fine, admirable. (Said ironically.)

HAMLET

    Ay, so, goodbye to you.—Now I am alone.

    Oh, what a rogue and peasant slave am I!

    Is it not monstrous that this player here,

    But in a fiction, in a dream of passion,   552

    Could force his soul so to his own conceit   553

    That from her working all his visage wanned,   554

    Tears in his eyes, distraction in his aspect,   555

    A broken voice, and his whole function suiting   556

    With forms to his conceit? And all for nothing!   557

    For Hecuba!

    What's Hecuba to him, or he to Hecuba,

    That he should weep for her? What would he do

    Had he the motive and the cue for passion

    That I have? He would drown the stage with tears

    And cleave the general ear with horrid speech,   563

    Make mad the guilty and appall the free,   564

    Confound the ignorant, and amaze indeed   565

    The very faculties of eyes and ears. Yet I,

    A dull and muddy-mettled rascal, peak   567

    Like John-a-dreams, unpregnant of my cause,   568

    And can say nothing—no, not for a king

    Upon whose property and most dear life   570

    A damned defeat was made. Am I a coward?   571

    Who calls me villain? Breaks my pate across?   572

    Plucks off my beard and blows it in my face?

    Tweaks me by the nose? Gives me the lie i'th' throat   574

    As deep as to the lungs? Who does me this?

    Ha, 'swounds, I should take it; for it cannot be   576

    But I am pigeon-livered and lack gall   577

    To make oppression bitter, or ere this   578

    I should ha' fatted all the region kites   579

    With this slave's offal. Bloody, bawdy villain!   580

    Remorseless, treacherous, lecherous, kindless villain!   581

    Oh, vengeance!

    Why, what an ass am I! This is most brave,   583

    That I, the son of a dear father murdered,

587 **drab** whore

588 **scullion** menial kitchen servant. (Apt to be foul-mouthed.)   **About** About it, to work

591 **cunning** art, skill.   **scene** dramatic presentation

592 **presently** at once

598 **tent** probe.   **the quick** the tender part of a wound, the core.   **blench** quail, flinch

603 **spirits** humors (of melancholy)

604 **Abuses** deludes

605 **relative** cogent, pertinent

3.1 *Location: The castle.*

1 **drift of conference** course of talk

7 **forward** willing.   **sounded** questioned

Prompted to my revenge by heaven and hell,
Must like a whore unpack my heart with words
And fall a-cursing, like a very drab,   587
A scullion! Fie upon't, foh! About, my brains!   588
Hum, I have heard
That guilty creatures sitting at a play
Have by the very cunning of the scene   591
Been struck so to the soul that presently   592
They have proclaimed their malefactions;
For murder, though it have no tongue, will speak
With most miraculous organ. I'll have these players
Play something like the murder of my father
Before mine uncle. I'll observe his looks;
I'll tent him to the quick. If 'a do blench,   598
I know my course. The spirit that I have seen
May be the devil, and the devil hath power
T'assume a pleasing shape; yea, and perhaps,
Out of my weakness and my melancholy,
As he is very potent with such spirits,   603
Abuses me to damn me. I'll have grounds   604
More relative than this. The play's the thing   605
Wherein I'll catch the conscience of the King.   *Exit.*

[3.1] ✣ *Enter King, Queen, Polonius, Ophelia,*
           Rosencrantz, Guildenstern, lords.

KING

And can you by no drift of conference   1
Get from him why he puts on this confusion,
Grating so harshly all his days of quiet
With turbulent and dangerous lunacy?

ROSENCRANTZ

He does confess he feels himself distracted,
But from what cause 'a will by no means speak.

GUILDENSTERN

Nor do we find him forward to be sounded,   7

12 **disposition** inclination.
13 **Niggard of question** Laconic.   **demands** questions
14 **assay** try to win
17 **o'erraught** overtook
26 **edge** incitement
29 **closely** privately
31 **Affront** confront, meet
32 **espials** spies

But with a crafty madness keeps aloof
When we would bring him on to some confession
Of his true state.

QUEEN   Did he receive you well?

ROSENCRANTZ   Most like a gentleman.

GUILDENSTERN
But with much forcing of his disposition.   12

ROSENCRANTZ
Niggard of question, but of our demands   13
Most free in his reply.

QUEEN   Did you assay him   14
To any pastime?

ROSENCRANTZ
Madam, it so fell out that certain players
We o'erraught on the way. Of these we told him,   17
And there did seem in him a kind of joy
To hear of it. They are here about the court,
And, as I think, they have already order
This night to play before him.

POLONIUS   'Tis most true,
And he beseeched me to entreat Your Majesties
To hear and see the matter.

KING
With all my heart, and it doth much content me
To hear him so inclined.
Good gentlemen, give him a further edge   26
And drive his purpose into these delights.

ROSENCRANTZ
We shall, my lord.

                    Exeunt Rosencrantz and Guildenstern.

KING   Sweet Gertrude, leave us too,
For we have closely sent for Hamlet hither,   29
That he, as 'twere by accident, may here
Affront Ophelia.   31
Her father and myself, lawful espials,   32

43 **Gracious** Your Grace (i.e., the King)

44 **bestow** conceal

45 **exercise** religious exercise. (The book she reads is one of devotion.)   **color** give a plausible appearance to

46 **loneliness** being alone.

47 **too much proved** too often shown to be true, too often practiced

53 **to . . . helps it** in comparison with the cosmetic that fashions the cheek's false beauty

54 **painted word** deceptive utterances.

56.1 *withdraw* (The King and Polonius may retire behind an arras. The stage directions specify that they "enter" again near the end of the scene.)

Will so bestow ourselves that seeing, unseen,
We may of their encounter frankly judge,
And gather by him, as he is behaved,
If't be th'affliction of his love or no
That thus he suffers for.

QUEEN   I shall obey you.
And for your part, Ophelia, I do wish
That your good beauties be the happy cause
Of Hamlet's wildness. So shall I hope your virtues
Will bring him to his wonted way again,
To both your honors.

OPHELIA   Madam, I wish it may.

[Exit Queen.]

POLONIUS
Ophelia, walk you here.—Gracious, so please you,   43
We will bestow ourselves. [To Ophelia] Read on this
     book,   [giving her a book]   44
That show of such an exercise may color   45
Your loneliness. We are oft to blame in this—   46
'Tis too much proved—that with devotion's visage   47
And pious action we do sugar o'er
The devil himself.

KING [aside]   Oh, 'tis too true!
How smart a lash that speech doth give my
     conscience!
The harlot's cheek, beautied with plast'ring art,
Is not more ugly to the thing that helps it   53
Than is my deed to my most painted word.   54
Oh, heavy burden!

POLONIUS
I hear him coming. Let's withdraw, my lord.   56

[The King and Polonius withdraw.]

Enter Hamlet. [Ophelia pretends to read a book.]

HAMLET
To be, or not to be, that is the question:

66 **rub** (Literally, an obstacle in the game of bowls.)

68 **shuffled** sloughed, cast.   **coil** turmoil

69 **respect** consideration

70 **of . . . life** so long-lived, something we willingly endure for so long. (Also suggesting that long life is itself a calamity.)

72 **contumely** insolent abuse

73 **disprized** unvalued

74 **office** officialdom.   **spurns** insults

75 **of . . . takes** receives from unworthy persons

76 **quietus** acquittance; here, death

77 **a bare bodkin** a mere dagger, unsheathed.   **fardels** burdens

80 **bourn** frontier, boundary

85 **native hue** natural color, complexion

86 **cast** tinge, shade of color

87 **pitch** height (as of a falcon's flight).   **moment** importance

88 **regard** respect, consideration.   **currents** courses

89 **Soft you** i.e., Wait a minute, gently

90–1 **in . . . remembered** i.e., pray for me, sinner that I am.

Whether 'tis nobler in the mind to suffer
The slings and arrows of outrageous fortune,
Or to take arms against a sea of troubles
And by opposing end them. To die, to sleep—
No more—and by a sleep to say we end
The heartache and the thousand natural shocks
That flesh is heir to. 'Tis a consummation
Devoutly to be wished. To die, to sleep;
To sleep, perchance to dream. Ay, there's the rub,   66
For in that sleep of death what dreams may come,
When we have shuffled off this mortal coil,   68
Must give us pause. There's the respect   69
That makes calamity of so long life.   70
For who would bear the whips and scorns of time,
Th'oppressor's wrong, the proud man's contumely,   72
The pangs of disprized love, the law's delay,   73
The insolence of office, and the spurns   74
That patient merit of th'unworthy takes,   75
When he himself might his quietus make   76
With a bare bodkin? Who would fardels bear,   77
To grunt and sweat under a weary life,
But that the dread of something after death,
The undiscovered country from whose bourn   80
No traveler returns, puzzles the will,
And makes us rather bear those ills we have
Than fly to others that we know not of?
Thus conscience does make cowards of us all;
And thus the native hue of resolution   85
Is sicklied o'er with the pale cast of thought,   86
And enterprises of great pitch and moment   87
With this regard their currents turn awry   88
And lose the name of action.—Soft you now,   89
The fair Ophelia.—Nymph, in thy orisons   90
Be all my sins remembered.

OPHELIA   Good my lord,   91
How does Your Honor for this many a day?

104 **honest** (1) truthful (2) chaste.

106 **fair** (1) beautiful (2) just, honorable.

108 **your honesty** your chastity

109 **discourse to** familiar dealings with

110 **commerce** dealings, intercourse

114 **his** its

115–16 **This . . . proof** This was formerly an unfashionable view, but now the present age confirms how true it is.

118–20 **virtue . . . of it** virtue cannot be grafted onto our sinful condition without our retaining some taste of the old stock.

122 **nunnery** convent. (With an awareness that the word was also used derisively to denote a brothel.)

HAMLET
I humbly thank you; well, well, well.

OPHELIA
My lord, I have remembrances of yours,
That I have longèd long to redeliver.
I pray you, now receive them.   [*She offers tokens.*]

HAMLET
No, not I, I never gave you aught.

OPHELIA
My honored lord, you know right well you did,
And with them words of so sweet breath composed
As made the things more rich. Their perfume lost,
Take these again, for to the noble mind
Rich gifts wax poor when givers prove unkind.
There, my lord.   [*She gives tokens.*]

HAMLET Ha, ha! Are you honest?   104

OPHELIA My lord?

HAMLET Are you fair?   106

OPHELIA What means Your Lordship?

HAMLET That if you be honest and fair, your honesty 108
should admit no discourse to your beauty.   109

OPHELIA Could beauty, my lord, have better commerce 110
than with honesty?

HAMLET Ay, truly, for the power of beauty will sooner
transform honesty from what it is to a bawd than the
force of honesty can translate beauty into his likeness. 114
This was sometime a paradox, but now the time gives 115
it proof. I did love you once.   116

OPHELIA Indeed, my lord, you made me believe so.

HAMLET You should not have believed me, for virtue 118
cannot so inoculate our old stock but we shall relish of 119
it. I loved you not.   120

OPHELIA I was the more deceived.

HAMLET Get thee to a nunnery. Why wouldst thou be a 122

123 **indifferent honest** reasonably virtuous

126 **beck** command

140 **monsters** (An illusion to the horns of a cuckold.)
     you i.e., you women

144 **paintings** use of cosmetics

146–8 **You jig . . . ignorance** i.e., You prance about frivo-
       lously and speak with affected coyness, you put new la-
       bels on God's creatures (by your use of cosmetics), and
       you excuse your affectations on the grounds of pre-
       tended ignorance.

148 **on't** of it

155 **Th'expectancy and rose** the hope and ornament

156 **The glass . . . form** the mirror of true self-fashioning
     and the pattern of courtly behavior

breeder of sinners? I am myself indifferent honest, but 123
yet I could accuse me of such things that it were better
my mother had not borne me: I am very proud,
revengeful, ambitious, with more offenses at my beck 126
than I have thoughts to put them in, imagination to
give them shape, or time to act them in. What should
such fellows as I do crawling between earth and
heaven? We are arrant knaves all; believe none of us.
Go thy ways to a nunnery. Where's your father?

OPHELIA   At home, my lord.

HAMLET   Let the doors be shut upon him, that he may
play the fool nowhere but in 's own house. Farewell.

OPHELIA   Oh, help him, you sweet heavens!

HAMLET   If thou dost marry, I'll give thee this plague for
thy dowry: be thou as chaste as ice, as pure as snow,
thou shalt not escape calumny. Get thee to a nunnery,
farewell. Or, if thou wilt needs marry, marry a fool, for
wise men know well enough what monsters you 140
make of them. To a nunnery, go, and quickly too.
Farewell.

OPHELIA   Heavenly powers, restore him!

HAMLET   I have heard of your paintings too, well 144
enough. God hath given you one face, and you make
yourselves another. You jig, you amble, and you 146
lisp, you nickname God's creatures, and make your 147
wantonness your ignorance. Go to, I'll no more on't; 148
it hath made me mad. I say we will have no more
marriage. Those that are married already—all but
one—shall live. The rest shall keep as they are. To a
nunnery, go.   *Exit.*

OPHELIA
Oh, what a noble mind is here o'erthrown!
The courtier's, soldier's, scholar's, eye, tongue, sword,
Th'expectancy and rose of the fair state,   155
The glass of fashion and the mold of form,   156

157 **Th'observed ... observers** i.e., the center of attention and honor in the court

159 **music** musical, sweetly uttered

162 **blown** blossoming

163 **Blasted with ecstasy** blighted with madness.

165 **affections** emotions, feelings

168 **sits on brood** sits like a bird on a nest, about to *hatch* mischief (line 169)

169 **doubt** suspect, fear.   **disclose** disclosure, hatching

172 **set it down** resolved

175 **variable objects** various sights and surroundings to divert him

176 **This something ... heart** the strange matter settled in his heart

177 **still** continually

178 **From ... himself** out of his natural manner.

186 **round** blunt

188 **find him not** fails to discover what is troubling him

Th'observed of all observers, quite, quite down!   157
And I, of ladies most deject and wretched,
That sucked the honey of his music vows,   159
Now see that noble and most sovereign reason
Like sweet bells jangled out of tune and harsh,
That unmatched form and feature of blown youth   162
Blasted with ecstasy. Oh, woe is me,   163
T'have seen what I have seen, see what I see!

Enter King and Polonius.

KING
Love? His affections do not that way tend;   165
Nor what he spake, though it lacked form a little,
Was not like madness. There's something in his soul
O'er which his melancholy sits on brood,   168
And I do doubt the hatch and the disclose   169
Will be some danger; which for to prevent,
I have in quick determination
Thus set it down: he shall with speed to England   172
For the demand of our neglected tribute.
Haply the seas and countries different
With variable objects shall expel   175
This something-settled matter in his heart,   176
Whereon his brains still beating puts him thus   177
From fashion of himself. What think you on't?   178

POLONIUS
It shall do well. But yet do I believe
The origin and commencement of his grief
Sprung from neglected love.—How now, Ophelia?
You need not tell us what Lord Hamlet said;
We heard it all.—My lord, do as you please,
But, if you hold it fit, after the play
Let his queen-mother all alone entreat him
To show his grief. Let her be round with him;   186
And I'll be placed, so please you, in the ear
Of all their conference. If she find him not,   188

3.2 *Location: The castle.*

3   **our players** players nowadays.   **I had as lief** I would
    just as soon

9   **robustious** violent, boisterous.   **periwig-pated** wear-
    ing a wig

11 **groundlings** spectators who paid least and stood in the
    yard of the theater.   **capable of** able to understand

12 **dumb shows and noise** noisy spectacle (rather than
    thoughtful drama)

13–14 **Termagant** a supposed deity of the Mohammedans,
    not found in any English medieval play but elsewhere
    portrayed as violent and blustering

14 **Herod** Herod of Jewry. (A character in *The Slaughter of
    the Innocents* and other cycle plays. The part was played
    with great noise and fury.)

19 **modesty** restraint, moderation

20 **from** contrary to

23 `scorn` i.e., something foolish and deserving of scorn

23–4 **and the . . . pressure** and the present state of affairs
    its likeness as seen in an impression, such as wax.

25 **come tardy off** falling short

25–6 **the unskillful** those lacking in judgment

27 **the censure . . . one** the judgment of even one of
    whom.   **your allowance** your scale of values

To England send him, or confine him where
Your wisdom best shall think.

KING   It shall be so.
Madness in great ones must not unwatched go.

Exeunt.

[3.2] ❧ *Enter Hamlet and three of the Players.*

HAMLET   Speak the speech, I pray you, as I pronounced
it to you, trippingly on the tongue. But if you mouth
it, as many of our players do, I had as lief the town crier   3
spoke my lines. Nor do not saw the air too much with
your hand, thus, but use all gently; for in the very
torrent, tempest, and, as I may say, whirlwind of your
passion, you must acquire and beget a temperance
that may give it smoothness. Oh, it offends me to the
soul to hear a robustious periwig-pated fellow tear a   9
passion to tatters, to very rags, to split the ears of the
groundlings, who for the most part are capable of   11
nothing but inexplicable dumb shows and noise. I   12
would have such a fellow whipped for o'erdoing Ter-   13
magant. It out-Herods Herod. Pray you, avoid it.   14

FIRST PLAYER   I warrant Your Honor.

HAMLET   Be not too tame neither, but let your own
discretion be your tutor. Suit the action to the word,
the word to the action, with this special observance,
that you o'erstep not the modesty of nature. For   19
anything so o'erdone is from the purpose of playing,   20
whose end, both at the first and now, was and is to
hold as 'twere the mirror up to nature, to show virtue
her feature, scorn her own image, and the very age   23
and body of the time his form and pressure. Now this   24
overdone or come tardy off, though it makes the   25
unskillful laugh, cannot but make the judicious grieve,   26
the censure of the which one must in your allowance   27
o'erweigh a whole theater of others. Oh, there be play-

30 **not ... profanely** (Hamlet anticipates his idea in lines
    33–4 that some men were not made by God at all.)

31 **Christians** i.e., ordinary decent folk

32 **nor man** i.e., nor any human being at all

33 **journeymen** common workmen

35 **abominably** (Shakespeare's usual spelling, "abhom-
    inably," suggests a literal though etymologically incor-
    rect meaning, "removed from human nature.")

36 **indifferently** tolerably

40 **of them** some among them

41 **barren** i.e., of wit

48 **presently** at once.

54 **my ... withal** my dealings encountered.

ers that I have seen play, and heard others praise, and
that highly, not to speak it profanely, that, neither   30
having th'accent of Christians nor the gait of Chris-   31
tian, pagan, nor man, have so strutted and bellowed   32
that I have thought some of nature's journeymen had   33
made men and not made them well, they imitated
humanity so abominably.   35

FIRST PLAYER   I hope we have reformed that indifferently   36
with us, sir.

HAMLET   Oh, reform it altogether. And let those that play
your clowns speak no more than is set down for them;
for there be of them that will themselves laugh, to set   40
on some quantity of barren spectators to laugh too,   41
though in the meantime some necessary question of
the play be then to be considered. That's villainous,
and shows a most pitiful ambition in the fool that uses
it. Go make you ready.   [*Exeunt Players.*]

          Enter Polonius, Guildenstern, and Rosencrantz.

How now, my lord, will the King hear this piece of
work?

POLONIUS   And the Queen too, and that presently.   48

HAMLET   Bid the players make haste.   [*Exit Polonius.*]
Will you two help to hasten them?

ROSENCRANTZ
Ay, my lord.   *Exeunt they two.*

HAMLET   What ho, Horatio!

          Enter Horatio.

HORATIO   Here, sweet lord, at your service.

HAMLET
Horatio, thou art e'en as just a man
As e'er my conversation coped withal.   54

HORATIO
Oh, my dear lord—

HAMLET   Nay, do not think I flatter,
For what advancement may I hope from thee

59 **candied** sugared, flattering
60 **pregnant** compliant
61 **thrift** profit
63 **could ... election** could make distinguishing choices among persons
64 **sealed thee** (Literally, as one would seal a legal document to mark possession.)
68 **blood** passion.   **commeddled** commingled
70 **stop** hole in a wind instrument for controlling the sound
78 **very ... soul** your most penetrating observation and consideration
79 **occulted** hidden
80 **unkennel** (As one would say of a fox driven from its lair.)
83 **Vulcan's stithy** the smithy, the place of stiths (anvils) of the Roman god of fire and metalworking.
86 **censure of his seeming** judgment of his appearance or behavior.
87 **If 'a steal aught** If he gets away with anything

That no revenue hast but thy good spirits
To feed and clothe thee? Why should the poor be
    flattered?
No, let the candied tongue lick absurd pomp,   59
And crook the pregnant hinges of the knee   60
Where thrift may follow fawning. Dost thou hear?   61
Since my dear soul was mistress of her choice
And could of men distinguish her election,   63
Sh' hath sealed thee for herself, for thou hast been   64
As one, in suffering all, that suffers nothing,
A man that Fortune's buffets and rewards
Hast ta'en with equal thanks; and blest are those
Whose blood and judgment are so well commeddled   68
That they are not a pipe for Fortune's finger
To sound what stop she please. Give me that man   70
That is not passion's slave, and I will wear him
In my heart's core, ay, in my heart of heart,
As I do thee.—Something too much of this.—
There is a play tonight before the King.
One scene of it comes near the circumstance
Which I have told thee of my father's death.
I prithee, when thou see'st that act afoot,
Even with the very comment of thy soul   78
Observe my uncle. If his occulted guilt   79
Do not itself unkennel in one speech,   80
It is a damnèd ghost that we have seen,
And my imaginations are as foul
As Vulcan's stithy. Give him heedful note,   83
For I mine eyes will rivet to his face,
And after we will both our judgments join
In censure of his seeming.
HORATIO   Well, my lord.   86
If 'a steal aught the whilst this play is playing   87
And scape detecting, I will pay the theft.

        [Flourish.] Enter trumpets and kettledrums, King,
        Queen, Polonius, Ophelia, [Rosencrantz,

89 **idle** (1) unoccupied (2) mad.

91 **cousin** i.e., close relative

92 **chamelon's dish** (Chameleons were supposed to feed
on air. Hamlet deliberately misinterprets the King's *fares*
as "feeds." By his phrase *eat the air* he also plays on the
idea of feeding himself with the promise of succession,
of being the *heir.*)

93 **capons** roosters castrated and *crammed* with feed to
make them succulent

94 **have ... with** make nothing of, or gain nothing from

95 **are not mine** do not respond to what I asked.

96 **nor mine now** (Once spoken, words are proverbially
no longer the speaker's own—and hence should be uttered warily.)

101–2 **i'th' Capitol** (where Caesar was assassinated, according to *Julius Caesar,* 3.1, but see 1.3.126n in that play)

103 **brute** (The Latin meaning of *brutus,* "stupid," was often
used punningly with the name Brutus.)   **part** (1) deed
(2) role

104 **calf** fool

105 **stay upon** await

108 **metal** substance that is *attractive* i.e., magnetic, but with
suggestion also of *mettle,* "disposition"

110 **Lady ... lap?** Onstage, Hamlet often lies at Ophelia's
feet, but he could instead offer to do this and continue
to stand.

114 **country matters** sexual intercourse. (With a bawdy
pun on the first syllable of *country.*)

Guildenstern, and other lords, with guards
carrying torches].

HAMLET   They are coming to the play. I must be idle.   89
Get you a place.   [*The King, Queen, and courtiers sit.*]

KING   How fares our cousin Hamlet?   91

HAMLET   Excellent, i'faith, of the chameleon's dish: I eat   92
the air, promise-crammed. You cannot feed capons so.   93

KING   I have nothing with this answer, Hamlet. These   94
words are not mine.   95

HAMLET   No, nor mine now. [*To Polonius*] My lord, you   96
played once i'th'university, you say?

POLONIUS   That did I, my lord, and was accounted a
good actor.

HAMLET   What did you enact?

POLONIUS   I did enact Julius Caesar. I was killed i'th'   101
Capitol; Brutus killed me.   102

HAMLET   It was a brute part of him to kill so capital a   103
calf there.—Be the players ready?   104

ROSENCRANTZ   Ay, my lord. They stay upon your   105
patience.

QUEEN   Come hither, my dear Hamlet, sit by me.

HAMLET   No, good mother, here's metal more attractive.   108

POLONIUS   [*to the King*]   Oho, do you mark that?

HAMLET   Lady, shall I lie in your lap?   110
                    [*Lying down at Ophelia's feet.*]

OPHELIA   No, my lord.

HAMLET   I mean, my head upon your lap?

OPHELIA   Ay, my lord.

HAMLET   Do you think I meant country matters?   114

OPHELIA   I think nothing, my lord.

HAMLET   That's a fair thought to lie between maids'
legs.

119 **Nothing** The figure zero or naught, suggesting the female sexual anatomy. (*Thing* not infrequently has a bawdy connotation of male or female anatomy, and the reference here could be male.)

123 **only jig maker** very best composer of jigs, i.e., pointless merriment. (Hamlet replies sardonically to Ophelia's observation that he is merry by saying, "If you're looking for someone who is really merry, you've come to the right person.")

125 **within 's** within this (i.e., these)

128 **suit of sables** garments trimmed with the dark fur of the sable and hence suited for a person in mourning.

132 **suffer . . . on** undergo oblivion

133 **"For . . . forgot"** (Verse of a song occurring also in *Love's Labor's Lost*, 3.1.27–8. The hobbyhorse was a character made up to resemble a horse and rider, appearing in the morris dance and such May-game sports. This song laments the disappearance of such customs under pressure from the Puritans.)

133.12 *condole with* offer sympathy to

135 **this' miching mallico** this is sneaking mischief

OPHELIA   What is, my lord?

HAMLET   Nothing.   119

OPHELIA   You are merry, my lord.

HAMLET   Who, I?

OPHELIA   Ay, my lord.

HAMLET   Oh, God, your only jig maker. What should a   123
man do but be merry? For look you how cheerfully my
mother looks, and my father died within 's two hours.   125

OPHELIA   Nay, 'tis twice two months, my lord.

HAMLET   So long? Nay then, let the devil wear black, for
I'll have a suit of sables. O heavens! Die two months   128
ago, and not forgotten yet? Then there's hope a great
man's memory may outlive his life half a year. But, by'r
Lady, 'a must build churches, then, or else shall 'a
suffer not thinking on, with the hobbyhorse, whose   132
epitaph is "For oh, for oh, the hobbyhorse is forgot."   133

The trumpets sound. Dumb show follows.

*Enter a King and a Queen [very lovingly]; the
Queen embracing him, and he her. [She kneels,
and makes show of protestation unto him.] He
takes her up, and declines his head upon her neck.
He lies him down upon a bank of flowers. She,
seeing him asleep, leaves him. Anon comes in
another man, takes off his crown, kisses it, pours
poison in the sleeper's ears, and leaves him. The
Queen returns, finds the King dead, makes
passionate action. The Poisoner with some three or
four come in again, seem to condole with her. The
dead body is carried away. The Poisoner woos the
Queen with gifts; she seems harsh awhile, but in
the end accepts love.*

[Exeunt players.]

OPHELIA   What means this, my lord?

HAMLET   Marry, this' miching mallico; it means mis-   135
chief.

137 **Belike** Probably.   **argument** plot

140 **counsel** secret

142–3 **Be not you** Provided you are not

145 **naught** indecent. (Ophelia is reacting to Hamlet's pointed remarks about not being ashamed to show all.)

148 **stooping** bowing

150 **posy ... ring** brief motto in verse inscribed in a ring.

153 **Phoebus' cart** the sun-god's chariot, making its yearly cycle

154 **salt wash** the sea.   **Tellus** goddess of the earth, of the *orbèd ground*

155 **borrowed** i.e., reflected

157 **Hymen** god of matrimony

158 **commutual** mutually.   **bands** bonds.

163 **distrust** am anxious about

164 **Discomfort ... must** it must not distress you at all.

165 **hold quantity** keep proportion with one another

OPHELIA   Belike this show imports the argument of the   137
play.

  Enter Prologue.

HAMLET   We shall know by this fellow. The players cannot keep counsel; they'll tell all.   140

OPHELIA   Will 'a tell us what this show meant?

HAMLET   Ay, or any show that you will show him. Be   142
not you ashamed to show, he'll not shame to tell you   143
what it means.

OPHELIA   You are naught, you are naught. I'll mark the   145
play.

PROLOGUE
  For us, and for our tragedy,
  Here stooping to your clemency,   148
  We beg your hearing patiently.   [*Exit.*]

HAMLET   Is this a prologue, or the posy of a ring?   150

OPHELIA   'Tis brief, my lord.

HAMLET   As woman's love.

  Enter [two Players as] King and Queen.

PLAYER KING
  Full thirty times hath Phoebus' cart gone round   153
  Neptune's salt wash and Tellus' orbèd ground,   154
  And thirty dozen moons with borrowed sheen   155
  About the world have times twelve thirties been,
  Since love our hearts and Hymen did our hands   157
  Unite commutual in most sacred bands.   158

PLAYER QUEEN
  So many journeys may the sun and moon
  Make us again count o'er ere love be done!
  But, woe is me, you are so sick of late,
  So far from cheer and from your former state,
  That I distrust you. Yet, though I distrust,   163
  Discomfort you, my lord, it nothing must.   164
  For women's fear and love hold quantity;   165

166 **In ... extremity** (women feel) either no anxiety if they
do not love or extreme anxiety if they do love.

167 **proof** experience

169 **the littlest** even the littlest

172 **My ... to do** my vital functions are shutting down.

173 **behind** after I have gone

178 **None** (1) Let no woman; or (2) No woman does.   **but
who** except the one who

179 **Wormwood** i.e., How bitter. (Literally, a bitter-tasting
plant.)

180 **instances** motives.   **move** motivate

181 **base ... thrift** ignoble considerations of material pros-
perity

186 **Purpose ... memory** Our good intentions are subject
to forgetfulness

187 **validity** strength, durability

188 **Which** i.e., purpose

190–1 **Most ... debt** It's inevitable that in time we forget the
obligations we have imposed on ourselves

195 **enactures** fulfillments

196–7 **Where ... accident** The capacity for extreme joy
and grief go together, and often one extreme is instantly
changed into its opposite on the slightest provocation.

In neither aught, or in extremity.   166
Now, what my love is, proof hath made you know,   167
And as my love is sized, my fear is so.
Where love is great, the littlest doubts are fear;   169
Where little fears grow great, great love grows there.

PLAYER KING
Faith, I must leave thee, love, and shortly too;
My operant powers their functions leave to do.   172
And thou shalt live in this fair world behind,   173
Honored, beloved; and haply one as kind
For husband shalt thou—

PLAYER QUEEN   Oh, confound the rest!
Such love must needs be treason in my breast.
In second husband let me be accurst!
None wed the second but who killed the first.   178

HAMLET   Wormwood, wormwood.   179

PLAYER QUEEN
The instances that second marriage move   180
Are base respects of thrift, but none of love.   181
A second time I kill my husband dead
When second husband kisses me in bed.

PLAYER KING
I do believe you think what now you speak,
But what we do determine oft we break.
Purpose is but the slave to memory,   186
Of violent birth, but poor validity,   187
Which now, like fruit unripe, sticks on the tree,   188
But fall unshaken when they mellow be.
Most necessary 'tis that we forget   190
To pay ourselves what to ourselves is debt.   191
What to ourselves in passion we propose,
The passion ending, doth the purpose lose.
The violence of either grief or joy
Their own enactures with themselves destroy.   195
Where joy most revels, grief doth most lament;   196
Grief joys, joy grieves, on slender accident.   197

198 **aye** ever

202 **down** fallen in fortune

203 **The poor . . . enemies** when one of humble station is promoted, you see his enemies suddenly becoming his friends.

204 **hitherto** up to this point in the argument, or, to this extent.   **tend** attend

205 **who not needs** he who is not in need (of wealth)

206 **who in want** he who, being in need.   **try** test (his generosity)

207 **seasons him** ripens him into

209 **Our . . . run** what we want and what we get go so contrarily

210 **devices** intentions.   **still** continually

211 **ends** results

214 **Nor** Let neither

215 **Sport . . . night** may day deny me its pastimes and night its repose

217 **anchor's cheer** anchorite's or hermit's fare.   **my scope** the extent of my happiness.

218–19 **Each . . . destroy!** May every adverse thing that causes the face of joy to turn pale meet and destroy everything that I desire to see prosper!

220 **hence** in the life hereafter

224 **spirits** vital spirits

228 **doth . . . much** makes too many promises and protestations

This world is not for aye, nor 'tis not strange   198
That even our loves should with our fortunes change;
For 'tis a question left us yet to prove,
Whether love lead fortune, or else fortune love.
The great man down, you mark his favorite flies;   202
The poor advanced makes friends of enemies.   203
And hitherto doth love on fortune tend;   204
For who not needs shall never lack a friend,   205
And who in want a hollow friend doth try   206
Directly seasons him his enemy.   207
But, orderly to end where I begun,
Our wills and fates do so contrary run   209
That our devices still are overthrown;   210
Our thoughts are ours, their ends none of our own.   211
So think thou wilt no second husband wed,
But die thy thoughts when thy first lord is dead.

PLAYER QUEEN
Nor earth to me give food, nor heaven light,   214
Sport and repose lock from me day and night,   215
To desperation turn my trust and hope,
An anchor's cheer in prison be my scope!   217
Each opposite that blanks the face of joy   218
Meet what I would have well and it destroy!   219
Both here and hence pursue me lasting strife   220
If, once a widow, ever I be wife!

HAMLET   If she should break it now!

PLAYER KING
'Tis deeply sworn. Sweet, leave me here awhile;
My spirits grow dull, and fain I would beguile   224
The tedious day with sleep.

PLAYER QUEEN   Sleep rock thy brain,
And never come mischance between us twain!
          [He sleeps.] Exit [Player Queen].

HAMLET   Madam, how like you this play?

QUEEN   The lady doth protest too much, methinks.   228

230 **argument** plot.

232 **jest** make believe.

232–3 **offense** crime, injury. (Hamlet playfully alters the King's use of the word in line 231 to mean "cause for objection.")

235 **Tropically** Figuratively. (The first quarto reading, "trapically," suggests a pun on *trap* in *Mousetrap*.)

237 **Duke's** i.e., King's. (An inconsistency that may be due to Shakespeare's possible acquaintance with a historical incident, the alleged murder of the Duke of Urbino by Luigi Gonzaga in 1538.)

239 **free** guiltless

240 **galled jade** horse whose hide is rubbed by saddle or harness.   **withers** the part between the horse's shoulder blades

241 **unwrung** not rubbed sore.

243 **chorus** (In many Elizabethan plays, the forthcoming action was explained by an actor known as the "chorus"; at a puppet show, the actor who spoke the dialogue was known as an "interpreter," as indicated by the lines following.)

244 **interpret** (1) ventriloquize the dialogue, as in puppet show (2) act as pander

245 **puppets dallying** (With suggestion of sexual play, continued in *keen*, "sexually aroused," *groaning*, "moaning in pregnancy," and *edge*, "sexual desire" or "impetuosity.")

246 **keen** sharp, bitter

249 **Still . . . worse** More keen, always *bettering* what other people say with witty wordplay, but at the same time more offensive.

250 **So** Even thus (in marriage).   **mis-take** take falseheartedly and cheat on. (The marriage vows say "for better, for worse.")

254 **Confederate . . . seeing** the time and occasion conspiring (to assist me), and also no one seeing me

256 **Hecate's ban** the curse of Hecate, the goddess of witchcraft

257 **dire property** baleful quality

HAMLET   Oh, but she'll keep her word.

KING   Have you heard the argument? Is there no 230
offense in't?

HAMLET   No, no, they do but jest, poison in jest. No of- 232
fense i'th' world. 233

KING   What do you call the play?

HAMLET   *The Mousetrap.* Marry, how? Tropically. 235
This play is the image of a murder done in Vienna.
Gonzago is the Duke's name, his wife, Baptista. You 237
shall see anon. 'Tis a knavish piece of work, but what
of that? Your Majesty, and we that have free souls, it 239
touches us not. Let the galled jade wince, our withers 240
are unwrung. 241

        Enter Lucianus.

This is one Lucianus, nephew to the King.

OPHELIA   You are as good as a chorus, my lord. 243

HAMLET   I could interpret between you and your love, 244
if I could see the puppets dallying. 245

OPHELIA   You are keen, my lord, you are keen. 246

HAMLET   It would cost you a groaning to take off mine
edge.

OPHELIA   Still better, and worse. 249

HAMLET   So you mis-take your husbands.—Begin, mur- 250
derer; leave thy damnable faces and begin. Come, the
croaking raven doth bellow for revenge.

LUCIANUS
Thoughts black, hands apt, drugs fit, and time
    agreeing,
Confederate season, else no creature seeing, 254
Thou mixture rank, of midnight weeds collected,
With Hecate's ban thrice blasted, thrice infected, 256
Thy natural magic and dire property 257
On wholesome life usurp immediately.
        [*He pours the poison into the sleeper's ear.*]

259 **estate** i.e., the kingship.   **His** i.e., the King's

264 **false fire** the blank discharge of a gun loaded with powder but no shot.

269–72 **Why ... away** (Perhaps from an old ballad, with allusion to the popular belief that a wounded deer retires to weep and die; compare with *As You Like It*, 2.1.33–66.)

270 **ungallèd** unafflicted

271 **watch** remain awake

272 **Thus ... away** Thus the world goes.

273 **this** i.e., this success with the play I have just presented. **feathers** (Allusion to the plumes that Elizabethan actors were fond of wearing.)

274 **turn Turk with** turn renegade against, go back on

275 **Provincial roses** rosettes of ribbon, named for roses grown in a part of France.   **razed** with ornamental slashing

275–6 **fellowship ... players** partnership in a theatrical company.

276 **cry** pack (of hounds, etc.)

279 **Damon** the friend of Pythias, as Horatio is friend of Hamlet; or, a traditional pastoral name

280–2 **This realm ... pajock** i.e., Jove, representing divine authority and justice, has abandoned this realm to its own devices, leaving in his stead only a peacock or vain pretender to virtue (though the rhyme-word expected in place of *pajock or* "peacock" suggests that the realm is now ruled over by an "ass").

280 **dismantled** stripped, divested

HAMLET   'A poisons him i'th' garden for his estate. His 259
name's Gonzago. The story is extant, and written in
very choice Italian. You shall see anon how the
murderer gets the love of Gonzago's wife.

[Claudius rises.]

OPHELIA   The King rises.

HAMLET   What, frighted with false fire?   264

QUEEN   How fares my lord?

POLONIUS   Give o'er the play.

KING   Give me some light. Away!

POLONIUS   Lights, lights, lights!

Exeunt all but Hamlet and Horatio.

HAMLET
   "Why, let the strucken deer go weep,   269
      The hart ungallèd play.   270
   For some must watch, while some must sleep;   271
      Thus runs the world away."   272
   Would not this, sir, and a forest of feathers—if the 273
   rest of my fortunes turn Turk with me—with two 274
   Provincial roses on my razed shoes, get me a fellow- 275
   ship in a cry of players?   276

HORATIO   Half a share.

HAMLET   A whole one, I.
   "For thou dost know, O Damon dear,   279
      This realm dismantled was   280
   Of Jove himself, and now reigns here   281
      A very, very—pajock."   282

HORATIO   You might have rhymed.

HAMLET   Oh, good Horatio, I'll take the ghost's word for
a thousand pound. Didst perceive?

HORATIO   Very well, my lord.

HAMLET   Upon the talk of the poisoning?

HORATIO   I did very well note him.

Enter Rosencrantz and Guildenstern.

292 **perdy** (A corruption of the French *par dieu,* "by God.")

299 **retirement** withdrawal to his chambers

299–300 **distempered** out of humor. (But Hamlet deliberately plays on the wider application to any illness of mind or body, as in lines 335–6, especially to drunkenness.)

302 **choler** anger. (But Hamlet takes the word in its more basic humoral sense of "bilious disorder.")

305 **purgation** (Hamlet hints at something going beyond medical treatment to bloodletting and the extraction of confession.)

308 **frame** order. **start** shy or jump away (like a horse; the opposite of *tame* in line 309)

314 **breed** (1) kind (2) breeding, manners.

316 **pardon** permission to depart

HAMLET   Aha! Come, some music! Come, the re-
corders.
"For if the King like not the comedy,
Why then, belike, he likes it not, perdy."   292
Come, some music.

GUILDENSTERN   Good my lord, vouchsafe me a word
with you.

HAMLET   Sir, a whole history.

GUILDENSTERN   The King, sir—

HAMLET   Ay, sir, what of him?

GUILDENSTERN   Is in his retirement marvelous dis-   299
tempered.   300

HAMLET   With drink, sir?

GUILDENSTERN   No, my lord, with choler.   302

HAMLET   Your wisdom should show itself more richer
to signify this to the doctor, for for me to put him to his
purgation would perhaps plunge him into more   305
choler.

GUILDENSTERN   Good my lord, put your discourse into
some frame and start not so wildly from my affair.   308

HAMLET   I am tame, sir. Pronounce.

GUILDENSTERN   The Queen, your mother, in most great
affliction of spirit, hath sent me to you.

HAMLET   You are welcome.

GUILDENSTERN   Nay, good my lord, this courtesy is not
of the right breed. If it shall please you to make me a   314
wholesome answer, I will do your mother's commandment; if not, your pardon and my return shall be the   316
end of my business.

HAMLET   Sir, I cannot.

ROSENCRANTZ   What, my lord?

HAMLET   Make you a wholesome answer; my wit's diseased. But, sir, such answer as I can make, you shall

325 **admiration** bewilderment.

330 **closet** private chamber

334 **pickers and stealers** i.e., hands. (So called from the catechism, "to keep my hands from picking and stealing.")

337 **liberty** i.e., being freed from *distemper,* line 336; but perhaps with a veiled threat as well.   **deny** refuse to share

342 **"While ... grows"** (The rest of the proverb is "the silly horse starves"; Hamlet implies that his hopes of succession are distant in time at best.)

343 **something** somewhat

343.1 *Players* actors

345 **withdraw** speak privately

345–6 **recover the wind** get to the windward side (thus allowing the game to scent the hunter and thereby be driven in the opposite direction into the *toil* or net)

346 **toil** snare.

347–8 **if ... unmannerly** if I am using an unmannerly boldness, it is my love that occasions it.

349 **I ... that** i.e., I don't understand how genuine love can be unmannerly.

command, or rather, as you say, my mother. Therefore
no more, but to the matter. My mother, you say—

ROSENCRANTZ   Then thus she says: your behavior hath
struck her into amazement and admiration.   325

HAMLET   Oh, wonderful son, that can so 'stonish a mother!
But is there no sequel at the heels of this mother's admiration? Impart.

ROSENCRANTZ   She desires to speak with you in her
closet ere you go to bed.   330

HAMLET   We shall obey, were she ten times our mother.
Have you any further trade with us?

ROSENCRANTZ   My lord, you once did love me.

HAMLET   And do still, by these pickers and stealers.   334

ROSENCRANTZ   Good my lord, what is your cause of
distemper? You do surely bar the door upon your own
liberty if you deny your griefs to your friend.   337

HAMLET   Sir, I lack advancement.

ROSENCRANTZ   How can that be, when you have the
voice of the King himself for your succession in
Denmark?

HAMLET   Ay, sir, but "While the grass grows"—the   342
proverb is something musty.   343

Enter the Players with recorders.

Oh, the recorders. Let me see one. [*He takes a recorder.*]
To withdraw with you: why do you go about to recover   345
the wind of me, as if you would drive me into a toil?   346

GUILDENSTERN   Oh, my lord, if my duty be too bold, my   347
love is too unmannerly.   348

HAMLET   I do not well understand that. Will you play   349
upon this pipe?

GUILDENSTERN   My lord, I cannot.

HAMLET   I pray you.

356 **ventages** finger-holes or *stops* (line 359) of the recorder

365 **sound** (1) fathom (2) produce sound in

366 **compass** range (of voice)

367 **organ** musical instrument

370 **fret** irritate. (With a quibble on the *frets* or ridges on the fingerboard of some stringed instruments to regulate the fingering.)

374 **presently** at once.

383 **They fool . . . bent** They humor my odd behavior to the limit of my ability or endurance. (Literally, the extent to which a bow may be bent.)

GUILDENSTERN Believe me, I cannot.

HAMLET I do beseech you.

GUILDENSTERN I know no touch of it, my lord.

HAMLET It is as easy as lying. Govern these ventages 356
with your fingers and thumb, give it breath with your
mouth, and it will discourse most eloquent music.
Look you, these are the stops.

GUILDENSTERN But these cannot I command to any
utterance of harmony. I have not the skill.

HAMLET Why, look you now, how unworthy a thing
you make of me! You would play upon me, you would
seem to know my stops, you would pluck out the heart
of my mystery, you would sound me from my lowest 365
note to the top of my compass, and there is much 366
music, excellent voice, in this little organ, yet cannot 367
you make it speak. 'Sblood, do you think I am easier
to be played on than a pipe? Call me what instrument
you will, though you can fret me, you cannot play 370
upon me.

  Enter Polonius.

God bless you, sir!

POLONIUS My lord, the Queen would speak with you,
and presently.   374

HAMLET Do you see yonder cloud that's almost in
shape of a camel?

POLONIUS By th' Mass, and 'tis, like a camel indeed.

HAMLET Methinks it is like a weasel.

POLONIUS It is backed like a weasel.

HAMLET Or like a whale.

POLONIUS Very like a whale.

HAMLET Then I will come to my mother by and by.
[*Aside*] They fool me to the top of my bent.—I will 383
come by and by.

387 **witching time** time when spells are cast and evil is abroad

392 **nature** natural feeling.

393 **Nero** (This infamous Roman emperor put to death his mother, Agrippina, who had murdered her husband, Claudius.)

397–8 **How ... consent!** however much she is to be rebuked by my words, may my soul never consent to ratify those words with deeds of violence!

3.3 *Location: The castle.*

1 **him** i.e., his behavior

3 **dispatch** prepare, cause to be drawn up

5 **terms of our estate** circumstances of my royal position

7 **Out ... brows** i.e., from his brain, in the form of plots and threats. **We ... provide** We'll put ourselves in readiness.

8 **religious fear** sacred concern

11 **single and peculiar** individual and private

13 **noyance** harm

POLONIUS   I will say so.   [*Exit.*]

HAMLET   "By and by" is easily said. Leave me, friends.

                                    [*Exeunt all but Hamlet.*]

'Tis now the very witching time of night,   387
When churchyards yawn and hell itself breathes out
Contagion to this world. Now could I drink hot
    blood
And do such bitter business as the day
Would quake to look on. Soft, now to my mother.
O heart, lose not thy nature! Let not ever   392
The soul of Nero enter this firm bosom.   393
Let me be cruel, not unnatural;
I will speak daggers to her, but use none.
My tongue and soul in this be hypocrites:
How in my words somever she be shent,   397
To give them seals never my soul consent!   *Exit.*   398

[3.3] ❧ *Enter King, Rosencrantz, and Guildenstern.*

KING

I like him not, nor stands it safe with us   1
To let his madness range. Therefore prepare you.
I your commission will forthwith dispatch,   3
And he to England shall along with you.
The terms of our estate may not endure   5
Hazard so near 's as doth hourly grow
Out of his brows.

GUILDENSTERN   We will ourselves provide.   7
Most holy and religious fear it is   8
To keep those many many bodies safe
That live and feed upon Your Majesty.

ROSENCRANTZ

The single and peculiar life is bound   11
With all the strength and armor of the mind
To keep itself from noyance, but much more   13

14   **weal** well-being

15   **cess** decease, cessation

16   **gulf** whirlpool

17   **massy** massive

20   **mortised** fastened (as with a fitted joint).   **when it falls** i.e., when it descends, like the wheel of Fortune, bringing a king down with it

21   **Each ... consequence** i.e., every hanger-on and unimportant person or thing connected with the King

22   **Attends** participates in

24   **Arm** Provide, prepare

28   **arras** screen of tapestry placed around the walls of household apartments. (On the Elizabethan stage, the arras was presumably over a door or aperture in the tiring-house facade.)

29   **process** proceedings.   **tax him home** reprove him severely

31   **meet** fitting

33   **of vantage** from an advantageous place, or, in addition.

37   **the primal eldest curse** the curse of Cain, the first murderer; he killed his brother Abel

39   **Though ... will** though my desire is as strong as my determination

41   **bound** (1) destined (2) obliged. (The King wants to repent and still enjoy what he has gained.)

That spirit upon whose weal depends and rests   14
The lives of many. The cess of majesty   15
Dies not alone, but like a gulf doth draw   16
What's near it with it; or it is a massy wheel   17
Fixed on the summit of the highest mount,
To whose huge spokes ten thousand lesser things
Are mortised and adjoined, which, when it falls,   20
Each small annexment, petty consequence,   21
Attends the boist'rous ruin. Never alone   22
Did the King sigh, but with a general groan.

KING
Arm you, I pray you, to this speedy voyage,   24
For we will fetters put about this fear,
Which now goes too free-footed.

ROSENCRANTZ   We will haste us.
   Exeunt gentlemen [Rosencrantz and Guildenstern].

   Enter Polonius.

POLONIUS
My lord, he's going to his mother's closet.
Behind the arras I'll convey myself   28
To hear the process. I'll warrant she'll tax him home,   29
And, as you said—and wisely was it said—
'Tis meet that some more audience than a mother,   31
Since nature makes them partial, should o'erhear
The speech of vantage. Fare you well, my liege.   33
I'll call upon you ere you go to bed
And tell you what I know.

KING   Thanks, dear my lord.
        Exit [Polonius].
Oh, my offense is rank! It smells to heaven.
It hath the primal eldest curse upon't,   37
A brother's murder. Pray can I not,
Though inclination be as sharp as will;   39
My stronger guilt defeats my strong intent,
And like a man to double business bound   41

46-7 **Whereto . . . offense?** What function does mercy serve other than to meet sin face to face?

49 **forestallèd** prevented (from sinning)

56 **th' offense** the thing for which one offended.

57 **currents** courses of events

58 **gilded hand** hand offering gold as a bribe.   **shove by** thrust aside

59 **wicked prize** prize won by wickedness

61 **There . . . lies** There in heaven can be no evasion, there the deed lies exposed to view

62 **his** its

63 **to the teeth and forehead** face to face, concealing nothing

64 **give in** provide.   **rests** remains.

68 **limèd** caught as with birdlime, a sticky substance used to ensnare birds

69 **engaged** entangled.   **assay** trial. (Said to himself, or to the angels to try him.)

73 **pat** opportunely

I stand in pause where I shall first begin,
And both neglect. What if this cursèd hand
Were thicker than itself with brother's blood,
Is there not rain enough in the sweet heavens
To wash it white as snow? Whereto serves mercy   46
But to confront the visage of offense?   47
And what's in prayer but this twofold force,
To be forestallèd ere we come to fall,   49
Or pardoned being down? Then I'll look up.
My fault is past. But oh, what form of prayer
Can serve my turn? "Forgive me my foul murder"?
That cannot be, since I am still possessed
Of those effects for which I did the murder:
My crown, mine own ambition, and my queen.
May one be pardoned and retain th' offense?   56
In the corrupted currents of this world   57
Offense's gilded hand may shove by justice,   58
And oft 'tis seen the wicked prize itself   59
Buys out the law. But 'tis not so above.
There is no shuffling, there the action lies   61
In his true nature, and we ourselves compelled,   62
Even to the teeth and forehead of our faults,   63
To give in evidence. What then? What rests?   64
Try what repentance can. What can it not?
Yet what can it, when one cannot repent?
O wretched state, O bosom black as death,
O limèd soul that, struggling to be free,   68
Art more engaged! Help, angels! Make assay.   69
Bow, stubborn knees, and heart with strings of steel,
Be soft as sinews of the newborn babe!
All may be well.   [He kneels.]

        Enter Hamlet.

HAMLET
Now might I do it pat, now 'a is a-praying;   73
And now I'll do't. [He draws his sword.] And so 'a goes
    to heaven,

75 **would be scanned** needs to be looked into, or, would be interpreted as follows

80 **grossly, full of bread** i.e., enjoying his worldly pleasures rather than fasting. (See Ezekiel 16:49.)

81 **crimes broad blown** sins in full bloom.   **flush** vigorous

82 **audit** account.   **save** except for

83 **in … thought** as we see it from our mortal perspective

86 **seasoned** matured, readied

88 **know … hent** await to be grasped by me on a more horrid occasion. (*Hent* means "act of seizing.")

89 **drunk … rage** dead drunk, or in a fit of sexual passion

91 **game** gambling

92 **relish** trace, savor

95 **stays** awaits (me).

96 **physic** purging (by prayer), or, Hamlet's postponement of the killing

3.4 *Location: The Queen's private chamber.*

1 **lay home** reprove him soundly

2 **broad** unrestrained

4 **Much heat** i.e., the King's anger.   **I'll silence me** I'll quietly conceal myself. (Ironic, since it is his crying out at line 24 that leads to his death. Some editors emend *silence* to "sconce." The first quarto's reading, "shroud," is attractive.)

5 **round** blunt

And so am I revenged. That would be scanned: 75
A villain kills my father, and for that,
I, his sole son, do this same villain send
To heaven.
Why, this is hire and salary, not revenge.
'A took my father grossly, full of bread,   80
With all his crimes broad blown, as flush as May;   81
And how his audit stands who knows save heaven?   82
But in our circumstance and course of thought   83
'Tis heavy with him. And am I then revenged,
To take him in the purging of his soul,
When he is fit and seasoned for his passage?   86
No!
Up, sword, and know thou a more horrid hent.   88
                              [He puts up his sword.]
When he is drunk asleep, or in his rage,   89
Or in th'incestuous pleasure of his bed,
At game, a-swearing, or about some act   91
That has no relish of salvation in't—   92
Then trip him, that his heels may kick at heaven,
And that his soul may be as damned and black
As hell, whereto it goes. My mother stays.   95
This physic but prolongs thy sickly days.   *Exit.*   96

KING
My words fly up, my thoughts remain below.
Words without thoughts never to heaven go.   *Exit.*

[3.4] ⁓ *Enter [Queen] Gertrude and Polonius.*

POLONIUS
'A will come straight. Look you lay home to him.   1
Tell him his pranks have been too broad to bear with,   2
And that Your Grace hath screened and stood
    between
Much heat and him. I'll silence me even here.   4
Pray you, be round with him.   5

10 **thy father** i.e., your stepfather, Claudius

12 **idle** foolish

15 **forgot me** i.e., forgotten that I am your mother.
    rood cross of Christ

18 **speak** i.e., speak to someone so rude.

25 **Dead for a ducat** i.e., I bet a ducat he's dead; or, a ducat
    is his life's fee.

HAMLET (*within*) Mother, mother, mother!

QUEEN   I'll warrant you, fear me not.
 Withdraw, I hear him coming.

> [*Polonius hides behind the arras.*]

 Enter Hamlet.

HAMLET   Now, mother, what's the matter?

QUEEN
 Hamlet, thou hast thy father much offended.   10

HAMLET
 Mother, you have my father much offended.

QUEEN
 Come, come, you answer with an idle tongue.   12

HAMLET
 Go, go, you question with a wicked tongue.

QUEEN
 Why, how now, Hamlet?

HAMLET   What's the matter now?

QUEEN
 Have you forgot me?

HAMLET   No, by the rood, not so: 15
 You are the Queen, your husband's brother's wife,
 And—would it were not so!—you are my mother.

QUEEN
 Nay, then, I'll set those to you that can speak.   18

HAMLET
 Come, come, and sit you down; you shall not budge.
 You go not till I set you up a glass
 Where you may see the inmost part of you.

QUEEN
 What wilt thou do? Thou wilt not murder me?
 Help, ho!

POLONIUS [*behind the arras*]   What ho! Help!

HAMLET [*drawing*]
 How now? A rat? Dead for a ducat, dead!   25

34 **busy** nosey

38 **damnèd custom** habitual wickedness.   **brazed**
brazened, hardened

39 **proof** impenetrable, like *proof* or tested armor.
sense feeling.

45 **sets a blister** i.e., brands as a harlot

47 **contraction** the marriage contract

48 **sweet religion makes** i.e., makes marriage vows

                    [*He thrusts his rapier through the arras.*]

POLONIUS [*behind the arras*]
   Oh, I am slain!   [*He falls and dies.*]

QUEEN   Oh, me, what hast thou done?

HAMLET   Nay, I know not. Is it the King?

QUEEN
   Oh, what a rash and bloody deed is this!

HAMLET
   A bloody deed—almost as bad, good mother,
   As kill a king, and marry with his brother.

QUEEN
   As kill a king!

HAMLET   Ay, lady, it was my word.
                    [*He parts the arras and discovers Polonius.*]
   Thou wretched, rash, intruding fool, farewell!
   I took thee for thy better. Take thy fortune.
   Thou find'st to be too busy is some danger.—   34
   Leave wringing of your hands. Peace, sit you down,
   And let me wring your heart, for so I shall,
   If it be made of penetrable stuff,
   If damnèd custom have not brazed it so   38
   That it be proof and bulwark against sense.   39

QUEEN
   What have I done, that thou dar'st wag thy tongue
   In noise so rude against me?

HAMLET   Such an act
   That blurs the grace and blush of modesty,
   Calls virtue hypocrite, takes off the rose
   From the fair forehead of an innocent love
   And sets a blister there, makes marriage vows   45
   As false as dicers' oaths. Oh, such a deed
   As from the body of contraction plucks   47
   The very soul, and sweet religion makes   48

49 **rhapsody** senseless string

49–52 **Heaven's . . . act** Heaven's face blushes at this solid
world compounded of the various elements, with sorrowful face as though the day of doom were near, and is
sick with horror at the deed (i.e., Gertrude's marriage).

53 **index** table of contents, prelude or preface.

55 **counterfeit presentment** representation in portraiture

57 **Hyperion's** the sun-god's.   **front** brow

58 **Mars** god of war

59 **station** manner of standing.   **Mercury** winged messenger of the gods

60 **New-lighted** newly alighted.   **heaven-kissing** reach-
ing to the sky

62 **set his seal** i.e., affix his approval

65 **ear** i.e., of grain

66 **Blasting** blighting

67 **leave** cease

68 **batten** gorge.   **moor** barren or marshy ground.
(Suggesting also "dark-skinned.")

70 **The heyday . . . blood** (The blood was thought to be
the source of sexual desire.)

72 **Sense** Perception through the five senses (the functions
of the middle or sensible soul)

74 **apoplexed** paralyzed.   **err** so err

75–7 **Nor . . . difference** nor could your physical senses
ever have been so enthralled to *ecstasy* or lunacy that
they could not distinguish to some degree between
Hamlet Senior and Claudius.

78 **cozened** cheated.   **hoodman-blind** blindman's buff.
(In this game, says Hamlet, the devil must have pushed
Claudius toward Gertrude while she was blindfolded.)

80 **sans** without

82 **mope** be dazed, act aimlessly.

A rhapsody of words. Heaven's face does glow   49
O'er this solidity and compound mass   50
With tristful visage, as against the doom,   51
Is thought-sick at the act.

QUEEN   Ay me, what act,   52
That roars so loud and thunders in the index?   53

HAMLET [showing her two likenesses]
Look here upon this picture, and on this,
The counterfeit presentment of two brothers.   55
See what a grace was seated on this brow:
Hyperion's curls, the front of Jove himself,   57
An eye like Mars to threaten and command,   58
A station like the herald Mercury   59
New-lighted on a heaven-kissing hill—   60
A combination and a form indeed
Where every god did seem to set his seal   62
To give the world assurance of a man.
This was your husband. Look you now what follows:
Here is your husband, like a mildewed ear,   65
Blasting his wholesome brother. Have you eyes?   66
Could you on this fair mountain leave to feed   67
And batten on this moor? Ha, have you eyes?   68
You cannot call it love, for at your age
The heyday in the blood is tame, it's humble,   70
And waits upon the judgment, and what judgment
Would step from this to this? Sense, sure, you have,   72
Else could you not have motion, but sure that sense
Is apoplexed, for madness would not err,   74
Nor sense to ecstasy was ne'er so thralled,   75
But it reserved some quantity of choice   76
To serve in such a difference. What devil was't   77
That thus hath cozened you at hoodman-blind?   78
Eyes without feeling, feeling without sight,
Ears without hands or eyes, smelling sans all,   80
Or but a sickly part of one true sense
Could not so mope. O shame, where is thy blush?   82

84 **mutine** mutiny

85–6 **To ... fire** when it comes to sexually passionate
youth, let virtue melt like a candle or stick of sealing
wax held over a candle flame. (There's no point in hop-
ing for self-restraint among young people when ma-
tronly women set such a bad example.)

86–9 **Proclaim ... will** Call it no shameful business when
the compelling ardor of youth delivers the attack, i.e.,
commits lechery, since the *frost* of advanced age burns
with as active a fire of lust and reason perverts itself by
fomenting lust rather than restraining it.

92 **grainèd** ingrained, indelible

93 **leave their tinct** surrender their dark stain.

94 **enseamèd** saturated in the grease and filth of passionate lovemaking

95 **Stewed** soaked, bathed. (With a suggestion of "stew,"
brothel.)

96 **Over ... sty** (Like barnyard animals.)

100 **tithe** tenth part

101 **precedent lord** former husband.   **vice** (From the
morality plays, a model of iniquity and a buffoon.)

105.1 *nightgown* a robe for indoor wear.

106 **A king ... patches** i.e., a king whose splendor is all
sham; a clown or fool dressed in motley

111 **lapsed ... passion** having let time and passion slip
away

Rebellious hell,
If thou canst mutine in a matron's bones,   84
To flaming youth let virtue be as wax   85
And melt in her own fire. Proclaim no shame   86
When the compulsive ardor gives the charge,   87
Since frost itself as actively doth burn,   88
And reason panders will.   89

QUEEN   Oh, Hamlet, speak no more!
Thou turn'st mine eyes into my very soul,
And there I see such black and grainèd spots   92
As will not leave their tinct.

HAMLET   Nay, but to live   93
In the rank sweat of an enseamèd bed,   94
Stewed in corruption, honeying and making love   95
Over the nasty sty!   96

QUEEN   Oh, speak to me no more!
These words like daggers enter in my ears.
No more, sweet Hamlet!

HAMLET   A murderer and a villain,
A slave that is not twentieth part the tithe   100
Of your precedent lord, a vice of kings,   101
A cutpurse of the empire and the rule,
That from a shelf the precious diadem stole
And put it in his pocket!

QUEEN   No more!   105

Enter Ghost [in his nightgown].

HAMLET   A king of shreds and patches—   106
Save me, and hover o'er me with your wings,
You heavenly guards! What would your gracious
    figure?

QUEEN   Alas, he's mad!

HAMLET
Do you not come your tardy son to chide,
That, lapsed in time and passion, lets go by   111

112 **Th'important** the importunate, urgent

115 **whet** sharpen

116 **amazement** distraction

118 **Conceit** Imagination

122 **th'incorporal** the immaterial

124 **as ... th'alarm** like soldiers called out of sleep by an alarum

125 **bedded** laid flat.   **like life in excrements** i.e., as though hair, an outgrowth of the body, had a life of its own. (Hair was thought to be lifeless because it lacks sensation, and so its standing on end would be unnatural and ominous.)

127 **distemper** disorder

130 **His ... conjoined** His appearance joined to his cause for speaking

131 **capable** capable of feeling, receptive.

132–3 **convert ... effects** divert me from my stern duty.

134 **want ... blood** lack plausibility so that (with a play on the normal sense of *color*) I shall shed colorless tears instead of blood.

141 **habit** clothes.   **as** as when

Th'important acting of your dread command?   112
Oh, say!

GHOST

Do not forget. This visitation
Is but to whet thy almost blunted purpose.   115
But look, amazement on thy mother sits.   116
Oh, step between her and her fighting soul!
Conceit in weakest bodies strongest works.   118
Speak to her, Hamlet.

HAMLET   How is it with you, lady?

QUEEN   Alas, how is't with you,
That you do bend your eye on vacancy,
And with th'incorporal air do hold discourse?   122
Forth at your eyes your spirits wildly peep,
And, as the sleeping soldiers in th'alarm,   124
Your bedded hair, like life in excrements,   125
Start up and stand on end. O gentle son,
Upon the heat and flame of thy distemper   127
Sprinkle cool patience. Whereon do you look?

HAMLET

On him, on him! Look you how pale he glares!
His form and cause conjoined, preaching to stones,   130
Would make them capable.—Do not look upon me,   131
Lest with this piteous action you convert   132
My stern effects. Then what I have to do   133
Will want true color—tears perchance for blood.   134

QUEEN   To whom do you speak this?

HAMLET   Do you see nothing there?

QUEEN

Nothing at all, yet all that is I see.

HAMLET   Nor did you nothing hear?

QUEEN   No, nothing but ourselves.

HAMLET

Why, look you there, look how it steals away!
My father, in his habit as he lived!   141

143 **very** mere

144–5 **This ... in** Madness is skillful in creating this kind of hallucination.

150 **reword** repeat word for word

151 **gambol** skip away

152 **unction** ointment

154 **skin** grow a skin over

155 **mining** working under the surface

158 **compost** manure

159 **this my virtue** my virtuous talk in reproving you

160 **fatness** grossness.   **pursy** flabby, out of shape

162 **curb** bow, bend the knee.   **leave** permission

168 **who ... eat** which consumes and overwhelms the physical senses

169 **Of habits devil** devil-like in prompting evil habits

171 **livery** an outer appearance, a customary garb (and hence a predisposition easily assumed in time of stress)

172 **aptly** readily

Look where he goes even now out at the portal!

Exit Ghost.

QUEEN

This is the very coinage of your brain.   143
This bodiless creation ecstasy   144
Is very cunning in.   145

HAMLET   Ecstasy?

My pulse as yours doth temperately keep time,
And makes as healthful music. It is not madness
That I have uttered. Bring me to the test,
And I the matter will reword, which madness   150
Would gambol from. Mother, for love of grace,   151
Lay not that flattering unction to your soul   152
That not your trespass but my madness speaks.
It will but skin and film the ulcerous place,   154
While rank corruption, mining all within,   155
Infects unseen. Confess yourself to heaven,
Repent what's past, avoid what is to come,
And do not spread the compost on the weeds   158
To make them ranker. Forgive me this my virtue;   159
For in the fatness of these pursy times   160
Virtue itself of vice must pardon beg,
Yea, curb and woo for leave to do him good.   162

QUEEN

Oh, Hamlet, thou hast cleft my heart in twain.

HAMLET

Oh, throw away the worser part of it,
And live the purer with the other half.
Good night. But go not to my uncle's bed;
Assume a virtue, if you have it not.
That monster, custom, who all sense doth eat,   168
Of habits devil, is angel yet in this,   169
That to the use of actions fair and good
He likewise gives a frock or livery   171
That aptly is put on. Refrain tonight,   172
And that shall lend a kind of easiness
To the next abstinence; the next more easy;

175 **use** habit.   **the stamp of nature** our inborn traits

176 **And either** (A defective line, often emended by insert-
ing the word "master" after *either,* following the third
quarto and early editors, or some other word such as
"shame," "lodge," "curb," or "house.")

178–9 **when ... you** i.e., when you are ready to be penitent
and seek God's blessing, I will ask your blessing as a du-
tiful son should.

181 **To punish ... with me** to seek retribution from me for
killing Polonius, and from him through my means

182 **their scourge and minister** i.e., agent of heavenly retribution.

183 **bestow** stow, dispose of.   **answer** account or pay for

186 **This** i.e., The killing of Polonius.   **behind** to come.

189 **bloat** bloated

190 **Pinch wanton** i.e., leave his love pinches on your
cheeks, branding you as wanton

191 **reechy** dirty, filthy

192 **paddling** fingering amorously

193 **ravel ... out** unravel, disclose

195 **in craft** by cunning.   **good** (Said sarcastically; also
the following eight lines.)

197 **paddock** toad.   **gib** tomcat

198 **dear concernings** important affairs

199 **sense and secrecy** secrecy that common sense requires

200 **Unpeg the basket** open the cage, i.e., let out the secret

201 **famous ape** (In a story now lost.)

202 **try conclusions** test the outcome (in which the ape apparently enters a cage from which birds have been released and then tries to fly out of the cage as they have
done, falling to its death)

203 **down** in the fall.

For use almost can change the stamp of nature,   175
And either... the devil, or throw him out   176
With wondrous potency. Once more, good night;
And when you are desirous to be blest,   178
I'll blessing beg of you. For this same lord,   179

                                  [pointing to Polonius]

I do repent; but heaven hath pleased it so
To punish me with this, and this with me,   181
That I must be their scourge and minister.   182
I will bestow him, and will answer well   183
The death I gave him. So, again, good night.
I must be cruel only to be kind.
This bad begins, and worse remains behind.   186
One word more, good lady.

QUEEN   What shall I do?

HAMLET

Not this by no means that I bid you do:
Let the bloat king tempt you again to bed,   189
Pinch wanton on your cheek, call you his mouse,   190
And let him, for a pair of reechy kisses,   191
Or paddling in your neck with his damned fingers,   192
Make you to ravel all this matter out   193
That I essentially am not in madness,
But mad in craft. 'Twere good you let him know,   195
For who that's but a queen, fair, sober, wise,
Would from a paddock, from a bat, a gib,   197
Such dear concernings hide? Who would do so?   198
No, in despite of sense and secrecy,   199
Unpeg the basket on the house's top,   200
Let the birds fly, and like the famous ape,   201
To try conclusions, in the basket creep   202
And break your own neck down.   203

QUEEN

Be thou assured, if words be made of breath,
And breath of life, I have no life to breathe
What thou hast said to me.

211–12 **sweep . . . knavery** sweep a path before me and conduct me to some *knavery* or treachery prepared for me.

212 **work** proceed.

213 **engineer** maker of *engines* of war.

214 **Hoist with** blown up by.   **petard** an explosive used to blow in a door or make a breach

214–15 **'t shall . . . will** unless luck is against me, I will

215 **mines** tunnels used in warfare to undermine the enemy's emplacements; Hamlet will countermine by going under their mines

217 **in one line** i.e., mines and countermines on a collision course, or the countermines directly below the mines. **crafts** acts of guile, plots

218 **set me packing** set me to making schemes, and set me to lugging (him), and, also, send me off in a hurry.

223 **draw . . . end** finish up. (With a pun on *draw*, "pull.")

4.1 *Location: The castle.*

0.1 **Enter . . . Queen** (Some editors argue that Gertrude does not in fact exit at the end of 3.4 and that the scene is continuous here. It is true that the Folio ends 3.4 with *"Exit Hamlet tugging in Polonius,"* not naming Gertrude, and opens 4.1 with *"Enter King."* Yet the second quarto concludes 3.4 with a simple *"Exit,"* which often stands ambiguously for a single exit or an exeunt in early modern texts, and then starts 4.1 with *"Enter King, and Queene, with Rosencraus and Guyldensterne."* The King's opening lines in 4.1 suggest that he has had time, during a brief intervening pause, to become aware of Gertrude's highly wrought emotional state. In line 35, the King refers to Gertrude's *closet* as though it were elsewhere. The differences between the second quarto and the Folio offer an alternative staging. In either case, 4.1 follows swiftly upon 3.4.)

1 **matter** significance.   **heaves** heavy sighs.

HAMLET
    I must to England. You know that?

QUEEN   Alack,
    I had forgot. 'Tis so concluded on.

HAMLET
    There's letters sealed, and my two schoolfellows,
    Whom I will trust as I will adders fanged,
    They bear the mandate; they must sweep my way   211
    And marshal me to knavery. Let it work.   212
    For 'tis the sport to have the engineer   213
    Hoist with his own petard, and 't shall go hard   214
    But I will delve one yard below their mines   215
    And blow them at the moon. Oh, 'tis most sweet
    When in one line two crafts directly meet.   217
    This man shall set me packing.   218
    I'll lug the guts into the neighbor room.
    Mother, good night indeed. This counselor
    Is now most still, most secret, and most grave,
    Who was in life a foolish prating knave.—
    Come, sir, to draw toward an end with you.—   223
    Good night, mother.
            Exeunt [separately, Hamlet dragging in Polonius].

[4.1] ◆◇ *Enter King and Queen, with Rosencrantz and
        Guildenstern.*

KING
    There's matter in these sighs, these profound heaves.   1
    You must translate; 'tis fit we understand them.
    Where is your son?

QUEEN
    Bestow this place on us a little while.
                    [Exeunt Rosencrantz and Guildenstern.]
    Ah, mine own lord, what have I seen tonight!

KING
    What, Gertrude? How does Hamlet?

11 **brainish apprehension** frenzied misapprehension
12 **heavy** grievous
13 **us** i.e., me. (The royal "we"; also in line 15.)
16 **answered** explained.
17 **providence** foresight
18 **short** i.e., on a short tether.   **out of haunt** secluded
22 **from divulging** from becoming publicly known
25 **ore** vein of gold
26 **mineral** mine
32 **countenance** put the best face on
36 **fair** gently, courteously

QUEEN

    Mad as the sea and wind when both contend
    Which is the mightier. In his lawless fit,
    Behind the arras hearing something stir,
    Whips out his rapier, cries, "A rat, a rat!"
    And in this brainish apprehension kills   11
    The unseen good old man.

KING   Oh, heavy deed!   12
    It had been so with us, had we been there.   13
    His liberty is full of threats to all—
    To you yourself, to us, to everyone.
    Alas, how shall this bloody deed be answered?   16
    It will be laid to us, whose providence   17
    Should have kept short, restrained, and out of haunt   18
    This mad young man. But so much was our love,
    We would not understand what was most fit,
    But, like the owner of a foul disease,
    To keep it from divulging, let it feed   22
    Even on the pith of life. Where is he gone?

QUEEN

    To draw apart the body he hath killed,
    O'er whom his very madness, like some ore   25
    Among a mineral of metals base,   26
    Shows itself pure: 'a weeps for what is done.

KING   Oh, Gertrude, come away!
    The sun no sooner shall the mountains touch
    But we will ship him hence, and this vile deed
    We must with all our majesty and skill
    Both countenance and excuse.—Ho, Guildenstern!   32

       Enter Rosencrantz and Guildenstern.

    Friends both, go join you with some further aid.
    Hamlet in madness hath Polonius slain,
    And from his mother's closet hath he dragged him.
    Go seek him out, speak fair, and bring the body   36
    Into the chapel. I pray you, haste in this.

40 **And ... done** (A defective line; conjectures as to the missing words include "So, haply, slander" [Capell and others]; "For, haply, slander" [Theobald and others]; and "So envious slander" [Jenkins].)

41 **diameter** extent from side to side

42 **As level** with as direct aim.   **his blank** its target at point-blank range

44 **woundless** invulnerable

4.2 *Location: The castle.*

12–13 **That ... own** i.e., Don't expect me to do as you bid me and not follow my own counsel.

13 **demanded of** questioned by

13–14 **replication** reply

16 **countenance** favor

17 **authorities** delegated power, influence.

[*Exeunt Rosencrantz and Guildenstern.*]
Come, Gertrude, we'll call up our wisest friends
And let them know both what we mean to do
And what's untimely done   40
Whose whisper o'er the world's diameter,   41
As level as the cannon to his blank,   42
Transports his poisoned shot, may miss our name
And hit the woundless air. Oh, come away!   44
My soul is full of discord and dismay.   *Exeunt.*

[4.2] ❧ *Enter Hamlet.*

HAMLET   Safely stowed.

ROSENCRANTZ, GUILDENSTERN *(within)*   Hamlet! Lord
Hamlet!

HAMLET   But soft, what noise? Who calls on Hamlet? Oh,
here they come.

        Enter Rosencrantz and Guildenstern.

ROSENCRANTZ
What have you done, my lord, with the dead body?

HAMLET
Compounded it with dust, whereto 'tis kin.

ROSENCRANTZ
Tell us where 'tis, that we may take it thence
And bear it to the chapel.

HAMLET   Do not believe it.

ROSENCRANTZ   Believe what?

HAMLET   That I can keep your counsel and not mine   12
own. Besides, to be demanded of a sponge, what rep-   13
lication should be made by the son of a king?   14

ROSENCRANTZ   Take you me for a sponge, my lord?

HAMLET   Ay, sir, that soaks up the King's countenance,   16
his rewards, his authorities. But such officers do do the 17

24 **sleeps in** has no meaning to

28–9 **The ... body** (Perhaps alludes to the legal common-
place of "the king's two bodies," which drew a distinc-
tion between the sacred office of kingship and the
particular mortal who possessed it at any given time.
Hence, although Claudius's body is necessarily a part of
him, true kingship is not contained in it. Similarly,
Claudius will have Polonius's body when it is found, but
there is no kingship in this business either.)

31 **Of nothing** (1) of no account (2) lacking the essence of
kingship, as in lines 28–9 and note.

31–2 **Hide ... after** (An old signal cry in the game of hide-
and-seek, suggesting that Hamlet now runs away from
them.)

4.3 *Location: The castle.*

4 **of** by.   **distracted** fickle, unstable

5 **Who ... eyes** who choose not by judgment but by appearance

6–7 **th'offender's ... offense** i.e., the populace often
takes umbrage at the severity of a punishment without
taking into account the gravity of the crime.

7 **To ... even** To manage the business in an unprovoca-
tive way

9 **Deliberate pause** carefully considered action.

10 **appliance** remedies

King best service in the end. He keeps them, like an
ape, an apple, in the corner of his jaw, first mouthed
to be last swallowed. When he needs what you have
gleaned, it is but squeezing you, and, sponge, you
shall be dry again.

ROSENCRANTZ   I understand you not, my lord.

HAMLET   I am glad of it. A knavish speech sleeps in a   24
foolish ear.

ROSENCRANTZ   My lord, you must tell us where the
body is and go with us to the King.

HAMLET   The body is with the King, but the King is not   28
with the body. The King is a thing—   29

GUILDENSTERN   A thing, my lord?

HAMLET   Of nothing. Bring me to him. Hide fox, and all   31
after!   *Exeunt* [*running*].   32

[4.3]   ✧   *Enter King, and two or three.*

KING
I have sent to seek him, and to find the body.
How dangerous is it that this man goes loose!
Yet must not we put the strong law on him.
He's loved of the distracted multitude,   4
Who like not in their judgment, but their eyes,   5
And where 'tis so, th'offender's scourge is weighed,   6
But never the offense. To bear all smooth and even,   7
This sudden sending him away must seem
Deliberate pause. Diseases desperate grown   9
By desperate appliance are relieved,   10
Or not at all.

          Enter Rosencrantz, [*Guildenstern,*]
          and all the rest.

          How now, what hath befall'n?

14 **Without** Outside

20 **politic worms** crafty worms (suited to a master spy
   like Polonius).   **e'en** even now

21 **Your worm** Your average worm. (Compare *your fat
   king and your lean beggar* in line 23.)   **diet** food, eating.
   (With a punning reference to the Diet of Worms, a famous *convocation* held in 1521.)

24 **service** food served at table. (Worms feed on kings and
   beggars alike.)

27 **eat** eaten. (Pronounced *et.*)

32 **progress** royal journey of state

37 **nose** smell

ROSENCRANTZ
  Where the dead body is bestowed, my lord,
  We cannot get from him.
KING   But where is he?
ROSENCRANTZ
  Without, my lord; guarded, to know your pleasure.   14
KING
  Bring him before us.
ROSENCRANTZ [*calling*]   Ho! Bring in the lord.

        They enter [*with Hamlet*].

KING   Now, Hamlet, where's Polonius?
HAMLET   At supper.
KING   At supper? Where?
HAMLET   Not where he eats, but where 'a is eaten. A
  certain convocation of politic worms are e'en at him.   20
  Your worm is your only emperor for diet. We fat all   21
  creatures else to fat us, and we fat ourselves for mag-
  gots. Your fat king and your lean beggar is but
  variable service—two dishes, but to one table. That's   24
  the end.
KING   Alas, alas!
HAMLET   A man may fish with the worm that hath eat   27
  of a king, and eat of the fish that hath fed of that
  worm.
KING   What dost thou mean by this?
HAMLET   Nothing but to show you how a king may go
  a progress through the guts of a beggar.   32
KING   Where is Polonius?
HAMLET   In heaven. Send thither to see. If your messenger find him not there, seek him i'th'other place yourself. But if indeed you find him not within this month,
  you shall nose him as you go up the stairs into the   37
  lobby.

42 **tender** regard, hold dear.   **dearly** intensely

45 **bark** sailing vessel

46 **tend** wait.   **bent** in readiness

52 **cherub** (Cherubim are angels of knowledge. Hamlet hints that both he and heaven are onto Claudius's tricks.)

58 **at foot** close behind, at heel

61 **leans on** bears upon, is related to

62 **England** i.e., King of England.   **at aught** at any value

63 **As ... sense** for so my great power may give you a just appreciation of the importance of valuing my love

64 **cicatrice** scar

65 **free awe** unconstrained show of respect

66 **coldly set** regard with indifference

67 **process** command.   **imports at full** conveys specific directions for

68 **congruing** agreeing

KING [to some attendants] Go seek him there.

HAMLET 'A will stay till you come. [Exeunt attendants.]

KING
  Hamlet, this deed, for thine especial safety—
  Which we do tender, as we dearly grieve   42
  For that which thou hast done—must send thee hence
  With fiery quickness. Therefore prepare thyself.
  The bark is ready, and the wind at help,   45
  Th'associates tend, and everything is bent   46
  For England.

HAMLET For England!

KING Ay, Hamlet.

HAMLET Good.

KING
  So is it, if thou knew'st our purposes.

HAMLET I see a cherub that sees them. But come, for   52
  England! Farewell, dear mother.

KING Thy loving father, Hamlet.

HAMLET My mother. Father and mother is man and
  wife, man and wife is one flesh, and so, my mother.
  Come, for England!   Exit.

KING
  Follow him at foot; tempt him with speed aboard.   58
  Delay it not. I'll have him hence tonight.
  Away! For everything is sealed and done
  That else leans on th'affair. Pray you, make haste. 61
                    [Exeunt all but the King.]
  And, England, if my love thou hold'st at aught—   62
  As my great power thereof may give thee sense,   63
  Since yet thy cicatrice looks raw and red   64
  After the Danish sword, and thy free awe   65
  Pays homage to us—thou mayst not coldly set   66
  Our sovereign process, which imports at full,   67
  By letters congruing to that effect,   68

69 **present** immediate
70 **hectic** persistent fever
72 **Howe'er . . . begun** whatever else happens, I cannot begin to be happy.

4.4 *Location: The coast of Denmark.*

2 **license** permission
3 **conveyance** unhindered passage
6 **We . . . eye** I will come pay my respects in person
9 **softly** slowly, circumspectly
10 **powers** forces
16 **main** main part
18 **addition** exaggeration
21 **To pay** i.e., For a yearly rental of.   **farm it** take a lease of it

The present death of Hamlet. Do it, England,   69
For like the hectic in my blood he rages,   70
And thou must cure me. Till I know 'tis done,
Howe'er my haps, my joys were ne'er begun.   *Exit.*   72

[4.4] ⤦ *Enter Fortinbras with his army over the stage.*

FORTINBRAS
Go, Captain, from me greet the Danish king.
Tell him that by his license Fortinbras   2
Craves the conveyance of a promised march   3
Over his kingdom. You know the rendezvous.
If that His Majesty would aught with us,
We shall express our duty in his eye;   6
And let him know so.
CAPTAIN   I will do't, my lord.
FORTINBRAS   Go softly on.   [*Exeunt all but the Captain.*]   9

     Enter Hamlet, Rosencrantz, [Guildenstern,] etc.

HAMLET   Good sir, whose powers are these?   10
CAPTAIN   They are of Norway, sir.
HAMLET   How purposed, sir, I pray you?
CAPTAIN   Against some part of Poland.
HAMLET   Who commands them, sir?
CAPTAIN
The nephew to old Norway, Fortinbras.
HAMLET
Goes it against the main of Poland, sir,   16
Or for some frontier?
CAPTAIN
Truly to speak, and with no addition,   18
We go to gain a little patch of ground
That hath in it no profit but the name.
To pay five ducats, five, I would not farm it;   21

23 **ranker** higher.   **in fee** fee simple, outright.

27 **debate . . . straw** argue about this trifling matter.

28 **th'impostume** the abscess

29 **inward breaks** festers within.   **without** externally

33 **inform against** denounce; take shape against

35 **market of** profit of

37 **discourse** power of reasoning

38 **Looking before and after** able to review past events and anticipate the future

40 **fust** grow moldy

41 **oblivion** forgetfulness.   **craven** cowardly

42 **precisely** scrupulously.   **th'event** the outcome

46 **Sith** since

47 **gross** obvious

48 **charge** expense

Nor will it yield to Norway or the Pole
A ranker rate, should it be sold in fee.   23

HAMLET
Why, then the Polack never will defend it.

CAPTAIN
Yes, it is already garrisoned.

HAMLET
Two thousand souls and twenty thousand ducats
Will not debate the question of this straw.   27
This is th'impostume of much wealth and peace,   28
That inward breaks, and shows no cause without   29
Why the man dies. I humbly thank you, sir.

CAPTAIN
God b'wi'you, sir.   [Exit.]

ROSENCRANTZ   Will't please you go, my lord?

HAMLET
I'll be with you straight. Go a little before.
                    [Exeunt all except Hamlet.]
How all occasions do inform against me   33
And spur my dull revenge! What is a man,
If his chief good and market of his time   35
Be but to sleep and feed? A beast, no more.
Sure he that made us with such large discourse,   37
Looking before and after, gave us not   38
That capability and godlike reason
To fust in us unused. Now, whether it be   40
Bestial oblivion, or some craven scruple   41
Of thinking too precisely on th'event—   42
A thought which, quartered, hath but one part
    wisdom
And ever three parts coward—I do not know
Why yet I live to say "This thing's to do,"
Sith I have cause, and will, and strength, and means   46
To do't. Examples gross as earth exhort me: 47
Witness this army of such mass and charge,   48

49 **delicate and tender** of fine and youthful qualities

51 **Makes mouths** makes scornful faces.   **invisible event** unforeseeable outcome

53 **dare** could do (to him)

54–7 **Rightly . . . stake** True greatness is not a matter of being moved to action solely by a great cause; rather, it is to respond greatly to an apparently trivial cause when honor is at the stake.

59 **blood** (The supposed seat of the passions.)

62 **fantasy** fanciful caprice, illusion.   **trick** trifle, deceit

63 **plot** plot of ground

64 **Whereon . . . cause** on which there is insufficient room for the soldiers needed to fight for it

65 **continent** receptacle, container

4.5 *Location: The castle.*

2 **distract** out of her mind.

5 **tricks** deceptions.   **hems** clears her throat, makes "hmm" sounds.   **heart** i.e., breast

6 **Spurns . . . straws** kicks spitefully, takes offense at trifles.   **in doubt** of obscure meaning

8 **unshapèd use** incoherent manner

9 **collection** inference, a guess at some sort of meaning. **yawn** gape, wonder; grasp. (The Folio reading, "aim," is possible.)

Led by a delicate and tender prince,   49
Whose spirit with divine ambition puffed
Makes mouths at the invisible event,   51
Exposing what is mortal and unsure
To all that fortune, death, and danger dare,   53
Even for an eggshell. Rightly to be great   54
Is not to stir without great argument,   55
But greatly to find quarrel in a straw   56
When honor's at the stake. How stand I, then,   57
That have a father killed, a mother stained,
Excitements of my reason and my blood,   59
And let all sleep, while to my shame I see
The imminent death of twenty thousand men
That for a fantasy and trick of fame   62
Go to their graves like beds, fight for a plot   63
Whereon the numbers cannot try the cause,   64
Which is not tomb enough and continent   65
To hide the slain? Oh, from this time forth
My thoughts be bloody or be nothing worth!   *Exit.*

[4.5] ❧ *Enter Horatio, [Queen] Gertrude, and a Gentleman.*

QUEEN
I will not speak with her.

GENTLEMAN   She is importunate,
Indeed distract. Her mood will needs be pitied.   2

QUEEN   What would she have?

GENTLEMAN
She speaks much of her father, says she hears
There's tricks i'th' world, and hems, and beats her
    heart,   5
Spurns enviously at straws, speaks things in doubt   6
That carry but half sense. Her speech is nothing,
Yet the unshapèd use of it doth move   8
The hearers to collection; they yawn at it,   9

10 **botch** patch

11 **Which** which words.   **yield** deliver, represent

12–13 **there might . . . unhappily** that a great deal could be guessed at of a most unfortunate nature, even if one couldn't be at all sure.

15 **ill-breeding** prone to suspect the worst and to make mischief

18 **toy** trifle.   **amiss** calamity.

19–20 **So . . . spilt** Guilt is so burdened with conscience and guileless fear of detection that it reveals itself through apprehension of disaster.

20.1 ***Enter Ophelia*** (In the first quarto, Ophelia enters *"playing on a lute, and her hair down, singing."*)

25 **cockle hat** hat with cockleshell stuck in it as a sign that the wearer had been a pilgrim to the shrine of Saint James of Compostella in Spain

26 **shoon** shoes.

33 **Oho!** (Perhaps a sigh.)

And botch the words up fit to their own thoughts,   10
Which, as her winks and nods and gestures yield
     them,   11
Indeed would make one think there might be thought,   12
Though nothing sure, yet much unhappily.   13

HORATIO
'Twere good she were spoken with, for she may strew
Dangerous conjectures in ill-breeding minds.   15

QUEEN   Let her come in.   [Exit Gentleman.]
[Aside] To my sick soul, as sin's true nature is,
Each toy seems prologue to some great amiss.   18
So full of artless jealousy is guilt,   19
It spills itself in fearing to be spilt.   20

     Enter Ophelia [distracted].

OPHELIA
Where is the beauteous majesty of Denmark?

QUEEN   How now, Ophelia?

OPHELIA (she sings)
     "How should I your true love know
          From another one?
     By his cockle hat and staff,   25
          And his sandal shoon."   26

QUEEN   Alas, sweet lady, what imports this song?

OPHELIA   Say you? Nay, pray you, mark.
     "He is dead and gone, lady,   (Song.)
          He is dead and gone;
     At his head a grass-green turf,
          At his heels a stone."
Oho!   33

QUEEN   Nay, but Ophelia—

OPHELIA   Pray you, mark.
[Sings] "White his shroud as the mountain snow"—

     Enter King.

38 **Larded** strewn, bedecked
40 **showers** i.e., tears.
42 **God 'ild** God yield or reward.   **owl** (Refers to a leg-
    end about a baker's daughter who was turned into an
    owl for being ungenerous when Jesus begged a loaf of
    bread.)
45 **Conceit** Fancy, brooding
49 **betime** early
53 **dupped** did up, opened
59 **Gis** Jesus
62 **Cock** (A perversion of "God" in oaths; here also with a
    quibble on the slang word for penis.)
67 **An** if

QUEEN   Alas, look here, my lord.

OPHELIA
> "Larded with sweet flowers;   (*Song.*)   38
> Which bewept to the ground did not go
>   With true-love showers."   40

KING   How do you, pretty lady?

OPHELIA   Well, God 'ild you! They say the owl was a   42
baker's daughter. Lord, we know what we are, but
know not what we may be. God be at your table!

KING   Conceit upon her father.   45

OPHELIA   Pray let's have no words of this; but when
they ask you what it means, say you this:
> "Tomorrow is Saint Valentine's day,   (*Song.*)
>   All in the morning betime,   49
> And I a maid at your window,
>   To be your Valentine.
> Then up he rose, and donned his clothes,
>   And dupped the chamber door,   53
> Let in the maid, that out a maid
>   Never departed more."

KING   Pretty Ophelia—

OPHELIA   Indeed, la, without an oath, I'll make an end
on't:
> [*Sings*] "By Gis and by Saint Charity,   59
>   Alack, and fie for shame!
> Young men will do't, if they come to't;
>   By Cock, they are to blame.   62
> Quoth she, 'Before you tumbled me,
>   You promised me to wed.'"
He answers:
> "'So would I ha' done, by yonder sun,
>   An thou hadst not come to my bed.'"   67

KING   How long hath she been thus?

OPHELIA   I hope all will be well. We must be patient,
but I cannot choose but weep to think they would lay

79 **spies** scouts sent in advance of the main force

82 **remove** removal.   **muddied** stirred up, confused

84 **greenly** foolishly

85 **hugger-mugger** secret haste

88 **as much containing** as full of serious matter

90 **Feeds . . . clouds** feeds his resentment on this whole shocking turn of events, keeps himself aloof and mysterious

91 **wants** lacks.   **buzzers** gossipers, informers

93 **necessity** i.e., the need to invent some plausible explanation.   **of matter beggared** unprovided with facts

94–5 **Will . . . ear** will not hesitate to accuse my (royal) person in everybody's ears.

96 **murd'ring piece** cannon loaded so as to scatter its shot

97 **Gives . . . death** kills me over and over.

99 **Attend!** Guard me!

100 **Switzers** Swiss guards, mercenaries.

him i'th' cold ground. My brother shall know of it.
And so I thank you for your good counsel. Come, my
coach! Good night, ladies, good night, sweet ladies,
good night, good night.   [Exit.]

KING [to Horatio]
Follow her close. Give her good watch, I pray you.
                              [Exit Horatio.]
Oh, this is the poison of deep grief; it springs
All from her father's death—and now behold!
Oh, Gertrude, Gertrude,
When sorrows come, they come not single spies,   79
But in battalions. First, her father slain;
Next, your son gone, and he most violent author
Of his own just remove; the people muddied,   82
Thick and unwholesome in their thoughts and
    whispers
For good Polonius' death—and we have done but
    greenly,   84
In hugger-mugger to inter him; poor Ophelia   85
Divided from herself and her fair judgment,
Without the which we are pictures or mere beasts;
Last, and as much containing as all these,   88
Her brother is in secret come from France,
Feeds on this wonder, keeps himself in clouds,   90
And wants not buzzers to infect his ear   91
With pestilent speeches of his father's death,
Wherein necessity, of matter beggared,   93
Will nothing stick our person to arraign   94
In ear and ear. Oh, my dear Gertrude, this,   95
Like to a murd'ring piece, in many places   96
Gives me superfluous death.   A noise within.   97

QUEEN Alack, what noise is this?

KING Attend!   99
Where is my Switzers? Let them guard the door.   100

102 **overpeering of his list** overflowing its shore, boundary

103 **flats** i.e., flatlands near shore.   **impetuous** violent
(perhaps also with the meaning of *impiteous* ["impitious," Q2], "pitiless")

104 **riotous head** insurrectionary advance

106–8 **And . . . word** and, as if the world were to be started
all over afresh, utterly setting aside all ancient traditional customs that should confirm and underprop our
every word and promise

110 **Caps** (The caps are thrown in the air.)

113 **counter** (A hunting term, meaning to follow the trail in
a direction opposite to that which the game has taken.)

123 **between** amidst

Enter a Messenger.

What is the matter?

MESSENGER   Save yourself, my lord!
The ocean, overpeering of his list,   102
Eats not the flats with more impetuous haste   103
Than young Laertes, in a riotous head,   104
O'erbears your officers. The rabble call him lord,
And, as the world were now but to begin,   106
Antiquity forgot, custom not known,   107
The ratifiers and props of every word,   108
They cry, "Choose we! Laertes shall be king!"
Caps, hands, and tongues applaud it to the clouds,   110
"Laertes shall be king, Laertes king!"

QUEEN
How cheerfully on the false trail they cry!
                                        A noise within.
Oh, this is counter, you false Danish dogs!   113

          Enter Laertes with others.

KING   The doors are broke.

LAERTES
Where is this King?—Sirs, stand you all without.

ALL   No, let's come in.

LAERTES   I pray you, give me leave.

ALL   We will, we will.

LAERTES   I thank you. Keep the door. [*Exeunt followers.*]
                              Oh, thou vile king,
Give me my father!

QUEEN [*restraining him*] Calmly, good Laertes.

LAERTES
That drop of blood that's calm proclaims me bastard,
Cries cuckold to my father, brands the harlot
Even here between the chaste unsmirchèd brow   123
Of my true mother.

KING   What is the cause, Laertes,

125 **giantlike** (Recalling the rising of the giants of Greek mythology against Olympus.)

126 **fear our** fear for my

127 **hedge** protect, as with a surrounding barrier

128 **can . . . would** can only peep furtively, as through a barrier, at what it would intend

129 **Acts . . . will** (but) performs little of what it intends.

133 **juggled with** cheated, deceived.

136 **To . . . stand** I am resolved in this

137 **both . . . negligence** i.e., both this world and the next are of no consequence to me

139 **throughly** thoroughly

141 **My will . . . world's** I'll stop (*stay*) when my will is accomplished, not for anyone else's.

142 **for** as for

146 **swoopstake** i.e., indiscriminately. (Literally, taking all stakes on the gambling table at once. *Draw* is also a gambling term, meaning "take from.")

That thy rebellion looks so giantlike?   125
Let him go, Gertrude. Do not fear our person.   126
There's such divinity doth hedge a king   127
That treason can but peep to what it would,   128
Acts little of his will. Tell me, Laertes,   129
Why thou art thus incensed. Let him go, Gertrude.
Speak, man.

LAERTES   Where is my father?

KING   Dead.

QUEEN
  But not by him.

KING   Let him demand his fill.

LAERTES
  How came he dead? I'll not be juggled with.   133
  To hell, allegiance! Vows, to the blackest devil!
  Conscience and grace, to the profoundest pit!
  I dare damnation. To this point I stand,   136
  That both the worlds I give to negligence,   137
  Let come what comes, only I'll be revenged
  Most throughly for my father.   139

KING   Who shall stay you?

LAERTES   My will, not all the world's.   141
  And for my means, I'll husband them so well   142
  They shall go far with little.

KING   Good Laertes,
  If you desire to know the certainty
  Of your dear father, is't writ in your revenge
  That, swoopstake, you will draw both friend and foe, 146
  Winner and loser?

LAERTES   None but his enemies.

KING   Will you know them, then?

LAERTES
  To his good friends thus wide I'll ope my arms,

151 **pelican** (Refers to the belief that the female pelican fed its young with its own blood.)

152 **Repast** feed

155 **sensibly** feelingly

156 **level** plain

160 **virtue** faculty, power

161 **paid with weight** repaid, avenged equally or more

162 **beam** crossbar of a balance.

166–8 **Nature . . . loves** Human nature is exquisitely sensitive in matters of love, and in cases of sudden loss it sends some precious part of itself after the lost object of that love. (In this case, Ophelia's sanity deserts her out of sorrow for her lost father and perhaps too out of her love for Hamlet.)

175–6 **You . . . a-down-a** (Ophelia assigns the singing of refrains, like her own "Hey non nonny," to others present.)

176 **wheel** spinning wheel as accompaniment to the song, or refrain

177 **false steward** (The story is unknown.)

And like the kind life-rendering pelican   151
Repast them with my blood.

KING   Why, now you speak   152
Like a good child and a true gentleman.
That I am guiltless of your father's death,
And am most sensibly in grief for it,   155
It shall as level to your judgment 'pear   156
As day does to your eye.   *A noise within.*

LAERTES
How now, what noise is that?

        Enter Ophelia.

KING   Let her come in.

LAERTES
O heat, dry up my brains! Tears seven times salt
Burn out the sense and virtue of mine eye!   160
By heaven, thy madness shall be paid with weight   161
Till our scale turn the beam. O rose of May!   162
Dear maid, kind sister, sweet Ophelia!
O heavens, is't possible a young maid's wits
Should be as mortal as an old man's life?
Nature is fine in love, and where 'tis fine   166
It sends some precious instance of itself   167
After the thing it loves.   168

OPHELIA
        "They bore him barefaced on the bier,   (*Song.*)
            Hey non nonny, nonny, hey nonny,
        And in his grave rained many a tear—"
Fare you well, my dove!

LAERTES
Hadst thou thy wits and didst persuade revenge,
It could not move thus.

OPHELIA You must sing "A-down a-down," and you   175
"call him a-down-a." Oh, how the wheel becomes it! It   176
is the false steward that stole his master's daughter.   177

178 **This...matter** This seeming nonsense is more eloquent than sane utterance.

179 **rosemary** (Used as a symbol of remembrance both at
weddings and at funerals.)

180 **pansies** (Emblems of love and courtship; perhaps from
French *pensèes*, "thoughts.")

182 **document** instruction, lesson

184 **There's fennel...columbines** (*Fennel* betokens flat-
tery; *columbines*, unchastity or ingratitude. Throughout,
Ophelia addresses her various listeners, giving one
flower to one and another to another, perhaps with particular symbolic significance in each case.)

185 **rue** (Emblem of repentance—a signification that is evident in its popular name, *herb of grace*.)

187 **with a difference** (A device used in heraldry to distinguish one family from another on the coat of arms, here
suggesting that Ophelia and the others have different
causes of sorrow and repentance; perhaps with a play
on *rue* in the sense of "ruth," "pity.")   **daisy** (Emblem
of love's victims and of faithlessness.)

188 **violets** (Emblems of faithfulness.)

191 **Thought** Melancholy.   **passion** suffering

192 **favor** grace, beauty

199 **poll** head.

207 **whom** whichever of

LAERTES   This nothing's more than matter.   178

OPHELIA   There's rosemary, that's for remembrance; 179
pray you, love, remember. And there is pansies; that's 180
for thoughts.

LAERTES   A document in madness, thoughts and re- 182
membrance fitted.

OPHELIA   There's fennel for you, and columbines. 184
There's rue for you, and here's some for me; we may 185
call it herb of grace o' Sundays. You must wear your
rue with a difference. There's a daisy. I would give 187
you some violets, but they withered all when my 188
father died. They say 'a made a good end—
[Sings] "For bonny sweet Robin is all my joy."

LAERTES
Thought and affliction, passion, hell itself,   191
She turns to favor and to prettiness.   192

OPHELIA
    "And will 'a not come again?   (Song.)
    And will 'a not come again?
      No, no, he is dead.
      Go to thy deathbed,
    He never will come again.

    "His beard was as white as snow,
    All flaxen was his poll.   199
      He is gone, he is gone,
      And we cast away moan.
    God ha' mercy on his soul!"
And of all Christian souls, I pray God. God b'wi'you.
        [Exit, followed by Gertrude.]

LAERTES   Do you see this, O God?

KING
Laertes, I must commune with your grief,
Or you deny me right. Go but apart,
Make choice of whom your wisest friends you will,   207

209 **collateral hand** indirect agency

210 **us touched** me implicated

217 **trophy** memorial.   **hatchment** tablet displaying the armorial bearings of a deceased person

218 **ostentation** ceremony

220 **That** so that.   **call't in question** demand an explanation.

4.6 *Location: The castle.*

  3 **letters** a letter

  9 **an't** if it

 10 **th'ambassador** (Hamlet's ostensible role; see 3.1.172–3.)

And they shall hear and judge twixt you and me.
If by direct or by collateral hand   209
They find us touched, we will our kingdom give,   210
Our crown, our life, and all that we call ours
To you in satisfaction; but if not,
Be you content to lend your patience to us,
And we shall jointly labor with your soul
To give it due content.

LAERTES   Let this be so.
His means of death, his obscure funeral—
No trophy, sword, nor hatchment o'er his bones,   217
No noble rite, nor formal ostentation—   218
Cry to be heard, as 'twere from heaven to earth,
That I must call't in question.

KING   So you shall,   220
And where th'offense is, let the great ax fall.
I pray you, go with me.   *Exeunt.*

[4.6] ✧ *Enter Horatio and others.*

HORATIO
What are they that would speak with me?

GENTLEMAN   Seafaring men, sir. They say they have
letters for you.   3

HORATIO   Let them come in.   [*Exit Gentleman.*]
I do not know from what part of the world
I should be greeted, if not from Lord Hamlet.

        Enter Sailors.

FIRST SAILOR   God bless you, sir.

HORATIO   Let him bless thee too.

FIRST SAILOR   'A shall, sir, an't please him. There's a   9
letter for you sir—it came from th'ambassador that   10
was bound for England—if your name be Horatio, as
I am let to know it is.   [*He gives a letter.*]

13–14 **overlooked** looked over
14 **means** means of access
16 **appointment** equipage
21 **thieves of mercy** merciful thieves
23 **repair** come
26 **bore** caliber, i.e., importance
31 **way** means of access

4.7 *Location: The castle.*
1 **my acquittance seal** confirm or acknowledge my innocence
3 **Sith** since
6 **feats** acts
7 **capital** punishable by death
9 **mainly** greatly

HORATIO [*reads*] "Horatio, when thou shalt have over-   13
    looked this, give these fellows some means to the King;   14
    they have letters for him. Ere we were two days old at
    sea, a pirate of very warlike appointment gave us   16
    chase. Finding ourselves too slow of sail, we put on a
    compelled valor, and in the grapple I boarded them.
    On the instant they got clear of our ship, so I alone
    became their prisoner. They have dealt with me like
    thieves of mercy, but they knew what they did: I am to   21
    do a good turn for them. Let the King have the letters
    I have sent, and repair thou to me with as much speed   23
    as thou wouldest fly death. I have words to speak in
    thine ear will make thee dumb, yet are they much too
    light for the bore of the matter. These good fellows will   26
    bring thee where I am. Rosencrantz and Guildenstern
    hold their course for England. Of them I have much to
    tell thee. Farewell.

                He that thou knowest thine, Hamlet."
Come, I will give you way for these your letters,   31
And do't the speedier that you may direct me
To him from whom you brought them.   *Exeunt.*

[4.7] ᭀᒋ *Enter King and Laertes.*

KING
    Now must your conscience my acquittance seal,   1
    And you must put me in your heart for friend,
    Sith you have heard, and with a knowing ear,   3
    That he which hath your noble father slain
    Pursued my life.

LAERTES   It well appears. But tell me
    Why you proceeded not against these feats   6
    So crimeful and so capital in nature,   7
    As by your safety, greatness, wisdom, all things else,
    You mainly were stirred up.   9

11 **unsinewed** weak

15 **conjunctive** closely united. (An astronomical metaphor.)

16 **his** its.   **sphere** one of the hollow spheres in which, according to Ptolemaic astronomy, the planets were supposed to move

18 **count** account, reckoning, indictment

19 **general gender** common people

21 **Work** operate, act.   **spring** i.e., a spring with such a concentration of lime that it coats a piece of wood with limestone, in effect gilding and petrifying it

22 **gyves** fetters (which, gilded by the people's praise, would look like badges of honor)

23 **Too . . . wind** with too light a shaft for so powerful a gust (of popular sentiment)

27 **terms** state, condition

28 **go back** recall what she was

29 **on mount** set up on high

KING   Oh, for two special reasons,
    Which may to you perhaps seem much unsinewed,   11
    But yet to me they're strong. The Queen his mother
    Lives almost by his looks, and for myself—
    My virtue or my plague, be it either which—
    She is so conjunctive to my life and soul   15
    That, as the star moves not but in his sphere,   16
    I could not but by her. The other motive
    Why to a public count I might not go   18
    Is the great love the general gender bear him,   19
    Who, dipping all his faults in their affection,
    Work like the spring that turneth wood to stone,   21
    Convert his gyves to graces, so that my arrows,   22
    Too slightly timbered for so loud a wind,   23
    Would have reverted to my bow again
    But not where I had aimed them.

LAERTES
    And so have I a noble father lost,
    A sister driven into desp'rate terms,   27
    Whose worth, if praises may go back again,   28
    Stood challenger on mount of all the age   29
    For her perfections. But my revenge will come.

KING
    Break not your sleeps for that. You must not think
    That we are made of stuff so flat and dull
    That we can let our beard be shook with danger
    And think it pastime. You shortly shall hear more.
    I loved your father, and we love ourself;
    And that, I hope, will teach you to imagine—

    Enter a Messenger with letters.

How now? What news?

MESSENGER   Letters, my lord, from Hamlet:
    This to Your Majesty, this to the Queen.
                              [He gives letters.]

45 **naked** destitute, unarmed, without following
47 **pardon** (for returning without authorization)
50 **abuse** deceit.   **no such thing** not what the letter says.
51 **character** handwriting.
53 **devise** explain to
57 **Thus didst thou** i.e., Here's for what you did to my father.
58 **As . . . otherwise?** how can this (Hamlet's return) be true? Yet how otherwise than true (since we have the evidence of his letter)?
60 **So** provided that
62 **checking at** i.e., turning aside from (like a falcon leaving the quarry to fly at a chance bird).   **that** if
64 **device** devising, invention

KING From Hamlet? Who brought them?

MESSENGER
Sailors, my lord, they say. I saw them not.
They were given me by Claudio. He received them
Of him that brought them.

KING   Laertes, you shall hear them.—
Leave us.   [*Exit Messenger.*]
[*He reads.*] "High and mighty, you shall know I am set
naked on your kingdom. Tomorrow shall I beg leave   45
to see your kingly eyes, when I shall, first asking your
pardon, thereunto recount the occasion of my sudden 47
and more strange return.   Hamlet."
What should this mean? Are all the rest come back?
Or is it some abuse, and no such thing?   50

LAERTES
Know you the hand?

KING   'Tis Hamlet's character. "Naked!"   51
And in a postscript here he says "alone."
Can you devise me?   53

LAERTES
I am lost in it, my lord. But let him come.
It warms the very sickness in my heart
That I shall live and tell him to his teeth,
"Thus didst thou."

KING   If it be so, Laertes—   57
As how should it be so? How otherwise?—   58
Will you be ruled by me?

LAERTES   Ay, my lord,
So you will not o'errule me to a peace.   60

KING
To thine own peace. If he be now returned,
As checking at his voyage, and that he means   62
No more to undertake it, I will work him
To an exploit, now ripe in my device,   64

67 **uncharge the practice** acquit the stratagem of being a plot

70 **organ** agent, instrument.

73 **Your . . . parts** All your other virtues

76 **unworthiest siege** least important rank.

79 **no less becomes** is no less adorned by

81–2 **his sables . . . graveness** its rich robes furred with sable and its garments denoting dignified well-being and seriousness.

85 **can well** are skilled

88–9 **As . . . beast** as if, centaurlike, he had been made into one body with the horse, possessing half its nature.

89 **topped** surpassed

90 **forgery** fabrication

Under the which he shall not choose but fall;
And for his death no wind of blame shall breathe,
But even his mother shall uncharge the practice   67
And call it accident.

LAERTES   My lord, I will be ruled,
  The rather if you could devise it so
  That I might be the organ.

KING   It falls right.   70
  You have been talked of since your travel much,
  And that in Hamlet's hearing, for a quality
  Wherein they say you shine. Your sum of parts   73
  Did not together pluck such envy from him
  As did that one, and that, in my regard,
  Of the unworthiest siege.   76

LAERTES   What part is that, my lord?

KING
  A very ribbon in the cap of youth,
  Yet needful too, for youth no less becomes   79
  The light and careless livery that it wears
  Than settled age his sables and his weeds   81
  Importing health and graveness. Two months since   82
  Here was a gentleman of Normandy.
  I have seen myself, and served against, the French,
  And they can well on horseback, but this gallant   85
  Had witchcraft in't; he grew unto his seat,
  And to such wondrous doing brought his horse
  As had he been incorpsed and demi-natured   88
  With the brave beast. So far he topped my thought   89
  That I in forgery of shapes and tricks   90
  Come short of what he did.

LAERTES   A Norman was't?

KING   A Norman.

LAERTES
  Upon my life, Lamord.

KING   The very same.

94 **brooch** ornament

96 **confession** testimonial, admission of superiority

98 **For...defense** with respect to your skill and practice with your weapon

101 **Th'escrimers** The fencers

106 **sudden** immediate.   **play** fence

112 **begun by time** i.e., created by the right circumstance and hence subject to change

113 **passages of proof** actual well-attested instances

114 **qualifies** weakens, moderates

116 **snuff** the charred part of a candlewick

117 **nothing...still** nothing remains at a constant level of perfection

118 **pleurisy** excess, plethora. (Literally, a chest inflammation.)

119 **in...much** of its own excess.   **That** That which

121 **abatements** diminutions

122 **As...accidents** as there are tongues to dissuade, hands to prevent, and chance events to intervene

LAERTES

    I know him well. He is the brooch indeed   94
    And gem of all the nation.

KING   He made confession of you,   96
    And gave you such a masterly report
    For art and exercise in your defense,   98
    And for your rapier most especial,
    That he cried out 'twould be a sight indeed
    If one could match you. Th'escrimers of their nation,   101
    He swore, had neither motion, guard, nor eye
    If you opposed them. Sir, this report of his
    Did Hamlet so envenom with his envy
    That he could nothing do but wish and beg
    Your sudden coming o'er, to play with you.   106
    Now, out of this—

LAERTES   What out of this, my lord?

KING

    Laertes, was your father dear to you?
    Or are you like the painting of a sorrow,
    A face without a heart?

LAERTES   Why ask you this?

KING

    Not that I think you did not love your father,
    But that I know love is begun by time,   112
    And that I see, in passages of proof,   113
    Time qualifies the spark and fire of it.   114
    There lives within the very flame of love
    A kind of wick or snuff that will abate it,   116
    And nothing is at a like goodness still,   117
    For goodness, growing to a pleurisy,   118
    Dies in his own too much. That we would do,   119
    We should do when we would; for this "would" changes
    And hath abatements and delays as many   121
    As there are tongues, are hands, are accidents,   122

123 **spendthrift sigh** (An allusion to the belief that sighs draw blood from the heart.)

124 **hurts by easing** i.e., costs the heart blood and wastes precious opportunity even while it affords emotional relief.   **quick o'th'ulcer** i.e., heart of the matter

128 **sanctuarize** protect from punishment. (Alludes to the right of sanctuary with which certain religious places were invested.)

130 **Will you do this** if you wish to do this

132 **put on those shall** arrange for some to

134 **in fine** finally

135 **remiss** negligently unsuspicious

136 **generous** noble-minded

139 **unbated** not blunted, having no button.   **pass of practice** treacherous thrust in an arranged bout

142 **unction** ointment.   **mountebank** quack doctor

144 **cataplasm** plaster or poultice

145 **simples** herbs.   **virtue** potency

146 **Under the moon** i.e., anywhere (with reference perhaps to the belief that herbs gathered at night had a special power)

148 **gall** graze, wound

151 **shape** part we propose to act.

152 **drift . . . performance** intention should be made visible by our bungling

And then this "should" is like a spendthrift sigh,   123
That hurts by easing. But, to the quick o'th'ulcer: 124
Hamlet comes back. What would you undertake
To show yourself in deed your father's son
More than in words?

LAERTES   To cut his throat i'th' church.

KING
No place, indeed, should murder sanctuarize;   128
Revenge should have no bounds. But good Laertes,
Will you do this, keep close within your chamber.   130
Hamlet returned shall know you are come home.
We'll put on those shall praise your excellence   132
And set a double varnish on the fame
The Frenchman gave you, bring you in fine together,   134
And wager on your heads. He, being remiss,   135
Most generous, and free from all contriving,   136
Will not peruse the foils, so that with ease,
Or with a little shuffling, you may choose
A sword unbated, and in a pass of practice   139
Requite him for your father.

LAERTES   I will do't,
And for that purpose I'll anoint my sword.
I bought an unction of a mountebank   142
So mortal that, but dip a knife in it,
Where it draws blood no cataplasm so rare,   144
Collected from all simples that have virtue   145
Under the moon, can save the thing from death   146
That is but scratched withal. I'll touch my point
With this contagion, that if I gall him slightly,   148
It may be death.

KING   Let's further think of this,
Weigh what convenience both of time and means
May fit us to our shape. If this should fail,   151
And that our drift look through our bad performance,   152
'Twere better not assayed. Therefore this project

155 **blast in proof** come to grief when put to the test.

156 **cunnings** respective skills

159 **As** i.e., and you should

161 **nonce** occasion

162 **stuck** thrust. (From *stoccado*, a fencing term.)

167 **askant** aslant

168 **hoar leaves** white or gray undersides of the leaves

170 **long purples** early purple orchids

171 **liberal** free-spoken.   **a grosser name** (The testicle-resembling tubers of the orchid, which also in some cases resemble *dead men's fingers*, have earned various slang names like "dogstones" and "cullions.")

172 **cold** chaste

173 **pendent** overhanging.   **crownet** made into a chaplet or coronet

174 **envious sliver** malicious branch

175 **weedy** i.e., of plants

178 **lauds** hymns

179 **incapable of** lacking capacity to apprehend

180 **endued** adapted by nature

183 **lay** ballad, song

Should have a back or second, that might hold
If this did blast in proof. Soft, let me see.   155
We'll make a solemn wager on your cunnings—   156
I ha 't!
When in your motion you are hot and dry—
As make your bouts more violent to that end—   159
And that he calls for drink, I'll have prepared him
A chalice for the nonce, whereon but sipping,   161
If he by chance escape your venomed stuck,   162
Our purpose may hold there. [A cry within.] But stay,
   what noise?

   Enter Queen.

QUEEN
One woe doth tread upon another's heel,
So fast they follow. Your sister's drowned, Laertes.

LAERTES   Drowned! Oh, where?

QUEEN
There is a willow grows askant the brook,   167
That shows his hoar leaves in the glassy stream;   168
Therewith fantastic garlands did she make
Of crowflowers, nettles, daisies, and long purples,   170
That liberal shepherds give a grosser name,   171
But our cold maids do dead men's fingers call them.   172
There on the pendent boughs her crownet weeds   173
Clamb'ring to hang, an envious sliver broke,   174
When down her weedy trophies and herself   175
Fell in the weeping brook. Her clothes spread wide,
And mermaidlike awhile they bore her up,
Which time she chanted snatches of old lauds,   178
As one incapable of her own distress,   179
Or like a creature native and endued   180
Unto that element. But long it could not be
Till that her garments, heavy with their drink,
Pulled the poor wretch from her melodious lay   183
To muddy death.

188 **It is our trick** i.e., weeping is our natural way (when sad)

189–90 **When . . . out** When my tears are all shed, the woman in me will be expended, satisfied.

192 **douts** extinguishes. (The second quarto reads "drownes.")

5.1 *Location: A churchyard.*

0.1 *Clowns* rustics

2 **salvation** (A blunder for "damnation," or perhaps a suggestion that Ophelia was taking her own shortcut to heaven.)

4 **straight** straightaway, immediately. (But with a pun on *strait,* "narrow.")   **crowner** coroner.   **sat on her** conducted an inquest on her case

4–5 **finds it** gives his official verdict that her means of death was consistent with

8 **found so** determined so in the coroner's verdict.

9 *se offendendo* (A comic mistake for *se defendendo,* a term used in verdicts of self-defense.)

12 **Argal** (Corruption of *ergo,* "therefore.")

14 **goodman** (An honorific title often used with the name of a profession or craft.)

LAERTES   Alas, then she is drowned?

QUEEN   Drowned, drowned.

LAERTES
Too much of water hast thou, poor Ophelia,
And therefore I forbid my tears. But yet
It is our trick; nature her custom holds,   188
Let shame say what it will. [*He weeps.*] When these
   are gone,   189
The woman will be out. Adieu, my lord.   190
I have a speech of fire that fain would blaze,
But that this folly douts it.   *Exit.*

KING   Let's follow, Gertrude.   192
How much I had to do to calm his rage!
Now fear I this will give it start again;
Therefore let's follow.   *Exeunt.*

[5.1]   ❧ *Enter two Clowns [with spades and mattocks].*

FIRST CLOWN   Is she to be buried in Christian burial,
when she willfully seeks her own salvation?   2

SECOND CLOWN   I tell thee she is; therefore make her
grave straight. The crowner hath sat on her, and finds   4
it Christian burial.   5

FIRST CLOWN   How can that be, unless she drowned
herself in her own defense?

SECOND CLOWN   Why, 'tis found so.   8

FIRST CLOWN   It must be *se offendendo*, it cannot be else.   9
For here lies the point: if I drown myself wittingly,
it argues an act, and an act hath three branches—it is
to act, to do, and to perform. Argal, she drowned her-   12
self wittingly.

SECOND CLOWN   Nay, but hear you, goodman delver—   14

FIRST CLOWN   Give me leave. Here lies the water; good.
Here stands the man; good. If the man go to this

17 **will he, nill he** whether he will or no, willy-nilly

22 **quest** inquest

26 **there thou say'st** i.e., that's right.

27 **countenance** privilege

29 **even-Christian** fellow Christians.   **ancient** going back to ancient times

31 **hold up** maintain

33 **bore arms** (To be entitled to bear a coat of arms would make Adam a gentleman, but as one who bore a spade, our common ancestor was an ordinary delver in the earth.)

37 **arms** i.e., the arms of the body.

39 **confess thyself** (The saying continues, "and be hanged.")

43 **frame** (1) gallows (2) structure

46 **does well** (1) is an apt answer (2) does a good turn.

water and drown himself, it is, will he, nill he, he 17
goes, mark you that. But if the water come to him and
drown him, he drowns not himself. Argal, he that is
not guilty of his own death shortens not his own life.

SECOND CLOWN But is this law?

FIRST CLOWN Ay, marry, is't—crowner's quest law. 22

SECOND CLOWN Will you ha' the truth on't? If this had
not been a gentlewoman, she should have been
buried out o' Christian burial.

FIRST CLOWN Why, there thou say'st. And the more 26
pity that great folk should have countenance in this 27
world to drown or hang themselves, more than their
even-Christian. Come, my spade. There is no ancient 29
gentlemen but gardeners, ditchers, and grave makers.
They hold up Adam's profession. 31

SECOND CLOWN Was he a gentleman?

FIRST CLOWN 'A was the first that ever bore arms. 33

SECOND CLOWN Why, he had none.

FIRST CLOWN What, art a heathen? How dost thou
understand the Scripture? The Scripture says Adam
digged. Could he dig without arms? I'll put another 37
question to thee. If thou answerest me not to the
purpose, confess thyself— 39

SECOND CLOWN Go to.

FIRST CLOWN What is he that builds stronger than
either the mason, the shipwright, or the carpenter?

SECOND CLOWN The gallows maker, for that frame 43
outlives a thousand tenants.

FIRST CLOWN I like thy wit well, in good faith. The
gallows does well. But how does it well? It does well to 46
those that do ill. Now thou dost ill to say the gallows
is built stronger than the church. Argal, the gallows
may do well to thee. To't again, come.

52 **unyoke** i.e., after this great effort, you may unharness the team of your wits.

55 **Mass** By the Mass

60 **stoup** two-quart measure

61 **In...love** (This and the two following stanzas, with nonsensical variations, are from a poem attributed to Lord Vaux and printed in *Tottel's Miscellany,* 1557. The *oh* and *a* [for "ah"] seemingly are the grunts of the digger.)

63 **To contract...behove** i.e., to shorten the time for my own advantage. (Perhaps he means to *prolong* it.)

64 **meet** suitable, i.e., more suitable.

65 **'a** that he

67–8 **property of easiness** something he can do easily and indifferently.

70 **daintier sense** more delicate sense of feeling.

73 **into the land** i.e., toward my grave (?) (But note the lack of rhyme in *steps, land.*)

76 **jowls** dashes. (With a pun on *jowl,* "jawbone.")

SECOND CLOWN "Who builds stronger than a mason, a
  shipwright, or a carpenter?"

FIRST CLOWN Ay, tell me that, and unyoke.   52

SECOND CLOWN Marry, now I can tell.

FIRST CLOWN To't.

SECOND CLOWN Mass, I cannot tell.   55

  Enter Hamlet and Horatio [at a distance].

FIRST CLOWN Cudgel thy brains no more about it, for
  your dull ass will not mend his pace with beating; and
  when you are asked this question next, say "a grave
  maker." The houses he makes lasts till doomsday. Go
  get thee in and fetch me a stoup of liquor.   60
                    [Exit Second Clown. First Clown digs.]
                                                      Song.
    "In youth, when I did love, did love,   61
        Methought it was very sweet,
    To contract—oh—the time for—a—my behove,   63
        Oh, methought there—a—was nothing—a—
          meet."   64

HAMLET Has this fellow no feeling of his business, 'a   65
  sings in grave-making?

HORATIO Custom hath made it in him a property of   67
  easiness.   68

HAMLET 'Tis e'en so. The hand of little employment
  hath the daintier sense.   70

FIRST CLOWN   *Song.*
    "But age with his stealing steps
        Hath clawed me in his clutch,
    And hath shipped me into the land,   73
        As if I had never been such."
                              [He throws up a skull.]

HAMLET That skull had a tongue in it and could sing
  once. How the knave jowls it to the ground, as if   76
  'twere Cain's jawbone, that did the first murder! This

78 **politician** schemer, plotter

79 **o'erreaches** circumvents, gets the better of

89 **chapless** having no lower jaw.   **mazard** i.e., head.
    (Literally, a drinking vessel.)

90 **revolution** turn of Fortune's wheel, change.   **trick**
    knack

91–2 **cost ... but** involve so little expense and care in up-
    bringing that we may

92 **loggets** a game in which pieces of hard wood shaped
    like Indian clubs or bowling pins are thrown to lie as
    near as possible to a stake

95 **For and** and moreover

99–100 **his quiddities ... quillities** his subtleties, his legal
    niceties

100 **tenures** the holding of a piece of property or office, or
    the conditions or period of such holding

102 **sconce** head

103 **action of battery** lawsuit about physical assault.

104 **his statutes** his legal documents acknowledging obliga-
    tion of a debt

104–5 **recognizances** bonds undertaking to repay debts

105 **fines** procedures for converting entailed estates into
    "fee simple" or freehold.   **double vouchers** vouchers
    signed by two signatories guaranteeing the legality of
    real estate titles.   **recoveries** suits to obtain the au-
    thority of a court judgment for the holding of land.

106–7 **Is this ... dirt?** Is this the end of his legal maneuvers
    and profitable land deals, to have the skull of his elegant
    head filled full of minutely sifted dirt? (With multiple
    word-play on *fine* and *fines*.)

107–10 **Will ... indentures?** Will his vouchers, even double
    ones, guarantee him no more land than is needed to
    bury him in, being no bigger than the deed of con-
    veyance? (An *indenture* is literally a legal document
    drawn up in duplicate on a single sheet and then cut
    apart on a zigzag line so that each pair was uniquely
    matched.)

might be the pate of a politician, which this ass now   78
o'erreaches, one that would circumvent God, might   79
it not?

HORATIO   It might, my lord.

HAMLET   Or of a courtier, which could say, "Good
morrow, sweet lord! How dost thou, sweet lord?"
This might be my Lord Such-a-one, that praised my
Lord Such-a-one's horse when 'a meant to beg it,
might it not?

HORATIO   Ay, my lord.

HAMLET   Why, e'en so, and now my Lady Worm's,
chapless, and knocked about the mazard with a sex-   89
ton's spade. Here's fine revolution, an we had the trick   90
to see't. Did these bones cost no more the breeding   91
but to play at loggets with them? Mine ache to think   92
on't.

FIRST CLOWN   *Song.*
    "A pickax and a spade, a spade,
        For and a shrouding sheet;
    Oh, a pit of clay for to be made   95
        For such a guest is meet."

                            [*He throws up another skull.*]

HAMLET   There's another. Why may not that be the skull
of a lawyer? Where be his quiddities now, his quilli-   99
ties, his cases, his tenures, and his tricks? Why does   100
he suffer this mad knave now to knock him about the
sconce with a dirty shovel, and will not tell him of his   102
action of battery? Hum, this fellow might be in 's time   103
a great buyer of land, with his statutes, his recogni-   104
zances, his fines, his double vouchers, his recoveries.   105
Is this the fine of his fines and the recovery of his   106
recoveries, to have his fine pate full of fine dirt? Will   107
his vouchers vouch him no more of his purchases, and   108
double ones too, than the length and breadth of a   109
pair of indentures? The very conveyances of his lands   110

111 **box** (1) deed box (2) coffin.   **th'inheritor** the ac-
quirer, owner

116–17 **assurance in that** safety in legal parchments.

118 **sirrah** (A term of address to inferiors.)

126 **quick** living

137 **absolute** strict, precise

137–8 **by the card** i.e., with precision. (Literally, by the
mariner's compass-card, on which the points of the
compass were marked.)

138 **equivocation** ambiguity in the use of terms

139 **took** taken

139–41 **the age . . . kibe** i.e., the age has grown so finical and
mannered that the lower classes ape their social betters,
chafing at their heels. (*Kibes* are chilblains on the heels.)

will scarcely lie in this box, and must th'inheritor 111
himself have no more, ha?

HORATIO Not a jot more, my lord.

HAMLET Is not parchment made of sheepskins?

HORATIO Ay, my lord, and of calves' skins too.

HAMLET They are sheep and calves which seek out as- 116
surance in that. I will speak to this fellow.—Whose 117
grave's this, sirrah?   118

FIRST CLOWN Mine, sir.
 [Sings] "Oh, pit of clay for to be made
    For such a guest is meet."

HAMLET I think it be thine, indeed, for thou liest in't.

FIRST CLOWN You lie out on't, sir, and therefore 'tis
not yours. For my part, I do not lie in't, yet it is mine.

HAMLET Thou dost lie in't, to be in't and say it is
thine. 'Tis for the dead, not for the quick; therefore 126
thou liest.

FIRST CLOWN 'Tis a quick lie, sir; 'twill away again
from me to you.

HAMLET What man dost thou dig it for?

FIRST CLOWN For no man, sir.

HAMLET What woman, then?

FIRST CLOWN For none, neither.

HAMLET Who is to be buried in't?

FIRST CLOWN One that was a woman, sir, but, rest her
soul, she's dead.

HAMLET How absolute the knave is! We must speak by 137
the card, or equivocation will undo us. By the Lord, 138
Horatio, this three years I have took note of it: the age 139
is grown so picked that the toe of the peasant comes so 140
near the heel of the courtier he galls his kibe.—How 141
long hast thou been grave maker?

160 **ground** cause. (But, in the next line, the gravedigger takes the word in the sense of "land," "country.")

165 **pocky** rotten, diseased. (Literally, with the pox, or syphilis.)

166 **hold the laying in** hold together long enough to be interred.   **last you** last. (*You* is used colloquially here and in the following lines.)

171 **sore** keen, veritable.   **whoreson** (An expression of contemptuous familiarity.)

173 **lien you** lain. (See the note at line 166.)

FIRST CLOWN   Of all the days i'th' year, I came to't that
day that our last king Hamlet overcame Fortinbras.

HAMLET   How long is that since?

FIRST CLOWN   Cannot you tell that? Every fool can tell
that. It was that very day that young Hamlet was
born—he that is mad and sent into England.

HAMLET   Ay, marry, why was he sent into England?

FIRST CLOWN   Why, because 'a was mad. 'A shall
recover his wits there, or if 'a do not, 'tis no great
matter there.

HAMLET   Why?

FIRST CLOWN   'Twill not be seen in him there. There the
men are as mad as he.

HAMLET   How came he mad?

FIRST CLOWN   Very strangely, they say.

HAMLET   How strangely?

FIRST CLOWN   Faith, e'en with losing his wits.

HAMLET   Upon what ground?   160

FIRST CLOWN   Why, here in Denmark. I have been
sexton here, man and boy, thirty years.

HAMLET   How long will a man lie i'th'earth ere he rot?

FIRST CLOWN   Faith, if 'a be not rotten before 'a die—as
we have many pocky corpses nowadays, that will   165
scarce hold the laying in—'a will last you some eight   166
year or nine year. A tanner will last you nine year.

HAMLET   Why he more than another?

FIRST CLOWN   Why, sir, his hide is so tanned with his
trade that 'a will keep out water a great while, and
your water is a sore decayer of your whoreson dead   171
body. [He picks up a skull.] Here's a skull now hath
lien you i'th'earth three-and-twenty years.   173

HAMLET   Whose was it?

179 **Rhenish** Rhine wine
185 **bore** borne
187 **My gorge rises** i.e., I feel nauseated
189 **gibes** taunts
192 **chopfallen** (1) lacking the lower jaw (2) dejected.
193 **favor** aspect, appearance
204 **bunghole** hole for filling or emptying a cask.
205 **curiously** minutely
208 **with . . . lead it** with moderation and plausibility.

FIRST CLOWN   A whoreson mad fellow's it was. Whose
   do you think it was?

HAMLET   Nay, I know not.

FIRST CLOWN   A pestilence on him for a mad rogue! 'A
   poured a flagon of Rhenish on my head once. This 179
   same skull, sir, was, sir, Yorick's skull, the King's jester.

HAMLET   This?

FIRST CLOWN   E'en that.

HAMLET   Let me see. [He takes the skull.] Alas, poor
   Yorick! I knew him, Horatio, a fellow of infinite jest, of
   most excellent fancy. He hath bore me on his back a 185
   thousand times, and now how abhorred in my
   imagination it is! My gorge rises at it. Here hung those 187
   lips that I have kissed I know not how oft. Where be
   your gibes now? Your gambols, your songs, your 189
   flashes of merriment that were wont to set the table on
   a roar? Not one now, to mock your own grinning?
   Quite chopfallen? Now get you to my lady's chamber 192
   and tell her, let her paint an inch thick, to this favor 193
   she must come. Make her laugh at that. Prithee,
   Horatio, tell me one thing.

HORATIO   What's that, my lord?

HAMLET   Dost thou think Alexander looked o' this
   fashion i'th'earth?

HORATIO   E'en so.

HAMLET   And smelt so? Pah! [He throws down the skull.]

HORATIO   E'en so, my lord.

HAMLET   To what base uses we may return, Horatio!
   Why may not imagination trace the noble dust of
   Alexander till 'a find it stopping a bunghole? 204

HORATIO   'Twere to consider too curiously to consider 205
   so.

HAMLET   No, faith, not a jot, but to follow him thither
   with modesty enough, and likelihood to lead it. As 208

211 **loam** a mixture of clay, straw, sand, etc. used to mold bricks, or, in this case, bungs for a beer barrel

213 **Imperious** Imperial

216 **flaw** gust of wind.

217 **soft** i.e., wait, be careful

219 **maimèd** mutilated, incomplete

221 **Fordo it** destroy its.   **estate** rank.

222 **Couch we** Let's hide, lie low

227 **warranty** i.e., ecclesiastical authority.

228 **order** (1) prescribed practice (2) religious order of clerics

229 **She should . . . lodged** she should have been buried in unsanctified ground

230 **For** In place of

231 **Shards** broken bits of pottery

232 **crants** garlands betokening maidenhood

233 **strewments** flowers strewn on a coffin

233–4 **bringing . . . burial** laying the body to rest, to the sound of the bell.

thus: Alexander died, Alexander was buried, Alexan-
der returneth to dust, the dust is earth, of earth we
make loam, and why of that loam whereto he was   211
converted might they not stop a beer barrel?
Imperious Caesar, dead and turned to clay,   213
Might stop a hole to keep the wind away.
Oh, that that earth which kept the world in awe
Should patch a wall t'expel the winter's flaw!   216

> *Enter King, Queen, Laertes, and the corpse [of
> Ophelia, in procession, with Priest, lords, etc.].*

But soft, but soft awhile! Here comes the King,   217
The Queen, the courtiers. Who is this they follow?
And with such maimèd rites? This doth betoken   219
The corpse they follow did with desperate hand
Fordo it own life. 'Twas of some estate.   221
Couch we awhile and mark.   222

> *[He and Horatio conceal themselves.
> Ophelia's body is taken to the grave.]*

LAERTES   What ceremony else?

HAMLET   [to Horatio]
    That is Laertes, a very noble youth. Mark.

LAERTES   What ceremony else?

PRIEST
    Her obsequies have been as far enlarged
    As we have warranty. Her death was doubtful,   227
    And but that great command o'ersways the order   228
    She should in ground unsanctified been lodged   229
    Till the last trumpet. For charitable prayers,   230
    Shards, flints, and pebbles should be thrown on her.   231
    Yet here she is allowed her virgin crants,   232
    Her maiden strewments, and the bringing home   233
    Of bell and burial.   234

237 **such rest** i.e., to pray for such rest

238 **peace-parted souls** those who have died at peace with God.

240 **violets** (See 4.5.188 and note.)

242 **howling** i.e., in hell.

248 **ingenious sense** a mind that is quick, alert, of fine qualities

253 **Pelion** a mountain in northern Thessaly; compare *Olympus* and *Ossa* in lines 254 and 286. (In their rebellion against the Olympian gods, the giants attempted to heap Ossa on Pelion in order to scale Olympus.)

255 **emphasis** i.e., rhetorical and florid emphasis. (*Phrase* has a similar rhetorical connotation.)

256 **wandering stars** planets

257 **wonder-wounded** struck with amazement

258 **the Dane** (This title normally signifies the King; see 1.1.17 and note.)

259 **s.d.** *grappling with him* The testimony of the first quarto that *"Hamlet leaps in after Laertes"* and of the ballad "Elegy on Burbage," published in *Gentleman's Magazine* in 1825 ("Oft have I seen him leap into a grave") seem to indicate one way in which this fight was staged; however, the difficulty of fitting two contenders and Ophelia's body into a confined space (probably the trapdoor) suggests to many editors the alternative, that Laertes jumps out of the grave to attack Hamlet.)

262 **splenitive** quick-tempered

LAERTES
    Must there no more be done?

PRIEST   No more be done.
    We should profane the service of the dead
    To sing a requiem and such rest to her   237
    As to peace-parted souls.

LAERTES   Lay her i'th'earth,   238
    And from her fair and unpolluted flesh
    May violets spring! I tell thee, churlish priest,   240
    A ministering angel shall my sister be
    When thou liest howling.

HAMLET [to Horatio]   What, the fair Ophelia!   242

QUEEN [scattering flowers]   Sweets to the sweet! Farewell. .
    I hoped thou shouldst have been my Hamlet's wife.
    I thought thy bride-bed to have decked, sweet maid,
    And not t' have strewed thy grave.

LAERTES   Oh, treble woe
    Fall ten times treble on that cursèd head
    Whose wicked deed thy most ingenious sense   248
    Deprived thee of! Hold off the earth awhile,
    Till I have caught her once more in mine arms.
            [He leaps into the grave and embraces Ophelia.]
    Now pile your dust upon the quick and dead,
    Till of this flat a mountain you have made
    T' o'ertop old Pelion or the skyish head   253
    Of blue Olympus.

HAMLET [coming forward]   What is he whose grief
    Bears such an emphasis, whose phrase of sorrow   255
    Conjures the wandering stars and makes them stand   256
    Like wonder-wounded hearers? This is I,   257
    Hamlet the Dane.   258

LAERTES [grappling with him]   The devil take thy soul!   259

HAMLET   Thou pray'st not well.
    I prithee, take thy fingers from my throat,
    For though I am not splenitive and rash,   262

270 **wag** move. (A fluttering eyelid is a conventional sign that life has not yet gone.)

276 **forbear him** leave him alone.

277 **'Swounds** By His (Christ's) wounds

278 **Woo't** Wilt thou

279 **Woo't ... eisel?** Will you drink up a whole draft of vinegar? (An extremely self-punishing task as a way of expressing grief.)   **crocodile** (Crocodiles were tough and dangerous, and were supposed to shed crocodile tears.)

282 **quick** alive

285 **his pate** its head, i.e., top.   **burning zone** zone in the celestial sphere containing the sun's orbit, between the tropics of Cancer and Capricorn

286 **Ossa** (See 253n.)   **an thou'lt mouth** if you want to rant

287 **mere** utter

Yet have I in me something dangerous,
Which let thy wisdom fear. Hold off thy hand.

KING   Pluck them asunder.

QUEEN   Hamlet, Hamlet!

ALL   Gentlemen!

HORATIO   Good my lord, be quiet.
                            [*Hamlet and Laertes are parted.*]

HAMLET
Why, I will fight with him upon this theme
Until my eyelids will no longer wag.   270

QUEEN   Oh, my son, what theme?

HAMLET
I loved Ophelia. Forty thousand brothers
Could not with all their quantity of love
Make up my sum. What wilt thou do for her?

KING   Oh, he is mad, Laertes.

QUEEN   For love of God, forbear him.   276

HAMLET
'Swounds, show me what thou'lt do.   277
Woo't weep? Woo't fight? Woo't fast? Woo't tear
    thyself?   278
Woo't drink up eisel? Eat a crocodile?   279
I'll do't. Dost come here to whine?
To outface me with leaping in her grave?
Be buried quick with her, and so will I.   282
And if thou prate of mountains, let them throw
Millions of acres on us, till our ground,
Singeing his pate against the burning zone,   285
Make Ossa like a wart! Nay, an thou'lt mouth,   286
I'll rant as well as thou.

QUEEN   This is mere madness,   287
And thus awhile the fit will work on him;
Anon, as patient as the female dove

290 **golden couplets** two baby pigeons, covered with yellow down.   **disclosed** hatched

294–5 **Let...day** i.e., (1) Even Hercules couldn't stop Laertes's theatrical rant (2) I, too, will have my turn; i.e., despite any blustering attempts at interference, every person will sooner or later do what he or she must do.

297 **in** i.e., by recalling

298 **present push** immediate test.

300 **living** lasting. (For Laertes's private understanding, Claudius also hints that Hamlet's death will serve as such a monument.)

301 **hour of quiet** time free of conflict

5.2 *Location: The castle.*

1 **see the other** hear the other news. (See 4.6.24–6.)

6 **mutines** mutineers.   **bilboes** shackles.   **Rashly** On impulse. (This adverb goes with lines 12 ff.)

7 **know** acknowledge

8 **indiscretion** lack of foresight and judgment (not an indiscreet act)

9 **pall** fail, falter, go stale.   **learn** teach

When that her golden couplets are disclosed,   290
His silence will sit drooping.
HAMLET   Hear you, sir.
What is the reason that you use me thus?
I loved you ever. But it is no matter.
Let Hercules himself do what he may,   294
The cat will mew, and dog will have his day.   295

Exit Hamlet.

KING
I pray thee, good Horatio, wait upon him.

[*Exit*] *Horatio.*

[*To Laertes*] Strengthen your patience in our last
    night's speech;   297
We'll put the matter to the present push.—   298
Good Gertrude, set some watch over your son.—
This grave shall have a living monument.   300
An hour of quiet shortly shall we see;   301
Till then, in patience our proceeding be.   *Exeunt.*

[5.2] ᕦ *Enter Hamlet and Horatio.*

HAMLET
So much for this, sir; now shall you see the other.   1
You do remember all the circumstance?
HORATIO   Remember it, my lord!
HAMLET
Sir, in my heart there was a kind of fighting
That would not let me sleep. Methought I lay
Worse than the mutines in the bilboes. Rashly,   6
And praised be rashness for it—let us know   7
Our indiscretion sometime serves us well   8
When our deep plots do pall, and that should learn us   9
There's a divinity that shapes our ends,

11 **Rough-hew** shape roughly

13 **sea-gown** seaman's coat.   **scarfed** loosely wrapped

14 **them** i.e., Rosencrantz and Guildenstern

15 **Fingered** pilfered, pinched.   **in fine** finally, in conclusion

20 **Larded** garnished.   **several** different

21 **Importing** relating to

22 **With ... life** i.e., with all sorts of warnings of imaginary dangers if I were allowed to continue living. (*Bugs* are bugbears, hobgoblins.)

23 **That ... bated** that on the reading of this commission, no delay being allowed

24 **stay** await

30–1 **Ere ... play** before I could consciously turn my brain to the matter, it had started working on a plan

32 **fair** in a clear hand.

33 **statists** politicians, men of public affairs

34 **A baseness** beneath my dignity

38 **conjuration** entreaty

Rough-hew them how we will—

HORATIO   That is most certain.   11

HAMLET   Up from my cabin,
My sea-gown scarfed about me, in the dark   13
Groped I to find out them, had my desire,   14
Fingered their packet, and in fine withdrew   15
To mine own room again, making so bold,
My fears forgetting manners, to unseal
Their grand commission; where I found, Horatio—
Ah, royal knavery!—an exact command,
Larded with many several sorts of reasons   20
Importing Denmark's health and England's too,   21
With, ho! such bugs and goblins in my life,   22
That on the supervise, no leisure bated,   23
No, not to stay the grinding of the ax,   24
My head should be struck off.

HORATIO   Is't possible?

HAMLET   [giving a document]
Here's the commission. Read it at more leisure.
But wilt thou hear now how I did proceed?

HORATIO   I beseech you.

HAMLET
Being thus benetted round with villainies—
Ere I could make a prologue to my brains,   30
They had begun the play—I sat me down,   31
Devised a new commission, wrote it fair.   32
I once did hold it, as our statists do,   33
A baseness to write fair, and labored much   34
How to forget that learning, but, sir, now
It did me yeoman's service. Wilt thou know
Th'effect of what I wrote?

HORATIO   Ay, good my lord.

HAMLET
An earnest conjuration from the King,   38
As England was his faithful tributary,

40 **palm** (An image of health; see Psalm 92:12.)
41 **still** always.   **wheaten garland** (Symbolic of fruitful agriculture, of peace and plenty.)
42 **comma** (Indicating continuity, link.)
43 **"as"es** (1) the "whereases" of a formal document (2) asses.   **charge** (1) import (2) burden (appropriate to asses)
47 **shriving time** time for confession and absolution
48 **ordinant** directing.
49 **signet** small seal
50 **model** replica
51 **writ** writing
52 **Subscribed** signed (with forged signature).   **impression** i.e., with a wax seal
53 **changeling** i.e., substituted letter. (Literally, a fairy child substituted for a human one.)
54 **was sequent** followed
58 **defeat** destruction
59 **insinuation** intrusive intervention, sticking their noses in my business
60 **baser** of lower social station
61 **pass** thrust.   **fell** fierce
62 **opposites** antagonists.
63 **stand me now upon** become incumbent on me now
65 **th'election** (The Danish monarch was "elected" by a small number of high-ranking electors.)
66 **angle** fishhook.   **proper** very
67 **coz'nage** trickery
68 **quit** requite, pay back

As love between them like the palm might flourish,   40
As peace should still her wheaten garland wear   41
And stand a comma 'tween their amities,   42
And many suchlike "as"es of great charge,   43
That on the view and knowing of these contents,
Without debatement further more or less,
He should those bearers put to sudden death,
Not shriving time allowed.

HORATIO   How was this sealed?   47

HAMLET
Why, even in that was heaven ordinant.   48
I had my father's signet in my purse,   49
Which was the model of that Danish seal;   50
Folded the writ up in the form of th'other,   51
Subscribed it, gave't th'impression, placed it safely,   52
The changeling never known. Now, the next day   53
Was our sea fight, and what to this was sequent   54
Thou knowest already.

HORATIO
So Guildenstern and Rosencrantz go to't.

HAMLET
Why, man, they did make love to this employment.
They are not near my conscience. Their defeat   58
Does by their own insinuation grow.   59
'Tis dangerous when the baser nature comes   60
Between the pass and fell incensèd points   61
Of mighty opposites.

HORATIO   Why, what a king is this!   62

HAMLET
Does it not, think thee, stand me now upon—   63
He that hath killed my king and whored my mother,
Popped in between th'election and my hopes,   65
Thrown out his angle for my proper life,   66
And with such coz'nage—is't not perfect conscience   67
To quit him with this arm? And is't not to be damned   68

69   **canker** ulcer

69–70 **come In** grow into

74   **a man's ... "one"** one's whole life occupies such a short time, only as long as it takes to count to one.

79   **bravery** bravado

86–8 **Let ... mess** i.e., If a man, no matter how beastlike, is as rich in livestock and possessions as Osric, he may eat at the King's table.

87   **crib** manger

88   **chuff** boor, churl. (The second quarto spelling, "chough," is a variant spelling that also suggests the meaning here of "chattering jackdaw.")

93   **bonnet** any kind of cap or hat.   **his** its

97   **indifferent** somewhat

To let this canker of our nature come   69
In further evil?   70

HORATIO
It must be shortly known to him from England
What is the issue of the business there.

HAMLET
It will be short. The interim is mine,
And a man's life's no more than to say "one."   74
But I am very sorry, good Horatio,
That to Laertes I forgot myself,
For by the image of my cause I see
The portraiture of his. I'll court his favors.
But, sure, the bravery of his grief did put me   79
Into a tow'ring passion.

HORATIO   Peace, who comes here?

Enter a Courtier [Osric].

OSRIC   Your Lordship is right welcome back to Denmark.

HAMLET   I humbly thank you, sir. [*To Horatio*] Dost
know this water fly?

HORATIO   No, my good lord.

HAMLET   Thy state is the more gracious, for 'tis a vice to
know him. He hath much land, and fertile. Let a beast   86
be lord of beasts, and his crib shall stand at the King's   87
mess. 'Tis a chuff, but, as I say, spacious in the   88
possession of dirt.

OSRIC   Sweet lord, if Your Lordship were at leisure, I
should impart a thing to you from His Majesty.

HAMLET   I will receive it, sir, with all diligence of spirit.
Put your bonnet to his right use; 'tis for the head.   93

OSRIC   I thank Your Lordship, it is very hot.

HAMLET   No, believe me, 'tis very cold. The wind is
northerly.

OSRIC   It is indifferent cold, my lord, indeed.   97

99   **complexion** constitution.

105   **for my ease** (A conventional reply declining the invitation to put the hat back on.)

107   **absolute** perfect

107–8 **differences** special qualities

108   **soft society** agreeable manners.   **great showing** distinguished appearance.

109   **feelingly** with just perception

109–10 **the card ... gentry** the model or paradigm (literally, a chart or directory) of good breeding

110–11 **the continent ... see** one who contains in himself all the qualities a gentleman would like to see. (A *continent* is that which contains.)

112–15 **his definement ... sail** the task of defining Laertes's excellences suffers no diminution in your description of him, though I know that to enumerate all his graces would stupify one's powers of memory, and even so could do no more than veer unsteadily off course in a vain attempt to keep up with his rapid forward motion. (Hamlet mocks Osric by parodying his jargon-filled speeches.)

115–20 **But ... more** But, in true praise of him, I take him to be a person of remarkable value, and his essence of such rarity and excellence as, to speak truly of him, none can compare with him other than his own mirror; anyone following in his footsteps can only hope to be the shadow to his substance, nothing more.

122   **concernancy** import, relevance

123   **rawer breath** unrefined speech that can only come short in praising him.

125–6 **Is't ... tongue?** i.e., Is it not possible for you, Osric, to understand and communicate in any other tongue than the overblown rhetoric you have used? (Alternatively, Horatio could be asking Hamlet to speak more plainly.)

126   **You will do't** i.e., You can if you try, or, you may well have to try (to speak plainly).

127   **nomination** naming

HAMLET   But yet methinks it is very sultry and hot for
   my complexion.   99

OSRIC   Exceedingly, my lord. It is very sultry, as
   'twere—I cannot tell how. My lord, His Majesty bade
   me signify to you that 'a has laid a great wager on your
   head. Sir, this is the matter—

HAMLET   I beseech you, remember.
                    [*Hamlet moves him to put on his hat.*]

OSRIC   Nay, good my lord; for my ease, in good faith. 105
   Sir, here is newly come to court Laertes—believe me,
   an absolute gentleman, full of most excellent differ- 107
   ences, of very soft society and great showing. Indeed, 108
   to speak feelingly of him, he is the card or calendar of 109
   gentry, for you shall find in him the continent of what 110
   part a gentleman would see.   111

HAMLET   Sir, his definement suffers no perdition in 112
   you, though I know to divide him inventorially would 113
   dozy th'arithmetic of memory, and yet but yaw 114
   neither in respect of his quick sail. But, in the verity of 115
   extolment, I take him to be a soul of great article, and 116
   his infusion of such dearth and rareness as, to make 117
   true diction of him, his semblable is his mirror and 118
   who else would trace him his umbrage, nothing 119
   more.   120

OSRIC   Your Lordship speaks most infallibly of him.

HAMLET   The concernancy, sir? Why do we wrap the 122
   gentleman in our more rawer breath?   123

OSRIC   Sir?

HORATIO   Is't not possible to understand in another 125
   tongue? You will do't, sir, really.   126

HAMLET   What imports the nomination of this gentle- 127
   man?

OSRIC   Of Laertes?

134–5 **I would ... approve me** (Responding to Osric's in-
completed sentence as though it were a complete state-
ment, Hamlet says, with mock politeness, "I wish you
did know me to be not ignorant [i.e., to be knowledge-
able] about matters," and then turns this into an insult:
"But if you did, your recommendation of me would be
of little value in any case.")

138–40 **I dare ... himself** I dare not boast of knowing
Laertes's excellence lest I seem to imply a comparable
excellence in myself. Certainly, to know another person
well, one must know oneself.

141–2 **I mean ... unfellowed** I mean his excellence with his
rapier, not his general excellence; in the reputation he
enjoys for use of his weapons, his merit is unequaled.

145 **but well** but never mind.

147 **he** i.e., Laertes.   **impawned** staked, wagered

148 **poniards** daggers.   **assigns** appurtenances

149 **hangers** straps on the sword belt (*girdle*), from which
the sword hung.   **and so** and so on.

149–52 **Three ... conceit** Three of the hangers, truly, are
very pleasing to the fancy, decoratively matched with
the hilts, delicate in workmanship, and made with elab-
orate ingenuity.

153 **What call you** What do you refer to when you say

155 **margent** margin of a book, place for explanatory notes

HORATIO [*to Hamlet*]   His purse is empty already; all 's
golden words are spent.

HAMLET   Of him, sir.

OSRIC   I know you are not ignorant—

HAMLET   I would you did, sir. Yet in faith if you did,   134
it would not much approve me. Well, sir?   135

OSRIC   You are not ignorant of what excellence Laertes
is—

HAMLET   I dare not confess that, lest I should compare   138
with him in excellence. But to know a man well were   139
to know himself.   140

OSRIC   I mean, sir, for his weapon; but in the imputation   141
laid on him by them, in his meed he's unfellowed.   142

HAMLET   What's his weapon?

OSRIC   Rapier and dagger.

HAMLET   That's two of his weapons—but well.   145

OSRIC   The King, sir, hath wagered with him six Barbary
horses, against the which he has impawned, as I take   147
it, six French rapiers and poniards, with their assigns,   148
as girdle, hangers, and so. Three of the carriages, in   149
faith, are very dear to fancy, very responsive to the   150
hilts, most delicate carriages, and of very liberal con-   151
ceit.   152

HAMLET   What call you the carriages?   153

HORATIO [*to Hamlet*]   I knew you must be edified by
the margent ere you had done.   155

OSRIC   The carriages, sir, are the hangers.

HAMLET   The phrase would be more germane to the
matter if we could carry a cannon by our sides; I would
it might be hangers till then. But, on: six Barbary horses
against six French swords, their assigns, and three lib-
eral-conceited carriages; that's the French bet against
the Danish. Why is this impawned, as you call it?

163 **laid** wagered

164 **passes** bouts. (The odds of the betting are hard to explain. Possibly the King bets that Hamlet will win at
least five out of twelve, at which point Laertes raises the
odds against himself by betting he will win nine.)

167 **vouchsafe the answer** be so good as to accept the challenge. (Hamlet deliberately takes the phrase in its literal
sense of replying.)

172 **breathing time** exercise period.   **Let** i.e., If

177 **deliver you** report what you say

180 **commend** commit to your favor. (A conventional salu-
tation, but Hamlet wryly uses a more literal meaning,
"recommend," "praise," in line 182.)

183 **for 's turn** for his purposes, i.e., to do it for him.

184 **lapwing** (A proverbial type of youthful forwardness.
Also, a bird that draws intruders away from its nest and
was thought to run about with its head in the shell
when newly hatched; a seeming reference to Osric's
hat.)

186 **comply ... dug** observe ceremonious formality toward
his nurse's or mother's teat

187–93 **Thus ... are out** Thus has he—and many like him
of the sort our frivolous age dotes on—acquired the
trendy manner of speech of the time, and, out of habitual conversation with courtiers of their own kind, have
collected together a kind of frothy medley of current
phrases, which enables such gallants to hold their own
among persons of the most select and well-sifted views;
and yet do but test them by merely blowing on them,
and their bubbles burst.

OSRIC The King, sir, hath laid, sir, that in a dozen 163
passes between yourself and him, he shall not exceed 164
you three hits. He hath laid on twelve for nine, and it
would come to immediate trial, if Your Lordship would
vouchsafe the answer.   167

HAMLET How if I answer no?

OSRIC I mean, my lord, the opposition of your person
in trial.

HAMLET Sir, I will walk here in the hall. If it please His
Majesty, it is the breathing time of day with me. Let 172
the foils be brought, the gentleman willing, and the
King hold his purpose, I will win for him an I can; if
not, I will gain nothing but my shame and the odd
hits.

OSRIC Shall I deliver you so?   177

HAMLET To this effect, sir—after what flourish your
nature will.

OSRIC I commend my duty to Your Lordship.   180

HAMLET Yours, yours.   [*Exit Osric.*]
'A does well to commend it himself; there are no tongues
else for 's turn.   183

HORATIO This lapwing runs away with the shell on his 184
head.

HAMLET 'A did comply with his dug before 'a sucked 186
it. Thus has he—and many more of the same breed 187
that I know the drossy age dotes on—only got the 188
tune of the time, and, out of an habit of encounter, a 189
kind of yeasty collection, which carries them through 190
and through the most fanned and winnowed opin- 191
ions; and do but blow them to their trial, the bubbles 192
are out.   193

Enter a Lord.

LORD My lord, His Majesty commended him to you by
young Osric, who brings back to him that you attend

197 **play** fence.   **that** if

200 **If . . . ready** If he declares his readiness, my convenience
waits on his

203 **In happy time** (A phrase of courtesy indicating that
the time is convenient.)

204–5 **entertainment** greeting

213–14 **gaingiving** misgiving

216 **repair** coming

217 **augury** the attempt to read signs of future events in order to avoid predicted trouble.

220–2 **Since . . . Let be** Since no one has knowledge of what
he is leaving behind, what does an early death matter after all? Enough; forbear.

222.1 ***trumpets, drums*** trumpeters, drummers

222.3 ***all the state*** the entire court

him in the hall. He sends to know if your pleasure
hold to play with Laertes, or that you will take longer 197
time.

HAMLET   I am constant to my purposes; they follow the
King's pleasure. If his fitness speaks, mine is ready; 200
now or whensoever, provided I be so able as now.

LORD   The King and Queen and all are coming down.

HAMLET   In happy time.   203

LORD   The Queen desires you to use some gentle enter- 204
tainment to Laertes before you fall to play.   205

HAMLET   She well instructs me.   [Exit Lord.]

HORATIO   You will lose, my lord.

HAMLET   I do not think so. Since he went into France, I
have been in continual practice; I shall win at the odds.
But thou wouldst not think how ill all's here about my
heart; but it is no matter.

HORATIO   Nay, good my lord—

HAMLET   It is but foolery, but it is such a kind of gain- 213
giving as would perhaps trouble a woman.   214

HORATIO   If your mind dislike anything, obey it. I will
forestall their repair hither and say you are not fit. 216

HAMLET   Not a whit, we defy augury. There is special 217
providence in the fall of a sparrow. If it be now, 'tis
not to come; if it be not to come, it will be now; if it
be not now; yet it will come. The readiness is all. Since 220
no man of aught he leaves knows, what is't to leave 221
betimes? Let be.   222

       A table prepared. [Enter] trumpets, drums, and
       officers with cushions; King, Queen, [Osric,] and
       all the state; foils, daggers, [and wine borne in;]
       and Laertes.

KING
Come, Hamlet, come and take this hand from me.
       [The King puts Laertes's hand into Hamlet's.]

226 **presence** royal assembly
227 **punished** afflicted
229 **exception** disapproval
236 **faction** party
242 **in nature** i.e., as to my personal feelings
243 **motive** prompting
247 **voice** authoritative pronouncement.   **of peace** for reconciliation
248 **name ungored** reputation unwounded.
251 **frankly** without ill feeling or the burden of rancor

HAMLET [to Laertes]
    Give me your pardon, sir. I have done you wrong,
    But pardon't as you are a gentleman.
    This presence knows,   226
    And you must needs have heard, how I am punished   227
    With a sore distraction. What I have done
    That might your nature, honor, and exception   229
    Roughly awake, I here proclaim was madness.
    Was't Hamlet wronged Laertes? Never Hamlet.
    If Hamlet from himself be ta'en away,
    And when he's not himself does wrong Laertes,
    Then Hamlet does it not, Hamlet denies it.
    Who does it, then? His madness. If't be so,
    Hamlet is of the faction that is wronged;   236
    His madness is poor Hamlet's enemy.
    Sir, in this audience
    Let my disclaiming from a purposed evil
    Free me so far in your most generous thoughts
    That I have shot my arrow o'er the house
    And hurt my brother.

LAERTES   I am satisfied in nature,   242
    Whose motive in this case should stir me most   243
    To my revenge. But in my terms of honor
    I stand aloof, and will no reconcilement
    Till by some elder masters of known honor
    I have a voice and precedent of peace   247
    To keep my name ungored. But till that time   248
    I do receive your offered love like love,
    And will not wrong it.

HAMLET   I embrace it freely,
    And will this brothers' wager frankly play.—   251
    Give us the foils. Come on.

LAERTES   Come, one for me.

253 **foil** thin metal background which sets a jewel off. (With pun on the blunted rapier for fencing.)

255 **Stick fiery off** stand out brilliantly

259 **laid ... side** backed the weaker side.

261 **is bettered** is the odds-on favorite. (Laertes's handicap is the "three hits" specified in line 165.)

263 **likes** pleases

267 **Or ... exchange** or draws even with Laertes by winning the third exchange

269 **better breath** improved vigor

270 **union** pearl. (So called, according to Pliny's *Natural History*, 9, because pearls are *unique*, never identical.)

273 **kettle** kettledrum

HAMLET
> I'll be your foil, Laertes. In mine ignorance   253
> Your skill shall, like a star i'th' darkest night,
> Stick fiery off indeed.

LAERTES   You mock me, sir.   255

HAMLET   No, by this hand.

KING
> Give them the foils, young Osric. Cousin Hamlet,
> You know the wager?

HAMLET   Very well, my lord.
> Your Grace has laid the odds o'th' weaker side.   259

KING
> I do not fear it; I have seen you both.
> But since he is bettered, we have therefore odds.   261

LAERTES
> This is too heavy. Let me see another.
>   [*He exchanges his foil for another.*]

HAMLET
> This likes me well. These foils have all a length?   263
>   [*They prepare to fence.*]

OSRIC   Ay, my good lord.

KING
> Set me the stoups of wine upon that table.
> If Hamlet give the first or second hit,
> Or quit in answer of the third exchange,   267
> Let all the battlements their ordnance fire.
> The King shall drink to Hamlet's better breath,   269
> And in the cup an union shall he throw   270
> Richer than that which four successive kings
> In Denmark's crown have worn. Give me the cups,
> And let the kettle to the trumpet speak,   273
> The trumpet to the cannoneer without,
> The cannons to the heavens, the heaven to earth,

282.2 *A piece* A cannon
289 **fat** not physically fit, out of training
290 **napkin** handkerchief
291 **carouses** drinks a toast

"Now the King drinks to Hamlet." Come, begin.

Trumpets the while.

And you, the judges, bear a wary eye.

HAMLET Come on, sir.

LAERTES Come, my lord. [*They fence. Hamlet scores a hit.*]

HAMLET One.

LAERTES No.

HAMLET Judgment.

OSRIC   A hit, a very palpable hit.   282

Drum, trumpets, and shot. Flourish.

A piece goes off.

LAERTES Well, again.

KING

Stay, give me drink. Hamlet, this pearl is thine.

[*He drinks, and throws a pearl in Hamlet's cup.*]

Here's to thy health. Give him the cup.

HAMLET

I'll play this bout first. Set it by awhile.

Come. [*They fence.*] Another hit; what say you?

LAERTES A touch, a touch, I do confess't.

KING

Our son shall win.

QUEEN   He's fat and scant of breath.   289

Here, Hamlet, take my napkin, rub thy brows.   290

The Queen carouses to thy fortune, Hamlet.   291

HAMLET Good madam!

KING Gertrude, do not drink.

QUEEN

I will, my lord, I pray you pardon me.   [*She drinks.*]

KING [*aside*]

It is the poisoned cup. It is too late.

HAMLET

I dare not drink yet, madam; by and by.

301 **pass** thrust

302 **make . . . me** i.e., treat me like a spoiled child, trifle with me.

305.1–2 *in scuffling, they change rapiers* (This stage direction occurs in the Folio. According to a widespread stage tradition, Hamlet receives a scratch, realizes that Laertes's sword is unbated, and accordingly forces an exchange.)

309 **woodcock** a bird, a type of stupidity or as a decoy. **springe** trap, snare

QUEEN   Come, let me wipe thy face.

LAERTES [*aside to the King*]
My lord, I'll hit him now.

KING   I do not think't.

LAERTES [*aside*]
And yet it is almost against my conscience.

HAMLET
Come, for the third, Laertes. You do but dally.
I pray you, pass with your best violence;   301
I am afeard you make a wanton of me.   302

LAERTES   Say you so? Come on.   [*They fence.*]

OSRIC   Nothing neither way.

LAERTES
Have at you now!
                    [*Laertes wounds Hamlet; then, in scuffling,
                    they change rapiers, and Hamlet wounds Laertes.*]

KING   Part them! They are incensed.   305

HAMLET
Nay, come, again.   [*The Queen falls.*]

OSRIC   Look to the Queen there, ho!

HORATIO
They bleed on both sides. How is it, my lord?

OSRIC   How is't, Laertes?

LAERTES
Why, as a woodcock to mine own springe, Osric;   309
I am justly killed with mine own treachery.

HAMLET
How does the Queen?

KING   She swoons to see them bleed.

QUEEN
No, no, the drink, the drink—Oh, my dear Hamlet—
The drink, the drink! I am poisoned.   [*She dies.*]

320 **Unbated** not blunted with a button.   **practice** plot

328 **union** pearl. (See line 270; with grim puns on the word's other meanings: marriage, shared death.)

330 **tempered** mixed

336 **chance** mischance

337 **mutes** silent observers. (Literally, actors with nonspeaking parts.)

338 **fell sergeant** remorseless arresting officer

339 **strict** (1) severely just (2) unavoidable.   **arrest** (1) taking into custody (2) stopping my speech

HAMLET

Oh, villainy! Ho, let the door be locked!
Treachery! Seek it out.   [*Laertes falls. Exit Osric.*]

LAERTES

It is here, Hamlet. Hamlet, thou art slain.
No med'cine in the world can do thee good;
In thee there is not half an hour's life.
The treacherous instrument is in thy hand,
Unbated and envenomed. The foul practice   320
Hath turned itself on me. Lo, here I lie,
Never to rise again. Thy mother's poisoned.
I can no more. The King, the King's to blame.

HAMLET

The point envenomed too? Then, venom, to thy work.
                    [*He stabs the King.*]

ALL Treason! Treason!

KING

Oh, yet defend me, friends! I am but hurt.

HAMLET [*forcing the King to drink*]

Here, thou incestuous, murderous, damnèd Dane,
Drink off this potion. Is thy union here?   328
Follow my mother.   [*The King dies.*]

LAERTES   He is justly served.
It is a poison tempered by himself.   330
Exchange forgiveness with me, noble Hamlet.
Mine and my father's death come not upon thee,
Nor thine on me!   [*He dies.*]

HAMLET

Heaven make thee free of it! I follow thee.
I am dead, Horatio. Wretched Queen, adieu!
You that look pale and tremble at this chance,   336
That are but mutes or audience to this act,   337
Had I but time—as this fell sergeant, Death,   338
Is strict in his arrest—oh, I could tell you—   339
But let it be. Horatio, I am dead;

343 **Roman** (Suicide was an honorable choice for many Romans as an alternative to a dishonorable life.)

355 **o'ercrows** triumphs over (like the winner in a cockfight)

358 **voice** vote.

359 **th'occurrents** the events, incidents

360 **solicited** moved, urged. (Hamlet doesn't finish saying what the events have prompted—presumably, his acts of vengeance, or his reporting of those events to Fortinbras.)

Thou livest. Report me and my cause aright
To the unsatisfied.

HORATIO   Never believe it.
I am more an antique Roman than a Dane.   343
Here's yet some liquor left.

           [He attempts to drink from the poisoned cup.
                        Hamlet prevents him.]

HAMLET   As thou'rt a man,
Give me the cup! Let go! By heaven, I'll ha 't.
Oh, God, Horatio, what a wounded name,
Things standing thus unknown, shall I leave behind
   me!
If thou didst ever hold me in thy heart,
Absent thee from felicity awhile,
And in this harsh world draw thy breath in pain
To tell my story.   *A march afar off [and a volley within].*
   What warlike noise is this?

     Enter Osric.

OSRIC
Young Fortinbras, with conquest come from Poland,
To th'ambassadors of England gives
This warlike volley.

HAMLET   Oh, I die, Horatio!
The potent poison quite o'ercrows my spirit.   355
I cannot live to hear the news from England,
But I do prophesy th'election lights
On Fortinbras. He has my dying voice.   358
So tell him, with th'occurrents more and less   359
Which have solicited. The rest is silence.   *[He dies.]* 360

HORATIO
Now cracks a noble heart. Good night, sweet prince,
And flights of angels sing thee to thy rest!

                      [March within.]

Why does the drum come hither?

366 **This … havoc** This heap of dead bodies loudly proclaims a general slaughter.

367 **feast** i.e., Death feasting on those who have fallen. **toward** in preparation

374 **his** Claudius's

377 **so jump … question** so hard on the heels of this bloody business

380 **stage** platform

384 **judgments** retributions.   **casual** occurring by chance

385 **put on** instigated.   **forced cause** contrivance

Enter Fortinbras, with the [English] Ambassadors
[with drum, colors, and attendants].

FORTINBRAS
  Where is this sight?

HORATIO   What is it you would see?
  If aught of woe or wonder, cease your search.

FORTINBRAS
  This quarry cries on havoc. O proud Death,   366
  What feast is toward in thine eternal cell,   367
  That thou so many princes at a shot
  So bloodily hast struck?

FIRST AMBASSADOR   The sight is dismal,
  And our affairs from England come too late.
  The ears are senseless that should give us hearing,
  To tell him his commandment is fulfilled,
  That Rosencrantz and Guildenstern are dead.
  Where should we have our thanks?

HORATIO   Not from his mouth,   374
  Had it th'ability of life to thank you.
  He never gave commandment for their death.
  But since, so jump upon this bloody question,   377
  You from the Polack wars and you from England
  Are here arrived, give order that these bodies
  High on a stage be placèd to the view,   380
  And let me speak to th' yet unknowing world
  How these things came about. So shall you hear
  Of carnal, bloody, and unnatural acts,
  Of accidental judgments, casual slaughters,   384
  Of deaths put on by cunning and forced cause,   385
  And, in this upshot, purposes mistook
  Fall'n on th'inventors' heads. All this can I
  Truly deliver.

FORTINBRAS   Let us haste to hear it,
  And call the noblest to the audience.
  For me, with sorrow I embrace my fortune.

391 **of memory** traditional, remembered, unforgotten
392 **vantage** favorable opportunity
394 **voice . . . more** vote will influence still others.
395 **presently** immediately
397 **On** on top of
399 **put on** i.e., invested in royal office and so put to the test
400 **for his passage** to mark his passing
402 **Speak** (let them) speak
404 **Becomes the field** suits the field of battle

I have some rights of memory in this kingdom,   391
Which now to claim my vantage doth invite me.   392

HORATIO
Of that I shall have also cause to speak,
And from his mouth whose voice will draw on more.   394
But let this same be presently performed,   395
Even while men's minds are wild, lest more mischance
On plots and errors happen.

FORTINBRAS   Let four captains   397
Bear Hamlet, like a soldier, to the stage,
For he was likely, had he been put on,   399
To have proved most royal; and for his passage,   400
The soldiers' music and the rite of war
Speak loudly for him.   402
Take up the bodies. Such a sight as this
Becomes the field, but here shows much amiss.   404
Go bid the soldiers shoot.

Exeunt [marching, bearing off the dead bodies;
a peal of ordnance is shot off].

DATE AND TEXT

Like everything else about *Hamlet*, the textual problem is complicated. On July 26, 1602, James Roberts entered in the Stationers' Register, the official record book of the London Company of Stationers (booksellers and printers), "A booke called the Revenge of Hamlett Prince Denmarke as yt was latelie Acted by the Lord Chamberleyne his servantes." For some reason, however, Roberts did not print his copy of *Hamlet* until 1604, by which time the following unauthorized edition had appeared:

THE Tragicall Historie of HAMLET *Prince of Denmarke*[.] By William Shake-speare. As it hath beene diuerse times acted by his Highnesse seruants in the Cittie of London: as also in the two Vniuersities of Cambridge and Oxford, and else-where At London printed for N. L. [Nicholas Ling] and Iohn Trundell. 1603.

This edition, the first quarto of *Hamlet*, seems to have been memorially reconstructed by actors who toured the provinces (note the references to Cambridge, Oxford, etc.), with some recollection of an earlier *Hamlet* play (the *Ur-Hamlet*) written before 1589 and acted during the 1590s. The actors seemingly had no recourse to an authoritative manuscript. One of these actors may have played Marcellus and possibly Lucianus and Voltimand. Their version seems to have been based on an adaptation of the company's original playbook, which itself stood once removed from Shakespeare's working papers by way of an intermediate manuscript. The resulting text is very corrupt, and yet it seems to have affected the more authentic text, because the compositors of the second quarto made use of it, especially when they typeset the first act.

The authorized quarto of *Hamlet* appeared in 1604. Roberts, the printer, seems to have reached some agreement with Ling, one of the publishers of the first quarto, for their initials are now paired on the title page:

> THE Tragicall Historie of HAMLET, *Prince of Denmarke*. By William Shakespeare. Newly imprinted and enlarged to almost as much againe as it was, according to the true and perfect Coppie. AT LONDON, Printed by I. R. [James Roberts] for N. L. [Nicholas Ling] and are to be sold at his shoppe vnder Saint Dunstons Church in Fleetstreet. 1604.

Some copies of this edition are dated 1605. This text was based seemingly on Shakespeare's own papers, with the bookkeeper's annotations, but is marred by printing errors and is at times contaminated by the first quarto—presumably when the printers found Shakespeare's manuscript unreadable. This second quarto served as copy for a third quarto in 1611, Ling having meanwhile transferred his rights in the play to John Smethwick. A fourth quarto, undated but before 1623, was based on the third.

The First Folio text of 1623 omits more than two hundred lines found in the second quarto. Yet it supplies some clearly authentic passages. It seems to derive from a transcript of Shakespeare's draft, in which cuts made by the author were observed—cuts made by Shakespeare quite possibly because he knew the draft to be too long for performance, and which had either not been marked in the second quarto copy or had been ignored there by the compositors. The Folio also incorporates other alterations seemingly made for clarity or in anticipation of performance. To this theatrically motivated transcript Shakespeare apparently contributed some revisions. Subsequently, this version evidently was copied again by a careless scribe who took many liberties with the text. Typesetting from this inferior manuscript, the Folio compositors occasionally consulted the second quarto, but not often enough. Thus, even though the Folio supplies some genuine readings, as does the first quarto when both the Folio and the second quarto are wrong, the second quarto remains the most authentic version of the text.

Since the text of the second quarto is too long to be accommodated in the two hours' traffic of the stage and since it becomes even longer when the words found only in the Folio are added, Shakespeare must have known it would have to be cut for performance and probably marked at least some omissions himself. As he may have consented to such cuts primarily because of the constraints of time, however, this present edition holds to the view that the passages in question should not be excised from the text we read. The *Hamlet* presented here is doubtless longer than any version ever acted in Shakespeare's day, and thus does not represent a script for any actual performance, but it may well represent the play as Shakespeare wrote it and then expanded it somewhat, while also including passages that he may reluctantly have consented to cut for performance. It is also possible that some cuts were artistically intended, but, in the face of real uncertainty in this matter, an editorial policy of inclusion gives to the reader those passages that would otherwise have to be excised or put in an appendix on questionable grounds of authorial "intent."

Hamlet must have been produced before the Stationers' Register entry of July 26, 1602. Francis Meres does not mention the play in 1598 in his *Palladis Tamia: Wit's Treasury* (a slender volume on contemporary literature and art; valuable because it lists most of the plays of Shakespeare that existed at that time). Gabriel Harvey attributes the "tragedy of Hamlet, Prince of Denmark" to Shakespeare in a marginal note in Harvey's copy of Speght's Chaucer; Harvey acquired the book in 1598 but could have written the note any time between then and 1601 or even 1603. More helpful in dating is *Hamlet*'s clear reference to the so-called "War of the Theaters," the rivalry between the adult actors and the boy actors whose companies had newly revived in 1598–1599 after nearly a decade of inactivity (see *Hamlet*, 2.2.337–62). The Children of the Chapel Royal began

acting at Blackfriars in 1598 and provided such keen competi-
tion in 1599–1601 that the adult actors were at times forced to
tour the provinces (see *Hamlet*, 2.2.332–62). *Hamlet*'s reference to the rivalry appears, however, only in the Folio text and
could represent a late addition. The reference to an "inhibition" imposed on acting companies "by the means of the late
innovation" (2.2.332–3), printed in the 1604 quarto, may possibly refer to the abortive uprising of the Earl of Essex on
February 8, 1601, or to a decree issued by the Privy Council on
June 22, 1600, restricting London companies to two performances a week in each of two playhouses. Revenge tragedy was
also in fashion during these years: John Marston's *Antonio's
Revenge*, for example, dates from 1599–1601, and *The Mal-
content* is from about the same time or slightly later, though it is
hard to tell who influenced whom. *Hamlet*'s apparent indebted-
ness to John Florio's translation of Montaigne suggests that
Shakespeare had access to that work in manuscript before its
publication in 1603; the Florio had been registered for publication in 1595 and 1600.

TEXTUAL NOTES

These textual notes are not a historical collation, either of the early quartos and the early folios or of more recent editions; they are simply a record of departures in this edition from the copy text. The reading adopted in this edition appears in boldface, followed by the rejected reading from the copy text, i.e., the second quarto of 1604. Only major alterations in punctuation are noted. Changes in lineation are not indicated, nor are some minor and obvious typographical errors.

Abbreviations used:
F the First Folio
Q quarto

Copy text: the second quarto of 1604–1605 [Q2]. The First Folio text also represents an independently authoritative text; although seemingly not the correct choice for copy text, the Folio text is considerably less marred by typographical errors than is Q2. The adopted readings in these notes are from F unless otherwise indicated; [eds.] means that the adopted reading was first proposed by some editor since the time of F. Some readings also are supplied from the first quarto of 1603 [Q1]. Act and scene divisions are missing in Q_q 1–2; the Folio provides such markings only through 1.3 and at Act 2.

1.1. 1 Who's Whose **19 soldier** [F, Q1] souldiers **44 off** [Q1] of **48 harrows** horrowes **67 sledded Polacks** [eds.] sleaded pollax **77 why** [F, Q1] with **cast** cost **91 heraldry** [F, Q1] heraldy **92 those** [F, Q1] these **95 returned** returne **97 cov'nant** comart **98 designed** [eds.] desseigne **112 e'en so** [eds.] enso **116 mote** [eds.] moth **119 tenantless** tennatlesse **125 feared** [eds.] feare

142 you [F, Q1] your   **144 at it** it   **181 conveniently** [F, Q1]
conuenient

1.2. 0.2 [and elsewhere] **Gertrude** *Gertrad*   **1 KING** *Claud.*   **67 so** so
much   **77 good** coold   **82 shapes** [Q3] chapes   **83 denote** deuote
96 a or   **105 corpse** [eds.] course   **112 you. For** you for
114 retrograde retrogard   **129 sullied** [eds.] sallied [Q2] solid [F]
132 self seale   **133 weary** wary   **137 to this** thus   **140 satyr** [F4]
satire   **143 would** [F, Q1] should   **149 even she** [F; not in Q2]
175 to drink deep [F, Q1] for to drinke   **178 to see** [F, Q1] to
199 waste [F2] wast [Q2, F]   **206 jelly with . . . fear,** gelly, with . . .
feare   **210 Where, as** [Q5] Whereas   **225 Indeed, indeed** [F, Q1]
Indeede   **241 Very like, very like** [F, Q1] Very like   **242 hundred**
hundreth   **243 MARCELLUS, BERNARDO** [eds.] *Both*   **247 tonight** to
nigh   **256 fare** farre   **257 eleven** a leauen   **259.1** *Exeunt* [at line
258 in Q2]   **262 Foul** [F, Q1] fonde

1.3. 3 convoy is conuay, in   **12 bulk** bulkes   **18** [F; not in Q2]
29 weigh way   **49 like a** a a   **74 Are** Or   **75 be** boy   **76 loan** loue
110 Running [eds.] Wrong [Q2] Roaming [F]   **116 springes** springs
126 tether tider   **130 implorators** imploratotors   **131 bawds** [eds.]
bonds   **132 beguile** beguide

1.4. 2 is a is   **6.1 go off** [eds.] *goes of*   **17 revel** [Q3] reueale   **19
clepe** clip   **36 evil** [eds.] eale [Q2] ease [Q3]   **37 often dout** [eds.] of
a doubt   **49 inurned** interr'd [Q2, Q1]   **61, 79 wafts** waues   **80 off**
of   **82 artery** arture   **86.1** *Exeunt Exit*   **87 imagination** [F, Q1]
imagion

1.5. 1 Whither [eds.] Whether   **20 on** [eds.] an   **21 fretful
porcupine** [F, Q1] fearfull Porpentine   **44 wit** [eds.] wits   **48 what a**
what   **56 lust** [F, Q1] but   **angel** Angle   **57 sate** [F] sort   **59 scent**
[eds.] sent   **68 alleys** [eds.] allies   **69 posset** possesse   **96 stiffly**
swiftly   **119 bird** and   **128 HORATIO, MARCELLUS** *Booth* [also at line
151] **heaven, my lord** heauen   **138 Look you, I'll** I will   **158 s.d.
cries** *Ghost cries*   **179 some'er** so mere   **185 Well** well, well [Q1,
Q2]

2.1. 0.1 *man* [eds.] *man or two*   **3 marvelous** meruiles   **29 Faith, no**
Fayth   **41 warrant** wit   **42 sullies** sallies   **43 wi' th'** with
60 o'ertook or tooke   **64 takes** take   **76 s.d.** *Exit Reynaldo. Enter
Ophelia* [after line 75 in Q2]   **107 passion** passions   **114 quoted**
[eds.] coted

2.2. 0.1 [and elsewhere] *Rosencrantz* Rosencraus   **57 o'erhasty**
hastie   **73 three** [F, Q1] threescore   **90 since brevity** breuitie
125 This [Q2 has a speech prefix: *Pol.* This]   **126 above** about
137 winking working   **143 his** her   **148 watch** wath   **149 to a** to
151 'tis [F, Q1; not in Q2]   **170.1** [at line 169 in Q2]   *Exeunt* [eds.]
Exit   **210 sanity** sanctity   **212–13 and suddenly ... him** [F; not in
Q2]   **213 honorable lord** Lord   **214 most humbly take** take   **215
cannot, sir** cannot   **216 more** not more   **224 excellent** extent
228–9 overhappy./ On euer happy on   **229 cap** lap   **240–70 Let ...
attended** [F; not in Q2]   **267 ROSENCRANTZ, GUILDENSTERN** *Both* [F]
273 even euer   **288 could** can   **292 off** of   **304 What a** What
306–7 admirable, in action how ... angel, in [F, subst.] admirable in
action, how ... Angell in   **310 no, nor** nor   **314 you** yee   **321 of**
on   **324–5 the clown ... sear** [F; not in Q2]   **tickle** [eds.] tickled [F]
326 blank black   **337–62 How ... too** [F; not in Q2]   **342 berattle**
[eds.] be-ratled [F]   **349 most like** [eds.] like most [F]   **373 lest my**
let me   **381 too** to   **398–9 tragical-historical, tragical-comical-
historical-pastoral** [F; not in Q2]   **401 light ... these** [eds.] light for
the lawe of writ, and the liberty: these   **425 By'r** by   **429 e'en to 't**
ento't   **French falconers** friendly Fankners   **433 [and elsewhere]**
FIRST PLAYER *Player*   **436–7 caviare** cauiary   **443 affectation**
affection   **446 tale** [F, Q1] talke   **456 heraldry** [F, Q1] heraldy
dismal. Head dismall head   **474 Then senseless Ilium** [F; not in Q2]
481 And, like Like   **495 fellies** [F4] follies [Q2] Fallies [F]
504 "Moblèd queen" is good [F; not in Q2; F reads "Inobled"]
506 bisson Bison   **514 husband's** [F, Q1] husband   **519 whe'er**
where   **540 a** [F; not in Q2]   **541 or** [F, Q1] lines, or   **546 s.d.**
Exeunt players [see textual note at line 548.1]   **547 till** tell
548.1 *Exeunt* [F; Q2 has "*Exeunt Pol. and Players*" after line 547]
554 his the   **556 and** an   **559 to Hecuba** [F, Q1] to her   **561 the**
cue that   **582 Oh, vengeance** [F; not in Q2]   **584 father** [Q1, Q3,
Q4; not in Q2, F]   **588 scullion** [F] stallyon [Q2] scalion [Q1]
600 the devil a deale   **the devil** the deale

3.1. 1 And An   **28 too** two   **32 lawful espials** [F; not in Q2]
33 Will Wee'le   **46 loneliness** lowlines   **to** too   **56 Let's withdraw**
with-draw   **56.2 Enter Hamlet** [after line 55 in Q2]   **65 wished. To**
wisht to   **73 disprized** despiz'd   **84 of us all** [F, Q1; not in Q2]
86 sicklied sickled   **93 well, well, well** well   **100 the** these
108 your honesty you   **119 inoculate** euocutat   **122 to a** a

130 knaves all knaues   **144 paintings too** [Q1] paintings   **146 jig, you amble** gig & amble   **147 lisp** list   **148 your ignorance** [F, Q1] ignorance   **155 Th'expectancy** Th'expectation   **159 music** musickt   **160 that** what   **161 tune** time   **162 feature** stature   **164** [Q2 has "*Exit*" at the end of this line]   **191 unwatched** vnmatcht

3.2. 10 tatters totters   **split** [F, Q1] spleet   **27 of the** of   **29 praise** praysd   **37 sir** [F; not in Q2]   **45.1 *Enter . . . Rosencrantz*** [after line 47 in Q2]   **88 detecting** detected   **96 now. My lord,** now my Lord.   **107** [and elsewhere] QUEEN *Ger.*   **108 metal** mettle   **112–13** [F; not in Q2]   **127 devil** deule [Q2] Diuel [F]   **133.1 *sound*** [eds.] *sounds*   **133.7 *Anon comes*** anon come   **135 miching** [F, Q1] munching   **140 keep counsel** [F, Q1] keepe   **153** [and throughout scene] PLAYER KING *King*   **154 orbèd** orb'd the   **159** [and throughout scene] PLAYER QUEEN *Quee.*   **162 your** our   **164** [Q2 follows here with an extraneous unrhymed line: "For women feare too much, euen as they loue"]   **165 For** And   **166 In** Eyther none, in   **167 love** Lord   **179 Wormwood, wormwood** That's wormwood   **180 PLAYER QUEEN** [not in Q2]   **188 like the**   **197 joys** joy   **217 An** And   **221 a widow** [F, Q1] I be a widow   **be** [F] be a   **226.1 *Exit*** [F, Q1] *Exeunt*   **240 wince** [Q1] winch [Q2, F]   **241.1** [after line 242 in Q2]   **254 Confederate** [F, Q1] Considerat   **256 infected** [F, Q1, Q4] inuected   **258 usurp** vsurps   **264** [F; not in Q2]   **274 with two** with   **288.1** [F; after line 293 in Q2]   **308 start** stare   **317 of my** of   **343.1** [after line 341 in Q2]   **357 thumb** the vmber   **366 to the top of** tò   **370 can fret me** [F] fret me not [Q2] can fret me, yet [Q1]   **371.1** [after line 372 in Q2]   **385 POLONIUS** [F; not in Q2]   **386 Leave me, friends** [so F; Q2 places before "I will say so," and assigns both to Hamlet]   **388 breathes** breakes   **390 bitter . . . day** business as the bitter day   **395 daggers** [F, Q1] dagger

3.3. 19 huge hough   **22 ruin** raine   **23 but with** but   **35.1 *Exit*** [after "I know" in F]   **50 pardoned** pardon   **58 Offense's** [eds.] Offences   **shove** showe   **73 pat . . . a-praying** but now a is a praying   **75 revenged** reuendge   **79 hire and salary** base and silly   **81 With all** Withall

3.4. 5–6 with him . . . Mother, mother, mother [F; not in Q2]   **7 warrant** wait   **8.1 *Enter Hamlet*** [at line 5 in Q2]   **21 inmost** most   **23 Help, ho!** Helpe how   **43 off** of   **51 tristful** heated   **53** [assigned in Q2 to Hamlet]   **60 heaven-kissing** heaue, a kissing

89 panders pardons   **91 mine . . . soul** my very eyes into my soule
92 grainèd greeued   **93 not leave** leaue there   **100 tithe** kyth
146 Ecstasy [F; not in Q2]   **150 I the** the   **165 live** leaue
172 Refrain tonight to refraine night   **193 ravel** rouell   **205 to
breathe** [eds.] to breath   **222 a** [F, Q1] a most   **224.1 *Exeunt*** [eds.]
Exit

4.1. 32.1 [at 31 in Q2]

4.2. 0.1 [Q2: "*Enter Hamlet, Rosencraus, and others.*"]   **2–3** [F; not in
Q2; the s.p. in F is "*Gentlemen*"]   **4 HAMLET** [not in Q2]   **5.1** [F; not
in Q2]   **7 Compounded** Compound   **18–19 an ape** [not in Q2]
31–2 Hide . . . after [F; not in Q2]

4.3. 44 With fiery quickness [F; not in Q2]   **56 and so** so   **72 were
will** begun begin

4.4. 20–1 name. To name To

4.5. 16 Let . . . in [assigned in Q2 to Horatio]   **20.1** [after line 16 in
Q2]   **38 with all** with   **52 clothes** close   **57 Indeed, la** Indeede
62 to too   **83 in their** in   **98** [F; not in Q2]   **100.1** [below line 97
in Q2]   **103 impetuous** [Q3, F2] impitious [Q2] impittious [F]
109 They The   **146 swoopstake** [eds.] soopstake [Q1 reads "Swoop-
stake-like"]   **158 Let her come in** [assigned in Q2 to Laertes and
placed before "How now, what noyse is that?"]   **s.d. *Enter Ophelia***
[after line 157 in Q2]   **162 Till** Tell   **165 an old** [F, Q1] a poore
166–8, 170 [F; not in Q2]   **186 must** [F, Q1] may   **191 affliction** [F,
Q1] afflictions   **199 All flaxen** Flaxen   **203 Christian** [F] Christians
souls, I pray God [F, Q1] soules   **204 you see** you   **217 trophy,
sword** trophe sword

4.6. 7, 9 FIRST SAILOR *Say*.   **9 an't** and   **22 good turn** turne
26 bore bord   **30 He** *So*   **31 will give** will

4.7. 6 proceeded proceede   **7 crimeful** criminall   **15 conjunctive**
concliue   **22 gyves** Giues   **23 loud a wind** loued Arm'd   **25 had**
haue   **37 How . . . Hamlet** [F; not in Q2]   **38 This** These
46–7 your pardon you pardon   **48 and more strange** [F; not in Q2]
Hamlet [F; not in Q2]   **56 shall live** [F, Q1] liue   **62 checking the**
King   **78 ribbon** [eds.] ribaud   **89 my** me   **101 escrimers** [eds.]
Scrimures   **116 wick** [eds.] weeke   **123 spendthrift** [Q5] spend
thrifts   **135 on** ore   **139 pass** pace   **141 for that** for   **151 shape.**

If shape if   157 ha't hate   160 prepared prefard   168 hoar horry
172 cold cull-cold   192 douts [F "doubts"] drownes

5.1. 1 [and throughout] FIRST CLOWN *Clowne*   3 [and throughout]
SECOND CLOWN *Other*   9 *se offendendo* so offended   12 and to to
Argal or all   34–7 SECOND CLOWN: Why . . . arms? [F, not in Q2]
43 that frame that   55.1 [before line 65 in Q2]   60 stoup soope
70 daintier dintier   85 meant [F, Q1, Q3] went   89 mazard massene
106–7 Is . . . recoveries [F; not in Q2]   107–8 Will his will
109 double ones too doubles   120 Oh or   121 [F; not in Q2]
143 Of all Of   165 nowadays [F; not in Q2]   183 Let me see [F;
not in Q]   192 chamber [F, Q1] table   208–9 As thus [F; not in Q2]
216 winter's waters   226, 235 PRIEST *Doct.*   231 Shards, flints
Flints   246 t'have haue   247 treble double   262 and rash rash
288 thus this   296.1 [*Exit*] Horatio *and Horatio*   301 shortly
thereby 302 Till Tell

5.2. 5 Methought my thought   6 bilboes bilbo   9 pall fall
17 unseal vnfold   19 Ah, [eds.] A   29 villainies villaines   30 Ere
Or   43 "as"es as sir   52 Subscribed Subscribe   57, 68–80 [F; not
in Q2]   73 interim is [eds.] *interim's* [F]   78 court [eds.] count [F]
81 [and throughout] OSRIC *Cour.*   82 humbly humble   93 Put
your your   98 sultry sully   for or   107 gentleman [eds.] gentlemen
109 feelingly [Q4] fellingly   114 dozy [eds.] dazzie   yaw [eds.] raw
141 his [eds.] this   142 him by them, him, by them   149 hangers
hanger   156 carriages carriage   159 might be be might
162 impawned, as [eds.] all [Q2] impon'd, as [F]   174 purpose, I
purpose; I   181–2 Yours, yours. 'A does Yours doo's   186 comply
so sir   190 yeasty histy   191 fanned [eds.] prophane [Q2] fond [F]
winnowed trennowed   210 But thou thou   218 be now be
220 will come well come   238 [F; not in Q2]   248 To keep To
till all   252 foils. Come on foiles.   255 off of   261 bettered better
270 union Vnice ["Onixe" in some copies]   288 A touch, a touch,
I I   302 afeard sure   316 Hamlet, Hamlet *Hamlet*   319 thy [F,
Q1] my   327 murderous [F; not in Q2]   328 off of   thy union [F,
Q1] the Onixe   345 ha 't [eds.] hate [Q2] have 't [F]   366 proud
prou'd   369 FIRST AMBASSADOR *Embas.*   381 th' yet yet
385 forced for no   394 on no

Passages contained only in F and omitted from Q2 are noted in the textual notes above. Listed below are the more important instances in which Q2 contains words, lines, and passages omitted in F.

1.1. 112–29 BERNARDO I think...countrymen

1.2. 58–60 wrung...consent

1.3. 9 perfume and

1.4. 17–38 This heavy-headed...scandal   75–8 The very...beneath

2.1. 122 Come

2.2. 17 Whether...thus   217 except my life   363 very   366 'Sblood (and some other profanity passim)   371 then   444–5 as wholesome...fine   521–2 of this   589 Hum

3.2. 169–70 Where...there   216–17 To...scope

3.4. 72–7 Sense...difference   79–82 Eyes...mope   168–72 That monster...put on   174–7 the next...potency   187 One word... lady   209–17 There's...meet

4.1. 4 Bestow...while   41–4 Whose...air

4.2. 4 But soft

4.3. 26–9 KING Alas...worm

4.4. 9–67 *Enter Hamlet*...worth

4.5. 33 Oho

4.7. 68–82 LAERTES My lord...graveness   101–3 Th' escrimers... them   115–24 There...ulcer

5.1. 154 There

5.2. 106–42 here is...unfellowed (replaced in F by "you are not ignorant of what excellence Laertes is at his weapon")
154–5 HORATIO [*to Hamlet*] I knew...done   193–207 *Enter a Lord*...lose, my lord (replaced in F by "You will lose this wager, my lord")   222 Let be

SHAKESPEARE'S SOURCES

The ultimate source of the *Hamlet* story is Saxo Grammaticus's *Historia Danica* (1180–1208), the saga of one Amlothi or (as Saxo calls him) Amlethus. The outline of the story is essentially that of Shakespeare's play, even though the emphasis of the Danish saga is overwhelmingly on cunning, brutality, and bloody revenge. Amlethus' father is Horwendil, a Governor of Jutland, who bravely kills the King of Norway in single combat and thereby wins the hand in marriage of Gerutha, daughter of the King of Denmark. This good fortune goads the envious Feng into slaying his brother Horwendil and marrying Gerutha, "capping unnatural murder with incest." Though the deed is known to everyone, Feng invents excuses and soon wins the approbation of the fawning courtiers. Young Amlethus vows revenge, but, perceiving his uncle's cunning, he feigns madness. His mingled words of craft and candor awaken suspicions that he may be playing a game of deception.

Two attempts are made to lure Amlethus into revealing that he is actually sane. The first plan is to tempt him into lechery, on the theory that one who lusts for women cannot be truly insane. Feng causes an attractive woman to be placed in a forest where Amlethus will meet her as though by chance; but Amlethus, secretly warned of the trap by a kindly foster brother, spirits the young lady off to a hideaway where they can make love unobserved by Feng's agents. She confesses the plot to Amlethus. In a second stratagem, a courtier who is reported to be "gifted with more assurance than judgment" hides himself under some straw in the Queen's chamber in order to overhear her private conversations with Amlethus. The hero, suspecting just such a trap, feigns madness and begins crowing like a noisy rooster, bouncing up and down on the straw until he finds the eavesdropper. Amlethus stabs the man to death, drags him forth, cuts the body into morsels, boils them, and flings the bits "through the mouth of an open sewer for the swine to eat." Thereupon he returns to his mother to accuse her of being an infamous harlot. He wins her over to repentant virtue and even cooperation. When Feng, returning from a journey, looks around for his counselor, Amlethus jestingly (but in part truly) suggests that the man went to the sewer and fell in.

Feng now sends Amlethus to the King of Britain with secret orders for his execution. However, Amlethus finds the letter to the British King in the coffers of the two unnamed retainers accompanying him on the journey, and substitutes a new letter ordering their execution instead. The new letter, purportedly written and signed by Feng, goes on to urge that the King of Britain marry his daughter to a young Dane being sent from the Danish court. By this means Amlethus gains an English wife and rids himself of the escorts. A year later Amlethus returns to Jutland, gets the entire court drunk, flings a tapestry (knitted for him by his mother) over the prostrate courtiers, secures the tapestry with stakes, and then sets fire to the palace. Feng escapes this holocaust, but Amlethus cuts him down with the King's own sword. (Amlethus exchanges swords because his own has been nailed fast into its scabbard by his enemies.) Subsequently, Amlethus convinces the people of the justice of his cause and is chosen King of Jutland. After ruling for several years, he returns to Britain, bigamously marries a Scottish queen, fights a battle with his first father-in-law, is betrayed by his second wife, and is finally killed in battle.

In Saxo's account we thus find the prototypes of Hamlet, Claudius, Gertrude, Polonius, Ophelia, Rosencrantz, and Guildenstern. Several episodes are close in narrative detail to Shakespeare's play: the original murder and incestuous marriage, the feigned madness, the woman used as a decoy, the eavesdropping counselor, and especially the trip to England. A translation of Saxo into French by François de Belleforest, in *Histories Tragiques* (1576 edition), adds a few details, such as Gertrude's adultery before the murder and Hamlet's melancholy. Belleforest's version is longer than Saxo's, with more psychological and moral observation and more dialogue. Shakespeare probably consulted it.

Shakespeare need not have depended extensively on these older versions of his story, however. His main source was almost certainly an old play of *Hamlet*. Much evidence testifies to the existence of such a play. The *Diary* of Philip Henslowe, a theater owner and manager, records a performance, not marked as "new," of a *Hamlet* at Newington Butts on June 11, 1594, by "my Lord Admiral's men" or "my Lord Chamberlain's men," probably the latter. Thomas Lodge's pamphlet *Wit's Misery and the World's Madness* (1596) refers to "the vizard of the ghost which cried so miserably at the theater, like an oyster wife, 'Hamlet, revenge!'" And Thomas Nashe, in his *Epistle* prefixed to Robert Greene's romance *Menaphon* (1589), offers the following observation:

> It is a common practice nowadays amongst a sort of shifting companions, that run through every art and thrive by none, to leave the trade of noverint, whereto they were born, and busy themselves with the endeavors of art, that could scarcely Latinize their neck verse if they should have need; yet English Seneca read by candlelight yields many good sentences, as "Blood is a beggar" and so forth; and if you entreat him fair in a frosty morning, he will afford you whole *Hamlets*, I should say handfuls, of tragical speeches. But O grief! *Tempus edax rerum*, what's that will last always? The sea exhaled by drops will in continuance be dry, and Seneca, let blood line by line and page by page, at length must needs die to our stage; which makes his famished followers to imitate the Kid in Aesop, who, enamored with the Fox's newfangles, forsook all hopes of life to leap into a new occupation; and these men, renouncing all possibilities of credit or estimation, to intermeddle with Italian translations...

Nashe's testimonial describes a *Hamlet* play, written in the Senecan style by some person born to the trade of "noverint," or scrivener, who has turned to hack writing and translation. The description has often been fitted to Thomas Kyd, though this identification is not certain. (Nashe could be punning on Kyd's name when he refers to "the Kid in Aesop.") Certainly Thomas Kyd's *The Spanish Tragedy* (c. 1587) shows many affinities with Shakespeare's play, and provides many Senecan ingredients missing from Saxo and Belleforest: the ghost, the difficulty in ascertaining whether the ghost's words are believable, the resulting need for delay and a feigning of madness, the moral perplexities afflicting a sensitive man called upon to revenge, the play within the play, the clever reversals and ironically caused deaths in the catastrophe, the rhetoric of tragical passion. Whether or not Kyd in fact wrote the *Ur-Hamlet*, his extant play enables us to see more clearly what that lost play must have contained. The unauthorized first quarto of *Hamlet* (1603) also offers a few seemingly authentic details that are not found in the authoritative second quarto but are found in the earlier sources and may have been a part of the *Ur-Hamlet*. For example, after Hamlet has killed Corambis (corresponding to Polonius), the Queen vows to assist Hamlet in his strategies against the King; and later, when Hamlet has returned to England, the Queen sends him a message by Horatio warning him to be careful.

One last document sheds light on the *Ur-Hamlet*. A German play, *Der bestrafte Brudermord* (*Fratricide Punished*), from a now-lost manuscript dated 1710, seems to have been based on a text used by English actors traveling in Germany in 1586 and afterward. Though changed by translation and manuscript transmission, and too entirely different from Shakespeare's play to have been based on it, this German version may well have been based on Shakespeare's source play. Polonius's name in this text, Corambus, is the Corambis of the first quarto of 1603. (The name may mean "cabbage cooked twice," for *coramble-bis*, a proverbially dull dish.)

Der bestrafte Brudermord begins with a prologue in the Senecan manner, followed by the appearance of the ghost to Francisco, Horatio, and sentinels of the watch. Within the palace, meanwhile, the King carouses. Hamlet joins the watch, confiding to Horatio that he is "sick at heart" over his father's death and mother's hasty remarriage. The ghost appears to Hamlet, tells him how the juice of hebona was poured into his ear, and urges revenge. When Hamlet swears Horatio and Francisco to silence, the ghost (now invisible) says several times "We swear," his voice following the men as they move from place to place. Hamlet reveals to Horatio the entire circumstance of the murder. Later, in a formal session of the

court, the new King speaks hypocritically of his brother's death
and explains the reasons for his marriage to the Queen. Hamlet is
forbidden to return to Wittenberg, though Corambus's son Leonhardus has already set out for France.

Some time afterward, Corambus reports the news of Hamlet's
madness to the King and Queen, and presumes on the basis of his
own youthful passions to diagnose Hamlet's malady as lovesickness.
Concealed, he and the King overhear Hamlet tell Ophelia to "go to
a nunnery." When players arrive from Germany, Hamlet instructs
them in the natural style of acting, and then requests them to perform a play before the King about the murder of King Pyrrhus by his
brother. (Death is again inflicted by hebona poured in the ear.) After the King's guilty reaction to the play, Hamlet finds him alone at
prayers but postpones the killing lest the King's soul be sent to
heaven. Hamlet kills Corambus behind the tapestry in the Queen's
chamber, and is visited again by the ghost (who says nothing, however). Ophelia, her mind deranged, thinks herself in love with a
court butterfly named Phantasmo. (This creature is also involved in
a comic action to help the clown Jens with a tax problem.)

The King sends Hamlet to England with two unnamed
courtiers who are instructed to kill Hamlet after their arrival. A
contrary wind takes them instead to an island near Dover, where
Hamlet foils his two enemies by kneeling between them and asking them to shoot him on signal; at the proper moment, he ducks
and they shoot each other. He finishes them off with their own
swords, and discovers letters on their persons ordering Hamlet's
execution by the English King if the original plot should fail.
When Hamlet returns to Denmark, the King arranges a duel between him and Corambus's son Leonhardus. If Leonhardus's poisoned dagger misses its mark, a beaker of wine containing finely
ground oriental diamond dust is to do the rest. Hamlet is informed of the impending duel by Phantasmo (compare Osric),
whom Hamlet taunts condescendingly and calls "Signora Phantasmo." Shortly before the duel takes place, Ophelia is reported to
have thrown herself off a hill to her death. The other deaths oc-
cur much as in Shakespeare's play. The dying Hamlet bids that

the crown be conveyed to his cousin, Duke Fortempras of Norway, of whom we have not heard earlier.

From the extensive similarities between *Hamlet* and this German play, we can see that Shakespeare inherited his narrative material almost intact, though in a jumble and so pitifully mangled that the modern reader can only laugh at the contrast. No source study in Shakespeare reveals so clearly the extent of Shakespeare's wholesale borrowing of plot, and the incredible transformation he achieved in reordering his materials.

The following excerpt is from the English *The History of Hamlet*, 1608, an unacknowledged translation of Belleforest that in one or two places seems to have been influenced by Shakespeare's play—as when Hamlet beats his arms on the hangings of the Queen's apartment instead of jumping on the quilt or bed, as in Belleforest, and cries, "A rat! a rat!" It is otherwise a close translation and, although too late for Shakespeare to have used, provides an Elizabethan version of the account Shakespeare most likely used.

THE HISTORY OF HAMLET
PRINCE OF DENMARK

CHAPTER 1

How Horvendil and Fengon were made Governors of the Province of Ditmarse, and how Horvendil married Geruth, the daughter to Roderick, chief King of Denmark, by whom he had Hamlet; and how after his marriage his brother Fengon slew him traitorously and married his brother's wife, and what followed.

YOU must understand, that long time before the kingdom of Denmark received the faith of Jesus Christ and embraced the doctrine of the Christians, that the common people in those days were barbarous and uncivil and their princes cruel, without faith or loyalty, seeking nothing but murder and deposing or at the least offending each other either in honors, goods, or lives, not caring to ransom such as they took prisoners but rather sacrificing them to the cruel vengeance naturally imprinted in their hearts; in such sort that if there were sometimes a good prince or king among them who, being adorned with the most perfect gifts of nature, would addict himself to virtue and use courtesy, although the people held him in admiration (as virtue is admirable to the most wicked) yet the envy of his neighbors was so great that they never ceased until that virtuous man were dispatched out of the world.

King Roderick, as then reigning in Denmark, after he had appeased the troubles in the country and driven the Swethlanders and Slaveans from thence, he divided the kingdom into divers provinces, placing governors therein, who after (as the like happened in France) bare the names of dukes, marquesses, and earls, giving the government of Jutie (at this present called Ditmarse), lying upon the country of the Cimbrians in the straight or narrow part of land that showeth like a point or cape of ground upon the sea which northward* bordereth upon the country of Norway, to two* valiant and warlike lords, Horvendil and Fengon, sons to Gervendil, who likewise had been governor of that province.

Now the greatest honor that men of noble birth could at that time win and obtain was in exercising the art of piracy upon the seas, assailing their neighbors and the countries bordering upon them; and how much the more they used to rob, pill,[1] and spoil other provinces and islands far adjacent, so much the more their honors and reputation increased and augmented. Wherein Horvendil obtained the highest place in his time, being the most renowned pirate that in those days scoured the seas and havens of the north parts; whose great fame so moved the heart of Collere, King of Norway, that he was much grieved to hear that Horvendil surmounted*[2] him in feats of arms, thereby obscuring the glory by him already obtained upon the seas—honor more than covetousness of riches in those days being the reason that provoked those barbarian princes to overthrow and vanquish one the other, not caring[3] to be slain by the hands of a victorious person.

This valiant and hardy king having challenged Horvendil to

1 **pill** plunder   2 **surmounted** excelled   3 **not caring** i.e., not considering it dishonorable

fight with him body to body, the combat was by him accepted, with conditions that he which should be vanquished should lose all the riches he had in his ship and that the vanquisher should cause the body of the vanquished (that should be slain in the combat) to be honorably buried, death being the prize and reward of him that should lose the battle. And to conclude, Collere, King of Norway, although a valiant, hardy, and courageous prince, was in the end vanquished and slain by Horvendil, who presently caused a tomb to be erected and therein, with all honorable obsequies fit for a prince, buried the body of King Collere, according to their ancient manner and superstitions in these days and the conditions of the combat, bereaving the King's ships of all their riches; and, having slain the King's sister, a very brave and valiant warrior, and overrun all the coast of Norway and the Northern Islands, returned home again laden with much treasure, sending the most part thereof to his sovereign, King Roderick, thereby to procure his good liking and so to be accounted one of the greatest favorites about His Majesty.

The King, allured by those presents and esteeming himself happy to have so valiant a subject, sought by a great favor and courtesy to make him become bounden unto him perpetually, giving him Geruth his daughter to his wife, of whom he knew Horvendil to be already much enamored. And, the more to honor him, determined himself in person to conduct her into Jutie, where the marriage was celebrated according to the ancient manner. And, to be brief, of this marriage proceeded Hamlet, of whom I intend to speak, and for his cause have chosen to renew this present history.

Fengon, brother to this prince Horvendil, who, not only* fretting and despiting[4] in his heart at the great honor and reputation won by his brother in warlike affairs but solicited and provoked by a foolish jealousy to see him honored with royal alliance, and fearing thereby to be deposed from his part of the government—or rather desiring to be only governor, thereby to obscure the memory of the victories and conquests of his brother Horvendil—

4 **despiting** entertaining a grudge

determined, whatsoever happened, to kill him; which he effected in such sort that no man once so much as suspected him, every man esteeming that from such and so firm a knot of alliance and consanguinity there could proceed no other issue than the full effects of virtue and courtesy. But, as I said before, the desire of bearing sovereign rule and authority respecteth neither blood nor amity, nor caring for virtue, as being wholly without respect of laws or majesty divine; for it is not possible that he which invadeth the country and taketh away the riches of another man without cause or reason should know or fear God. Was not this a crafty and subtle counselor? But he might have thought that the mother, knowing her husband's case, would not cast her son into the danger of death.

But Fengon, having secretly assembled certain men, and perceiving himself strong enough to execute his enterprise, Horvendil his brother being at a banquet with his friends, suddenly set upon him, where he slew him as traitorously as cunningly he purged himself of so detestable a murder to his subjects; for that before he had any violent or bloody hands, or once committed parricide upon his brother, he had incestuously abused his wife, whose honor he ought as well to have sought and procured as traitorously he pursued and effected his destruction. And it is most certain that the man that abandoneth himself to any notorious and wicked action whereby he becometh a great sinner, he careth not to commit much more heinous and abominable offenses; and covered his boldness and wicked practice with so great subtlety and policy, and under a veil of mere simplicity, that, being favored for the honest love that he bare to his sister-in-law—for whose sake, he affirmed, he had in that sort murdered his brother—that his sin found excuse among the common people and of the nobility was esteemed for justice. For that Geruth, being as courteous a princess as any then living in the north parts, and one that had never once so much as offended any of her subjects, either commons or courtiers, this adulterer and infamous murderer slandered his dead brother that he would have slain his wife,[5] and that he,[6]

5 slandered...wife i.e., made the slanderous accusation that Horvendil intended to slay his wife, Geruth   6 he i.e., Fengon

by chance finding him upon the point ready to do it, in defense of the lady had slain him, bearing off the blows which as then he[7] struck at the innocent princess without any other cause of malice whatsoever. Wherein he wanted[8] no false witnesses to approve[9] his act, which deposed[10] in like sort as the wicked calumniator himself protested, being the same persons that had borne him company and were participants of his treason. So that instead of pursuing him as a parricide and an incestuous person, all the courtiers admired and flattered him in his good fortune, making more account of false witnesses and detestable wicked reporters, and more honoring the calumniators, than they esteemed of those that, seeking to call the matter in question and admiring the virtues of the murdered prince, would have punished the massacrers and bereavers of his life.

Which was the cause that Fengon, boldened and encouraged by such impunity, durst venture to couple himself in marriage with her whom he used as his concubine during good Horvendil's life, in that sort spotting his name with a double vice, and charging his conscience with abominable guilt and twofold impiety, as[11] incestuous adultery and parricide murder. And that[12] the unfortunate and wicked woman, that had received the honor to be the wife of one of the valiantest and wisest* princes in the north, embased[13] herself in such vile sort as to falsify her faith unto him and, which is worse, to marry him that had been the tyrannous murderer of her lawful husband; which made divers men think that she had been the causer of the murder, thereby to live in her adultery without control.

But where shall a man find a more wicked and bold woman than a great personage once having loosed the bonds of honor and honesty? This princess, who at the first for her rare virtues and courtesies was honored of all men and beloved of her husband, as soon as she once gave ear to the tyrant Fengon forgot both the rank she held among the greatest names and the duty of

7 he i.e., Horvendil   8 he wanted i.e., Fengon lacked   9 approve confirm   10 which deposed who testifed   11 as that is, to wit   12 And that i.e., And was the cause that   13 embased lowered, debased

an honest wife on her behalf. But I will not stand to gaze and
marvel at women, for that there are many which seek to blaze[14]
and set them forth, in which their writings they spare not to
blame them all for the faults of some one or few women. But I say
that either nature ought to have bereaved[15] man of that opinion
to accompany[16] with women, or else to endow them with such
spirits as that they may easily support the crosses they endure
without complaining so often and so strangely, seeing it is their
own beastliness that overthrows them. For if it be so that a
woman is so imperfect a creature as they make her to be, and that
they know this beast to be so hard to be tamed as they affirm,
why then are they so foolish to preserve them and so dull and
brutish as to trust their deceitful and wanton embracings? But let
us leave her in this extremity of lasciviousness, and proceed to
show you in what sort the young Prince Hamlet behaved himself
to escape the tyranny of his uncle.

CHAPTER 2

*How Hamlet counterfeited the madman to escape the tyranny of his
uncle, and how he was tempted by a woman through his uncle's pro-
curement, who thereby thought to undermine the Prince and by that
means to find out whether he counterfeited madness or not; and how
Hamlet would by no means be brought to consent unto her, and what
followed.*

GERUTH having, as I said before, so much forgotten herself, the
Prince Hamlet, perceiving himself to be in danger of his life, as
being abandoned of his own mother and forsaken of all men,
and assuring himself that Fengon would not detract[1] the time to
send him the same way his father Horvendil was gone, to beguile[2] the tyrant in his subtleties (that esteemed him to be of
such a mind that if he once attained to man's estate[3] he would
not long delay the time to revenge the death of his father),

14 **blaze** proclaim   15 **bereaved** deprived   16 **accompany** keep company
1 **detract** lengthen   2 **to beguile** in order to beguile   3 **man's estate**
manhood

counterfeited* the madman with such craft and subtle practices that he made show as if he had utterly lost his wits, and under that veil he covered his pretense and defended his life from the treasons and practices of the tyrant his uncle. And although[4] he had been at the school of[5] the Roman prince who, because he counterfeited himself to be a fool, was called Brutus[6] yet he imitated his fashions and his wisdom. For, every day being in the Queen's palace (who as then was more careful to please her whoremaster than ready to revenge the cruel death of her husband or to restore her son to his inheritance), he rent and tore his clothes, wallowing and lying in the dirt and mire, his face all filthy and black, running through the streets like a man distraught, not speaking one word but such as seemed to proceed of madness and mere[7] frenzy, all his actions and gestures being no other than the right countenances[8] of a man wholly deprived of all reason and understanding, in such sort that as then he seemed fit for nothing but to make sport[9] to the pages and ruffling[10] courtiers that attended in the court of his uncle and father-in-law.[11] But the young Prince noted them well enough, minding one day to be revenged in such manner that the memory thereof should remain perpetually to the world....

Hamlet, in this sort counterfeiting the madman, many times did divers actions of great and deep consideration, and often made such and so fit answers that a wise man would soon have judged from what spirit so fine an invention might proceed; for that standing by the fire and sharpening sticks like poniards and pricks, one in smiling manner asked him wherefore he made those little staves so sharp at the points? "I prepare," saith he, "piercing darts and sharp arrows to revenge my father's death."

4 **although** inasmuch as   5 **been at the school of** i.e., studied the method of   6 **Brutus** (Lucius Junius Brutus assumed the disguise of idiocy in order to escape the fate of his brother, whom their uncle Tarquinius Superbus had put to death. *Brutus* means "stupid.")   7 **mere** absolute   8 **right countenances** true demeanor   9 **make sport** serve as the butt of joking   10 **ruffling** swaggering   11 **father-in-law** i.e., stepfather

Fools, as I said before, esteemed those his words as nothing; but men of quick spirits and such as had a deeper reach[12] began to suspect somewhat, esteeming that under that kind of folly there lay hidden a great and rare subtlety such as one day might be prejudicial to their prince, saying that under color of such rudeness he shadowed a crafty policy and by his devised simplicity he concealed a sharp and pregnant[13] spirit.

For which cause they counseled the King to try and know, if it were possible, how to discover the intent and meaning of the young Prince. And they could find no better nor more fit invention to entrap him than to set some fair and beautiful woman in a secret place that, with flattering speeches and all the craftiest means she could use, should purposely seek to allure his mind to have his pleasure of her. For the nature of all young men, especially such as are brought up wantonly, is so transported with the desires of the flesh, and entereth so greedily into the pleasures thereof, that it is almost impossible to cover the foul affection, neither yet to dissemble or hide the same by art or industry, much less to shun it. What cunning or subtlety soever they use to cloak their pretense, seeing occasion offered, and that in secret, especially in the most enticing sin that reigneth in man, they cannot choose, being constrained by voluptuousness, but fall to natural effect and working.

To this end certain courtiers were appointed to lead Hamlet into a solitary place within the woods, whither they brought the woman, inciting him to take their pleasures together and to embrace one another—but the subtle practices used in these our days,[14] not to try if men of great account be extract[15] out of their wits but rather to deprive them of strength, virtue, and wisdom by means of such devilish practitioners and infernal* spirits, their domestical servants and ministers of corruption. And surely the poor Prince at this assault had been[16] in great danger, if a gentleman (that in Horvendil's time had been nourished

12 reach comprehension   13 pregnant fertile, intentive   14 but...
days i.e., machinations used often enough in more recent times. but
only   15 extract extracted, removed   16 had been would have been

with him) had not shown himself more affectioned to the bringing-up he had received with Hamlet than desirous to please the tyrant who by all means sought to entangle the son in the same nets wherein the father had ended his days. This gentleman bare the courtiers (appointed as aforesaid of this treason) company, more desiring to give the Prince instruction what he should do than to entrap him, making full account that the least show of perfect sense and wisdom[17] that Hamlet should make would be sufficient to cause him to lose his life. And therefore by certain signs he gave Hamlet intelligence in what danger he was like[18] to fall, if by any means he seemed to obey or once like the wanton toys[19] and vicious provocations of the gentlewoman sent thither by his uncle. Which much abashed the Prince, as then wholly being in affection to the lady; but by her he was likewise informed of the treason, as being one that from her infancy loved and favored him and would have been exceeding sorrowful for his misfortune, and much more[20] to leave his company without enjoying the pleasure of his body, whom she loved more than herself. The Prince in this sort having both deceived the courtiers and the lady's expectation, that affirmed and swore that he never once offered to have his pleasure of the woman, although in subtlety[21] he affirmed the contrary, every man thereupon assured themselves that without all doubt he was distraught of his senses, that his brains were as then wholly void of force and incapable of reasonable apprehension, so that as then[22] Fengon's practice took no effect. But for all that he left not off, still seeking by all means to find out Hamlet's subtlety, as in the next chapter you shall perceive.

CHAPTER 3

How Fengon, uncle to Hamlet, a second time to entrap him in his politic madness, caused one of his counselors to be secretly hidden in

17 the least ... wisdom (Hamlet's yielding to the lady's blandishments would be viewed as a proof of sanity and would thus betray him to his uncle.) 18 like likely 19 toys tricks 20 much more much more sorrowful 21 in subtlety in private 22 as then as of that time

the Queen's chamber, behind the arras, to hear what speeches passed
between Hamlet and the Queen; and how Hamlet killed him and
escaped that danger, and what followed.

AMONG the friends of Fengon there was one that above all the
rest doubted of Hamlet's practices in counterfeiting the madman, who for that cause said that it was impossible that so crafty
a gallant as Hamlet, that counterfeited the fool, should be discovered with so common and unskillful practices which might
easily be perceived, and that to find out his politic pretense it
were necessary to invent some subtle and crafty means more attractive whereby the gallant might not have the leisure to use
his accustomed dissimulation. Which to effect he said he knew
a fit way and a most convenient mean[1] to effect the King's desire and thereby to entrap Hamlet in his subtleties and cause
him of his own accord to fall into the net prepared for him, and
thereby evidently show his secret meaning.

His devise was thus: that King Fengon should make as though
he were to go some long voyage concerning affairs of great importance, and that in the meantime Hamlet should be shut up
alone in a chamber with his mother, wherein some other should
secretly be hidden behind the hangings, unknown either to him
or his mother, there to stand and hear their speeches and the
complots[2] by them to be taken[3] concerning the accomplishment
of the dissembling fool's pretense; assuring the King that if there
were any point of wisdom and perfect sense in the gallant's spirit,
that without all doubt he would easily discover[4] it to his mother,
as being devoid of all fear that she would utter or make known
his secret intent, being the woman that had borne him in her
body and nourished him so carefully; and withal[5] offered himself
to be the man that should stand to hearken and bear witness of
Hamlet's speeches with his mother, that he might not be esteemed a counselor in such a case wherein he refused to be the
executioner for the behoof and service of his prince.

1 **mean** means   2 **complots** conspiracy   3 **taken** undertaken   4 **dis-**
cover reveal   5 **withal** in addition

This invention pleased the King exceeding well, esteeming it as the only and sovereign remedy to heal the Prince of his lunacy, and to that end, making a long voyage, issued out of his palace and rode to hunt in the forest.

Meantime the counselor entered secretly into the Queen's chamber and there hid himself behind the arras not long before the Queen and Hamlet came thither, who, being crafty and politic, as soon as he was within the chamber, doubting[6] some treason and fearing if he should speak severely and wisely to his mother touching his secret practices he should be understood and by that means intercepted, used his ordinary manner of dissimulation and began to come like a cock,[7] beating with his arms (in such manner as cocks use to strike with their wings) upon the hangings of the chamber. Whereby, feeling something stirring under them, he cried, "A rat, a rat!" and presently drawing his sword thrust it into the hangings, which done, pulled the counselor (half dead) out by the heels, made an end of killing him, and, being slain, cut his body in pieces, which he caused to be boiled and then cast it into an open vault or privy that so it might serve for food to the hogs.

By which means having discovered the ambush and given the inventor thereof his just reward, he came again to his mother, who in the meantime wept and tormented herself to see all her hopes frustrate, for that what fault soever she had committed yet was she sore grieved to see her only child made a mere mockery—every man reproaching her with his folly, one point whereof she had as then seen before her eyes. Which was no small prick to her conscience, esteeming that the gods sent her that punishment for joining incestuously in marriage with the tyrannous murderer of her husband (who likewise ceased not to invent all the means he could to bring his nephew to his end), accusing her* own natural indiscretion, as being the ordinary guide of those that so much desire the pleasures of the body, who, shutting up the way to all reason, respect not what may ensue of their lightness and great inconstancy, and how a

6 doubting suspecting, fearing   7 come like a cock crow like a rooster

pleasure of small moment is sufficient to give them cause of repentance during their lives, and make them curse the day and
time that ever any such apprehensions entered into their minds
or that they closed their eyes to reject the honesty requisite in
ladies of her quality....

And while in this sort she sat tormenting herself, Hamlet
entered into the chamber, who, having once again searched
every corner of the same, distrusting his mother as well as the
rest, and perceiving himself to be alone, began in sober and dis-
creet manner to speak unto her, saying,

"What treason is this, O most infamous woman of all that
ever prostrated themselves to the will of an abominable whore-
monger, who, under the veil of a dissembling creature, covereth
the most wicked and detestable crime that man could ever
imagine or was committed! Now may I be assured to trust you
that, like a vile wanton adulteress altogether impudent and
given over to her pleasure, runs spreading forth her arms joyfully
to embrace the traitorous villainous tyrant that murdered my father, and most incestuously receivest the villain into the lawful
bed of your loyal spouse, imprudently entertaining him instead
of the dear father of your miserable and discomforted son—if
the gods grant him not the grace speedily to escape from a cap-
tivity so unworthy the degree he holdeth and the race and noble family of his ancestors. Is this the part of a queen and
daughter to a king? To live like a brute beast and like a mare
that yieldeth her body to the horse that hath beaten her companion away, to follow the pleasure of an abominable king that
hath murdered a far more honester and better man than himself
in massacring Horvendil, the honor and glory of the Danes?
Who are now esteemed of no force nor valor at all since the
shining splendor of knighthood was brought to an end by the
most wickedest and cruelest villain living upon earth.

"I for my part will never account him for my kinsman nor
once know him for mine uncle, nor you my dear mother, for not
having respect to the blood that ought to have united us so
straitly together, and who neither with your honor nor without

suspicion of consent to the death of your husband could ever have agreed to have married with his cruel enemy. O, Queen Geruth! It is the part of a bitch to couple with many and desire acquaintance of divers mastiffs. It is licentiousness only that hath made you deface out of your mind the memory of the valor and virtues of the good king your husband and my father. It was an unbridled desire that guided the daughter of Roderick to embrace the tyrant Fengon, and not to remember Horvendil (unworthy of so strange entertainment),[8] neither that he[9] killed his brother traitorously, and that she being his[10] father's wife betrayed him, although he[11] so well favored and loved her that for her sake he utterly bereaved Norway of her riches and valiant soldiers to augment the treasures of Roderick and make Geruth wife to the hardiest[12] prince in Europe. It is not the part of a woman, much less of a princess, in whom all modesty, courtesy, compassion, and love ought to abound, thus to leave her dear child to fortune in the bloody and murderous hands of a villain and traitor. Brute beasts do not so, for lions tigers, ounces,[13] and leopards fight for the safety and defense of their whelps; and birds that have beaks, claws, and wings resist such as would ravish them of their young ones. But you, to the contrary, expose and deliver me to death, whereas ye should defend me. Is not this as much as if you should betray me, when you, knowing the perverseness of the tyrant and his intents (full of deadly counsel as touching the race and image of his brother), have not once sought nor desired to find the means to save your child and only son by sending him into Swethland,[14] Norway, or England, rather than to leave him as a prey to your infamous adulterer?

"Be not offended, I pray you, madam, if, transported with dolor and grief, I speak so boldly unto you, and that I respect you less than duty requireth; for you, having forgotten me and wholly rejected the memory of the deceased king my father,

---

8 **entertainment** treatment   9 **neither that he** i.e., nor to remember that he, Fengon   10 **his** i.e., Hamlet's   11 **although he** i.e., although Horvendil   12 **hardiest** bravest   13 **ounces** lynxes, wildcats   14 **Swethland** Sweden

must not be abashed if I also surpass the bounds and limits of due consideration. Behold into what distress I am now fallen, and to what mischief my fortune and your over-great lightness[15] and want of wisdom have induced me, that I am constrained to play the madman to save my life instead of using and practicing arms, following adventures, and seeking all means to make myself known to be the true and undoubted heir of the valiant and virtuous King Horvendil! It was not without cause and just occasion that my gestures, countenances, and words seem all to proceed from a madman, and that I desire to have all men esteem me wholly deprived of sense and reasonable understanding, because I am well assured that he that hath made no conscience to kill his own brother (accustomed to murders and allured with desire of government without control in his treasons) will not spare to save himself with the like cruelty in the blood and flesh of the loins of his brother by him massacred. . . .

"To conclude, weep not, madam, to see my folly, but rather sigh and lament your own offense, tormenting your conscience in regard of the infamy that hath so defiled the ancient renown and glory that in times past honored Queen Geruth; for we are not to sorrow and grieve at other men's vices but for our own misdeeds and great follies. Desiring you for the surplus[16] of my proceedings, above all things, as you love your own life and welfare, that neither the King nor any other may by any means know mine intent; and let me alone with the rest, for I hope in the end to bring my purpose to effect."

[The Queen contritely asks Hamlet's understanding for a marriage that (she insists) she entered into under duress, implores his forgiveness, and declares that her fondest hope is to see her son restored to his rights as heir and monarch of Denmark. Hamlet pledges his faith to her, beseeching her to put aside her attachment to Fengon, whom Hamlet "will surely kill, or cause to be put to death, in despite of all the devils in hell,"

15 lightness wantonness **16 surplus** what remains still to be done

along with the flatterers who serve him. In doing so he will act as the true King of Denmark, he avers, killing a traitor, not a legitimate ruler, and crowning virtue with glory while punishing regicide with ignominious death.]

After this, Fengon, as if he had been out some long journey, came to the court again and asked for him that had received the charge to play the intelligencer to entrap Hamlet in his dissembled wisdom, was abashed to hear neither news nor tidings of him, and for that cause asked Hamlet what was become of him, naming the man. The Prince, that never used lying, and who in all the answers that ever he made during his counterfeit madness never strayed from the truth (as a generous[17] mind is a mortal enemy to untruth), answered and said that the counselor he sought for was gone down through the privy where, being choked by the filthiness of the place, the hogs meeting him had filled their bellies.

CHAPTER 4

How Fengon, the third time, devised to send Hamlet to the King of England with secret letters to have him put to death; and how Hamlet, when his companions slept, read the letters, and instead of them counterfeited others, willing the King of England to put the two messengers to death and to marry his daughter to Hamlet, which was effected; and how Hamlet escaped out of England.

A MAN would have judged anything rather than that Hamlet had committed that murder; nevertheless Fengon could not content himself, but still his mind gave him[1] that the fool would play him some trick of legerdemain, and willingly would have killed him; but he feared King Roderick, his grandfather, and further durst not offend the Queen, mother to the fool, whom she loved and much cherished, showing great grief and heaviness to see him so transported out of his wits. And in that

17 **generous** highborn, noble
1 **gave him** misgave him, made him apprehensive

conceit,[2] seeking to be rid of him, he determined* to find the means to do it by the aid of a stranger, making the King of England minister of his massacring resolution, choosing rather that his friend should defile his renown with so great a wickedness than himself to fall into perpetual infamy by an exploit of so great cruelty, to whom he purposed to send him and by letters desire him to put him to death.

Hamlet, understanding that he should be sent into England, presently doubted[3] the occasion of his voyage, and for that cause, speaking to the Queen, desired her not to make any show of sorrow or grief for his departure, but rather counterfeit a gladness as being rid of his presence whom, although she loved, yet she daily grieved to see him in so pitiful estate, deprived of all sense and reason; desiring her further that she should hang the hall with tapestry and make it fast with nails upon the walls and keep the brands[4] for him which he had sharpened at the points, then whenas[5] he said he made arrows to revenge the death of his father. Lastly he counseled her that, the year after his departure being accomplished, she should celebrate his funerals, assuring her that at the same instant she should see him return with great contentment and pleasure unto her from that his voyage.

Now, to bear him company were assigned two of Fengon's faithful ministers, bearing letters engraved in wood that contained Hamlet's death, in such sort as he had advertised[6] the King of England. But the subtle Danish Prince, being at sea, whilst his companions slept, having read the letters and known his uncle's great treason, with the wicked and villainous minds of the two courtiers that led him to the slaughter, rased[7] out the letters that concerned his death and instead thereof graved oth-

2 conceit frame of mind   3 presently doubted at once suspected
4 brands i.e., the staves or sticks that Hamlet sharpened as though in his madness; see Chapter 2. (A brand is usually a piece of wood that has been burning on the hearth or is to be used as a torch.)   5 then whenas on that occasion when   6 advertised given notice to, commanded
7 rased erased, or possibly razed, scraped

ers with commission to the King of England to hang his two companions; and not content to turn the death they had devised against him upon their own necks, wrote further that King Fengon willed him to give his daughter to Hamlet in marriage.

And so arriving in England, the messengers presented themselves to the King, giving him Fengon's letters, who, having read the contents, said nothing as then, but stayed[8] convenient time to effect Fengon's desire, meantime using the Danes familiarly, doing them that honor to sit at his table (for that kings as then were not so curiously nor solemnly[9] served as in these our days, for in these days mean[10] kings and lords of small revenue are as difficult and hard to be seen as in times past the monarchs of Persia used to be, or as it is reported of the great King of Ethiopia, who will not permit any man to see his face, which ordinarily he covereth with a veil). And as the messengers sat at the table with the King, subtle Hamlet was so far from being merry with them that he would not taste one bit of meat, bread, nor cup of beer whatsoever as then set upon the table, not without great wondering of the company, abashed to see a young man and a stranger not to esteem of the delicate meats and pleasant drinks served at the banquet, rejecting them as things filthy, evil of taste, and worse prepared. The King, who for that time dissembled what he thought, caused his guests to be conveyed into their chamber, willing one of his secret servants to hide himself therein and so to certify him what speeches passed among the Danes at their going to bed.

Now they were no sooner entered into the chamber, and those that were appointed to attend upon them gone out, but Hamlet's companions asked him why he refused to eat and drink of that which he found upon the table, not honoring the banquet of so great a king, that entertained them in friendly sort, with such honor and courtesy as it deserved? Saying further that he did not well but dishonored him that sent him, as if he sent men into England that feared to be poisoned by so great a

8 **stayed** awaited   9 **curiously nor solemnly** fastidiously or ceremoniously   10 **mean** insignificant

king. The Prince, that had done nothing without reason and prudent consideration, answered them and said: "What, think you that I will eat bread dipped in human blood, and defile my throat with the rust of iron, and use that meat that stinketh and savoreth of man's flesh already putrified and corrupted, and that scenteth like the savor of a dead carrion long since cast into a vault? And how would you have me to respect the King that hath the countenance of a slave, and the Queen, who instead of great majesty, hath done three things more like a woman of base parentage and fitter for a waiting-gentlewoman than beseeming a lady of her quality and estate?" And, having said so, used many injurious and sharp speeches as well against the King and Queen as others that had assisted at that banquet for the entertainment of the Danish ambassadors. And therein Hamlet said truth, as hereafter you shall hear, for that in those days, the north parts of the world, living as then under Satan's laws, were full of enchanters, so that there was not any young gentleman whatsoever that knew not something therein sufficient to serve his turn if need required, as yet in those days in Gotland[11] and Biarmy[12] there are many that knew not what the Christian religion permitteth, as by reading the histories of Norway and Gotland you may easily perceive. And so Hamlet, while his father lived, had been instructed in that devilish art whereby the wicked spirit abuseth mankind and advertiseth him (as he can) of things past.

[Hamlet, aided by the devilish power of magic he has learned, amazes the King of England by demonstrating the truth of the riddling and prophetic statements he has just uttered. It turns out that the King's bread is in fact defiled by human blood shed on the battlefield where the grain was grown, that his pork comes from hogs that have fed on a hanged thief, that his beer is brewed from a water supply polluted by rusty armor, and that, more distressingly, the King is the illegitimate son of a slave and the Queen of

11 **Gotland** an area in what is now southern Sweden   12 **Biarmy** a region in northern Lapland

no less base parentage. The King thereupon treats Hamlet with the respect that such awesome magical powers deserve.]

The King, admiring the young Prince and beholding in him some matter of greater respect than in the common sort of men, gave him his daughter in marriage, according to the counterfeit letters by him devised, and the next day caused the two servants of Fengon to be executed, to satisfy, as he thought, the King's desire. But Hamlet, although the sport[13] pleased him well, and that the King of England could not have done him a greater favor, made as though he had been much offended, threatening the King to be revenged; but the King, to appease him, gave him a great sum of gold, which Hamlet caused to be molten and put into two staves, made hollow for the same purpose, to serve his turn therewith as need should require. For of all the King's treasures he took nothing with him into Denmark but only those two staves, and as soon as the year began to be at an end, having somewhat before obtained license of the King his father-in-law to depart, went for Denmark, then with all the speed he could to return again into England to marry his daughter; and so set sail for Denmark.

CHAPTER 5

How Hamlet, having escaped out of England, arrived in Denmark the same day that the Danes were celebrating his funerals, supposing him to be dead in England; and how he revenged his father's death upon his uncle and the rest of the courtiers; and what followed.

HAMLET in that sort sailing into Denmark, being arrived in the country entered into the palace of his uncle the same day that they were celebrating his funerals, and, going into the hall, procured no small astonishment and wonder to them all—no man thinking other but that he had been dead. Among the which

13 the sport i.e., the execution of his two companions. (Hamlet pretends to be offended at this so that the King will pacify him with a large gift, as he does.)

many of them rejoiced not a little for the pleasure which they knew Fengon would conceive for so pleasant a loss,[1] and some were sad, as remembering the honorable King Horvendil, whose victories they could by no means forget, much less deface out of their memories that which appertained unto him, who[2] as then greatly rejoiced to see a false report spread[3] of Hamlet's death and that the tyrant had not as yet obtained his will of the heir of Jutie,[4] but rather hoped God would restore him to his senses again for the good and welfare of that province. Their amazement at the last[5] being turned into laughter, all that as then were assistant at the funeral banquet of him whom they esteemed dead mocked each at other for having been so simply deceived, and, wondering at the Prince, that in his so long a voyage he had not recovered any of his senses, asked what was become of them that had borne him company into Great Britain? To whom he made answer (showing them the two hollow staves wherein he had put his molten gold that the King of England had given him to appease his fury concerning the murder of his two companions) and said, "Here they are both." Whereat many that already knew his humors presently conjectured that he had played some trick of legerdemain, and to deliver himself out of danger had thrown them into the pit prepared for him; so that, fearing to follow after them and light upon some evil adventure, they went presently out of the court. And it was well for them that they did so, considering the tragedy acted by him the same day, being accounted his funeral but in truth their last days that as then rejoiced for his* overthrow.[6]

For when every man busied himself to make good cheer, and

1 rejoiced ... loss i.e., rejoiced greatly to think how Fengon had desired the loss of Hamlet and how he would now be frustrated   2 who i.e., the courtiers who admire Hamlet   3 rejoiced ... spread i.e., rejoiced to learn that the rumor was false   4 Jutie Jutland, Denmark   5 at the last finally   6 but in truth ... overthrow i.e., a day that was supposed to have been for Hamlet's funeral but that in truth became the day of doom for those who had rejoiced in his overthrow.

Hamlet's arrival provoked them more to drink and carouse, the Prince himself at that time played the butler and a gentleman attending on the tables, not suffering the pots nor goblets to be empty, whereby he gave the noblemen such store of liquor that all of them, being full laden with wine and gorged with meat, were constrained to lay themselves down in the same place where they had supped, so much their senses were dulled and overcome with the fire of overgreat drinking (a vice common and familiar among the Almains[7] and other nations inhabiting the north parts of the world). Which when Hamlet perceiving, and finding so good opportunity to effect his purpose and be revenged of his enemies, and, by the means to abandon the actions, gestures, and apparel of a madman, occasion so fitly finding his turn and as it were effecting itself, failed not to take hold thereof[8] and, seeing those drunken bodies filled with wine, lying like hogs upon the ground, some sleeping, others vomiting the over-great abundance of wine which without measure they had swallowed up, made the hangings about the hall to fall down and cover them all over, which he nailed to the ground, being boarded, and at the ends thereof he stuck the brands whereof I spake before, by him sharpened, which served for pricks,[9] binding and tying the hangings in such sort that, what force soever they used to loose themselves, it was unpossible to get from under them. And presently he set fire to the four corners of the hall in such sort that all that were as then therein not one escaped away, but were forced to purge their sins by fire and dry up the great abundance of liquor by them received into their bodies, all of them dying in the inevitable[10] and merciless flames of the hot and burning fire.

Which the Prince, perceiving, became wise; and knowing that his uncle, before the end of the banquet, had withdrawn himself into his chamber, which stood apart from the place where the fire burnt, went thither and, entering into the chamber, laid hand upon the sword of his father's murderer, leaving

7 **Almains** Germans   8 **take hold thereof** seize the opportunity
9 **pricks** skewers   10 **inevitable** irresistible

his own in the place (which, while he was at the banquet, some of the courtiers had nailed fast into the scabbard); and going to Fengon said: "I wonder, disloyal king, how thou canst sleep here at thine ease, and all thy palace is burnt, the fire thereof having burnt the greatest part of thy courtiers and ministers of thy cruelty and detestable tyrannies. And, which is more, I cannot imagine how thou shouldst well assure thyself and thy estate[11] as now to take thy ease, seeing Hamlet so near thee armed with the shafts by him prepared long since, and at this present is ready to revenge the traitorous injury by thee done to his lord and father."

Fengon, as then knowing the truth of his nephew's subtle practice, and hearing him speak with staid[12] mind, and, which is more, perceived a sword naked in his hand which he already lifted up to deprive him of his life, leaped quickly out of the bed, taking hold of Hamlet's sword that was nailed into the scabbard, which, as he sought to pull out, Hamlet gave him such a blow upon the chine[13] of the neck that he cut his head clean from his shoulders, and, as he fell to the ground, said, "This just and violent death is a just reward for such as thou art. Now go thy ways, and when thou comest in hell, see thou forget not to tell thy brother whom thou traitorously slewest that it was his son that sent thee thither with the message, to the end that, being comforted thereby, his soul may rest among the blessed spirits and quit[14] me of the obligation that bound me to pursue his vengeance upon mine own blood, that seeing it was by thee that I lost the chief thing that tied me to this alliance and consanguinity."

A man, to say the truth, hardy, courageous, and worthy of eternal commendation, who, arming himself with a crafty, dissembling, and strange show of being distract out of his wits, under that pretense deceived the wise, politic, and crafty, thereby not only preserving his life from the treasons and wicked practices of the tyrant, but, which is more, by a new and unexpected

11 **assure ... estate** feel confident about your situation   12 **staid** steady   13 **chine** back   14 **quit** acquit, free

kind of punishment revenged his father's death many years after the act committed, in such* sort that, directing his courses with such prudence and effecting his purposes with so great boldness, and constancy, he left a judgment to be decided among men of wisdom, which[15] was more commendable in him, his constancy, or magnanimity, or his wisdom in ordering his affairs according to the premeditable determination he had conceived....

Hamlet, having in this manner revenged himself, durst not presently declare his action to the people, but to the contrary determined to work by policy, so to give them intelligence what he had done and the reason that drew him thereunto; so that, being accompanied with such of his father's friends that then were rising,[16] he stayed to see what the people would do when they should hear of that sudden and fearful action. The next morning, the towns bordering thereabouts, desiring to know from whence the flames of fire proceeded the night before they had seen, came thither, and, perceiving the King's palace burnt to ashes and many bodies (most part consumed) lying among the ruins of the house, all of them were much abashed, nothing being left of the palace but the foundation. But they were much more amazed to behold the body of the King all bloody, and his head cut off lying hard by him; whereat some began to threaten revenge, yet not knowing against whom; others, beholding so lamentable a spectacle, armed themselves; the rest rejoicing, yet not daring to make any show thereof, some detesting the cruelty, others lamenting the death of their prince but the greatest part, calling Horvendil's murder to remembrance, acknowledging a just judgment from above that had thrown down the pride of the tyrant. And in this sort, the diversities of opinions among that multitude of people being many, yet every man ignorant what would be the issue of that tragedy, none stirred from thence, neither yet attempted to move[17] any tumult, every man fearing his own skin and distrusting his neighbor, esteeming each other to be consenting to the massacre.

15 which as to which   16 rising arising   17 move set in motion, instigate

[In the last three chapters of the story, Hamlet makes an oration to the Danes in defense of his conduct, wins the loyalty of one and all, and makes good his promise to return to England. There, threatened with a secret plot on the part of the King of England to avenge the death of Fengon, Hamlet slays the English king and returns to Denmark with two wives. He is betrayed by his second wife, Hermetrude, Queen of Scots, in league with his uncle Wiglerus, and is slain.]

Text based on *The History of Hamlet* [spelled *Hamblet* in the original]. *London: Imprinted by Richard Bradocke for Thomas Pavier, and are to be sold at his shop in Cornhill near to the Royal Exchange. 1608.*

In the following, departures from the original text appear in boldface; original readings are in roman.

p. 294 *northward neithward ***to two** two ***surmounted** surmounting **p. 295 *not only** onely **p. 297 *wisest** wiseth **p. 299 *counterfeited** counterfeiting **p. 300 *infernal** intefernal **p. 303 *accusing her** accusing his **p. 308 *he determined** determined **p. 312 *his** their **p. 315 *in such** in no such

FURTHER READING

Alexander, Nigel. *Poison, Play, and Duel: A Study in "Hamlet."* London: Routledge and Kegan Paul, 1971. Alexander argues that the play's representation of complex moral and psychological problems depends upon three dominant symbols—poison, play, and duel—that structure the play's action and language. Through these powerful images, which come together in the play's final scene, Shakespeare conveys a sense of the inescapable difficulties of moral choice and action.

Bevington, David. "'Maimed Rites': Violated Ceremony in *Hamlet*." *Action Is Eloquence: Shakespeare's Language of Gesture.* Cambridge and London: Harvard Univ. Press, 1984. Bevington traces how Shakespeare shapes our responses to the play through visual means. *Hamlet*, he argues, is a play of "maimed rites," perversions of ceremony that reflect the moral and social disruptions in Denmark. In the final scene, the solemnity with which Hamlet is borne offstage serves to rehabilitate ceremony, restoring "some hope of perceivable meaning in the ceremonial meanings that hold together the social and moral order."

Bohannan, Laura. "Shakespeare in the Bush." *Natural History* 75 (1966): 28–33. Rpt. in *Every Man His Way: Readings in Cultural Anthropology*, ed. Alan Dundes. Englewood Cliffs, N.J.: Prentice-Hall, 1968. Bohannan, a cultural anthropologist, narrates the response of the elders of the Tiv tribe of West Africa to her retelling of the story of *Hamlet*. Her lively essay is a lesson in cultural relativity: familiar critical issues like the ghost, the incestuous marriage, Ophelia's madness, and Hamlet's revenge are freshly viewed from the perspective of a culture with non-Western ethical values and practices.

Booth, Stephen. "On the Value of *Hamlet*." *Reinterpretations of Elizabethan Drama*, ed. Norman Rabkin. New York: Columbia Univ. Press, 1969. Booth focuses on the audience's experience of the play. His patient analysis of the opening scene sets forth the process whereby Hamlet's frustrated desire for certainty and coherence becomes the audience's own. The result for Booth is that "*Hamlet* is a tragedy of an audience that cannot make up its mind."

Bowers, Fredson. "Hamlet as Minister and Scourge." *PMLA* 70 (1955): 740–749. When Hamlet calls himself a "scourge and minister," Bowers argues, he signals his awareness of a conflict between his roles as private avenger and agent of providential design. By locating *Hamlet* within the moral and dramatic traditions of Elizabethan revenge tragedy, Bowers discovers the cause of the hero's delay in Hamlet's desire for heaven to define and facilitate his complex responsibility.

Bradlay, A. C. "*Hamlet.*" *Shakespearean Tragedy*, 1904. Rpt., New York: St. Martin's, 1985. Bradley explores the sources of Hamlet's delay, locating it not in a temperament characteristically resistant to action but in a "violent shock to his moral being" that produces an enervating melancholy. The Ghost's revelation and demand for revenge is "the last rivet in the melancholy which holds him bound," and the play presents "his vain efforts to fulfill this duty, his unconscious self-excuses and unavailing self-reproaches, and the tragic results of his delay."

Calderwood, James L. *To Be and Not to Be: Negation and Metadrama in "Hamlet."* New York: Columbia Univ. Press, 1983. Calderwood's metadramatic reading provocatively examines the tensions between illusion and reality, absence and presence, negation and assertion, inscribed into a play that relentlessly proliferates uncertainties and contradictions, but that, as Calderwood's title suggests, ultimately accepts and contains them.

Coleridge, Samuel Taylor. "*Hamlet.*" *Coleridge's Writings on Shakespeare*, ed. Terence Hawkes. New York: G. P. Putnam's Sons, 1959. Coleridge, along with other early nineteenth-century intellectuals, was strongly drawn to Hamlet ("I have a smack of Hamlet myself") and saw him as an agonizing intellectual, endlessly reasoning and hesitating, detached from the world of events. In Coleridge's influential psychological reading, Hamlet is a man both "amiable and excellent" who is defeated by his "aversion to action, which prevails among such as have a world in themselves."

Eliot, T. S. "Hamlet and His Problems." *Selected Essays, 1917–1932.* New York: Harcourt, Brace and Co., 1932. The "problems" Eliot identifies in his influential essay are not in Hamlet's character but in the play itself. Eliot believes that *Hamlet* is Shakespeare's revision of a lost revenge play onto which Shakespeare's main theme—the effect of a mother's guilt upon her son—is unsuccessfully grafted. Hamlet's emotions are "in excess of the facts as they appear," Eliot finds; Hamlet can neither understand nor objectify them, since Shakespeare himself is unable to find any "objective correlative" in his play for Hamlet's complex psychological state.

Frye, Roland Mushat. *The Renaissance "Hamlet."* Princeton, N.J.: Princeton Univ. Press, 1984. Drawing upon a rich array of historical, literary, and pictorial evidence, Frye seeks to reconstruct the challenges and excitement that *Hamlet* offered to Shakespeare's Elizabethan audience. The rich specificity of the background that Frye reconstructs acknowledges "the complex and sophisticated concerns of Elizabethan minds" and the complexity of the play itself.

Goldman, Michael. " 'To Be or Not to Be' and the Spectrum of Action." *Acting and Action in Shakespearean Tragedy.* Princeton, N.J.: Princeton Univ. Press, 1985. Goldman argues that the challenges the role of Hamlet poses to an actor are analogous to the challenges the play poses to an audience. Each must engage in an act of interpretation that will discover unity and coherence in the multiple and often contradictory evidence of language and action.

Granville-Barker, Harley. *Preface to "Hamlet."* Princeton, N.J.: Princeton Univ. Press, 1946. This book-length "Preface" draws upon Granville-Barker's insights as a theatrical director and literary critic in its focus on the structure and tone of *Hamlet*. The first half of the study contains a detailed analysis of the three distinct movements (rather than the imposed five-act structure) that govern the play's action. Granville-Barker concludes with a discussion of the characters in this "tragedy of thwarted thought and tortured spirit."

Greenblatt, Stephen. *Hamlet in Purgatory.* Princeton and Oxford: Princeton Univ. Press, 2001. Starting with an exploration of the Catholic doctrine of Purgatory, Greenblatt explores the play's focus on death and the human desire somehow to remain in contact with the dead. Not only a reconstruction of early modern religious belief, Greenblatt's book offers an extended reading of the play that attempts to account for its uncanny power to fascinate audiences and readers.

Jones, Ernest. *Hamlet and Oepidus*. New York: Norton, 1949; published in 1910 in an earlier essay form. Jones, a student of Freud, considers the personality of Hamlet from a psychoanalytic perspective and diagnoses his delay as symptomatic of an Oepidal complex. Hamlet is incapable of revenge because of his unconscious identification with Claudius, who has enacted Hamlet's unconscious wish to kill his father and marry his mother. Jones extends his provocative argument with the suggestion that the play's Oedipal aspects have their origin in Shakespeare's own psychology in 1601, the year the play was possibly written and in which Shakespeare's father died.

Kastan, David Scott, ed. *Critical Essays on Shakespeare's "Hamlet."* New York: G. K. Hall, 1995. A generous and thoughtful anthology of essential essays on the play, including Laura Bohannan's anthropological piece on *Hamlet* among the Tiv, and critical essays by, among others, Stephen Booth, Barbara Everett, Michael Goldman, Lisa Jardine, and Paul Werstine.

Kerrigan, William. *Hamlet's Perfection*. Baltimore and London: The Johns Hopkins University Press, 1995. A short, engaging book whose ambiguous title indicates Kerrigan's interest in both the aesthetic perfection of the play itself and the thwarted search for perfection by its title character.

Kliman, Bernice, ed. *Approaches to Teaching Shakespeare's "Hamlet."* New York: Modern Language Association of America, 2002. A remarkably useful selection of short essays on strategies for teaching the play, with essays considering various pedagogical problems, including considerations of how to teach metrics, how to think about the multiple texts of the play, how to incorporate perfomance into the classroom, how to use internet resources, as well as essays that engage more traditional critical concerns.

Levin, Harry. *The Question of "Hamlet."* New York: Oxford Univ. Press, 1959. Levin's rhetorical analysis of the play's tone and action focuses on three dominant figures of speech (which are simultaneously modes of thought): interrogation, doubt, and irony. These, Levin finds, are organized dialectically, with the play's and Hamlet's own pervasive irony serving as a synthesis that permits us to face—though never to solve—the contradictions that the play's questions and unexpected answers expose.

Lewis, C. S. "Hamlet: The Prince or the Poem?" *Proceedings of the British Academy* 28 (1943 for 1942): 11–18. Rpt. in *They Asked for a Paper*. London: Bles, 1962; and in part as "Death in *Hamlet*" in *Shakespeare, the Tragedies: A Collection of Critical Essays*, ed. Alfred Harbage. Englewood Cliffs, N.J.: Prentice-Hall, 1964. Lewis takes issue with the focus on Hamlet's character that has dominated critical discussion of the play since the nineteenth century. He argues that the true subject of the play is death. The fear of being dead, born of a failure to understand human nature or the nature of the universe, is, for Lewis, the source of the play's powerful presentation of doubt and dread.

Mack, Maynard. "The World of *Hamlet*." *Yale Review* 41 (1952): 502–523. Rpt. in *Shakespeare, the Tragedies: A Collection of Critical Essays*, ed. Alfred Harbage. Englewood Cliffs, N.J.: Prentice-Hall, 1964. Mack's sensitive account of the play's verbal texture establishes the "imaginative environment" of *Hamlet* that is dominated both by a deep and disabling inscrutability and by an overriding sense of morality. In the final act, Mack argues, Hamlet comes to understand what it means to live in such a world and to accept the mysterious condition of being human.

Nietzsche, Friedrich. "The Birth of Tragedy or: Hellenism and Pessimism" (1872). *The Birth of Tragedy and the Case of Wagner*, trans. Walter Kaufmann. New York: Vintage, 1967. Nietzsche rejects the common nineteenth-century notion that Hamlet fails to act because he is paralyzed by excessive thought in favor of a view of Hamlet's "nausea" induced by looking "truly into the nature of things." What inhibits Hamlet is his tragic knowledge of the futility and folly of action in a world that is out of joint. "Knowledge kills action," Nietzsche asserts; "action requires the veil of illusion."

Prosser, Eleanor. *Hamlet and Revenge*. Stanford, Calif.: Stanford Univ. Press, 1967. Surveying Renaissance ethical codes and dramatic conventions, Prosser examines *Hamlet* in light of the Elizabethan understanding of revenge and ghosts. She contends that once we accept that the moral universe of the play (as well as of the audience) is Christian, we must see the Ghost as "demonic" and Hamlet's commitment to revenge as immoral and appalling.

MEMORABLE LINES

A little more than kin, and less than kind.   (HAMLET 1.2.65)

Oh, that this too too sullied flesh would melt ...

    (HAMLET 1.2.129)

How weary, stale, flat, and unprofitable
Seem to me all the uses of this world!

    (HAMLET 1.2.133–4)

Frailty, thy name is woman!   (HAMLET 1.2.146)

'A was a man. Take him for all in all,
I shall not look upon his like again.   (HAMLET 1.2.187–8)

Neither a borrower nor a lender be.   (POLONIUS 1.3.75)

This above all: to thine own self be true.   (POLONIUS 1.3.78)

But to my mind, though I am native here
And to the manner born, it is a custom
More honored in the breach than the observance.

    (HAMLET 1.4.14–16)

Something is rotten in the state of Denmark.

    (MARCELLUS 1.4.90)

Murder most foul, as in the best it is ...   (GHOST 1.5.28)

Oh, my prophetic soul!   (HAMLET 1.5.42)

There are more things in heaven and earth, Horatio,
Than are dreamt of in your philosophy.

    (HAMLET 1.5.175–6)

The time is out of joint. Oh, cursèd spite
That ever I was born to set it right!   (HAMLET 1.5.197–8)

Brevity is the soul of wit ...   (POLONIUS 2.2.90)

More matter, with less art.   (QUEEN 2.2.95)

That he's mad, 'tis true; 'tis true 'tis pity,
And pity 'tis 'tis true.   (POLONIUS 2.2.97–8)

Words, words, words.   (HAMLET 2.2.193)

Though this be madness, yet there is method in't.

(POLONIUS 2.2.205–6)

There is nothing either good or bad but thinking makes it so.

(HAMLET 2.2.250–1)

What a piece of work is a man!   (HAMLET 2.2.304–5)

What's Hecuba to him, or he to Hecuba,
That he should weep for her?   (HAMLET 2.2.559–60)

                    The play's the thing
Wherein I'll catch the conscience of the King.

(HAMLET 2.2.605–6)

To be, or not to be, that is the question.   (HAMLET 3.1.57)

Whether 'tis nobler in the mind to suffer
The slings and arrows of outrageous fortune,
Or to take arms against a sea of troubles
And by opposing end them.   (HAMLET 3.1.58–61)

                    To die, to sleep;
To sleep, perchance to dream. Ay, there's the rub…

(HAMLET 3.1.65–6)

Thus conscience does make cowards of us all.

(HAMLET 3.1.84)

Get thee to a nunnery.   (HAMLET 3.1.122)

The glass of fashion and the mold of form,
Th'observed of all observers…   (OPHELIA 3.1.156–7)

I would have such a fellow whipped for o'erdoing Termagant.
It out-Herods Herod.   (HAMLET 3.2.12–14)

Suit the action to the word, the word to the action, with this
special observance, that you o'erstep not the modesty of nature.

(HAMLET 3.2.17–19)

...the purpose of playing, whose end, both at the first and now, was and is to hold as 'twere the mirror up to nature...

(HAMLET 3.2.20–2)

                    ...for thou hast been
As one, in suffering all, that suffers nothing,
A man that Fortune's buffets and rewards
Hast ta'en with equal thanks.   (HAMLET 3.2.64–7)

OPHELIA 'Tis brief, my lord.

HAMLET   As woman's love.   (3.2.151–2)

The lady doth protest too much, methinks.   (QUEEN 3.2.228)

'Tis now the very witching time of night.   (HAMLET 3.2.387)

                    The cess of majesty
Dies not alone, but like a gulf doth draw
What's near it with it.   (ROSENCRANTZ 3.3.15–17)

For 'tis the sport to have the engineer
Hoist with his own petard...   (HAMLET 3.4.213–14)

How all occasions do inform against me
And spur my dull revenge!   (HAMLET 4.4.33–4)

                    Rightly to be great
Is not to stir without great argument,
But greatly to find quarrel in a straw
When honor's at the stake.   (HAMLET 4.4.54–7)

When sorrows come, they come not single spies,
But in battalions.   (KING 4.5.79–80)

There's rosemary, that's for remembrance... And there is pansies; that's for thoughts.   (OPHELIA 4.5.179–81)

Alas, poor Yorick! I knew him, Horatio, a fellow of infinite jest, of most excellent fancy.   (HAMLET 5.1.183–5)

The cat will mew, and dog will have his day.

(HAMLET 5.1.295)

There's a divinity that shapes our ends,
Rough-hew them how we will.   (HAMLET 5.2.10–11)

Not a whit, we defy augury. There is special providence in the fall of a sparrow. If it be now, 'tis not to come; if it be not to come, it will be now; if it be not now, yet it will come. The readiness is all.   (HAMLET 5.2.217–20)

A hit, a very palpable hit.   (OSRIC 5.2.282)

　　　　　　　Good night, sweet prince,
And flights of angels sing thee to thy rest!

                                        (HORATIO 5.2.361–2)

SEE YOUR BOOKSELLER FOR THESE BANTAM CLASSICS

FIFTY GREAT AMERICAN SHORT STORIES, 0-553-27294-2
SHORT SHORTS, 0-553-27440-6
GREAT AMERICAN SHORT STORIES, 0-440-33060-2
SHORT STORY MASTERPIECES, 0-440-37864-8
THE VOICE THAT IS GREAT WITHIN US, 0-553-26263-7
THE BLACK POETS, 0-553-27563-1
THREE CENTURIES OF AMERICAN POETRY, (Trade) 0-553-37518-0,
    (Hardcover) 0-553-10250-8